Don't Panic

My Travels Through Anxiety
to a Life of Calm

Helga K. Beer

Table of Contents

Letter to my Younger Self

Dear younger Helga

I didn't realise when I started writing 'Don't Panic' that I was writing this book for you.

I had lofty ideals that this was a work that needed to be out there, but I realise now that it was always for you.

You who was at Glastonbury, feeling so afraid and sure you would die.

You who was sitting there, scared in the GP's office, being told to put a brown paper bag over your head.

You, sitting with your boss when she said it could take as long as a year to recover. Ha!

You who wanted to see Oma before she died but was too afraid to get on the plane.

You who could never sleep, phoning the Samaritans because you couldn't get past the night terrors.

You who panicked so intensely at The Grand Hotel, Torquay, that you felt you might drown.

You who was too scared to leave the house and cried under your duvet for weeks.

You who got up and tried again.

You who was so ecstatic when you got two stripes on your pregnancy tests.

You who bravely accepted the news that you had a tear to your carotid artery.

You who coped with that ovarian cancer scare, the wrong diagnosis that suggested you had months to live.

You who holidayed a few miles from home and still made special memories for your children.

You who wrote on a Facebook page in 2018 that you had to turn back from a trip to Exeter because your anxiety was so intense.

You who kept on trying all the therapies, reading the books, listening to the podcasts, and refusing to give up.

You who was in tears in Cockwood, when you couldn't go to the airport with your family for the Naples holiday in 2019.

You who flew to Naples on your own at night, despite your fears.

You who took that job that would push you out of your comfort zone every week.

You who punches the air with joy every time you have a breakthrough.

You who turned back at Exeter Railway station, unable to join your family on the trip to Grossbullesheim as recently as 2022.

You who went to Nice in 2023, despite the tears and terrors.

You who shakily got on the coach to London for BST Hyde Park, All Points East, and Taylor Swift

You who still says yes when your fear screams no.

This book is for you.

I know you're struggling and that things feel impossible.

Thank you for being brave. I love your tenacious, Weeble-like properties. No, I'm not insulting your fuller figure; I'm reminding you of that 1970s advert: 'Weebles wobble, but they never fall down.'

You will have a few wobbles, but everything, and I do mean everything, plays an important role in your journey.

You will always be okay.

You can cope with everything life throws at you. Cope is the wrong word. You thrive.

Sniff out the 'joy truffles.' Pockets of happiness hidden just under the surface. They are all around you. You just need to dig a little.

Lift your head, remove your paper bag, take a few calming breaths, and take one small step.

That's all I ask of you.

You are so much closer than you think.

All my love,

Helga

'The world is full of mystery and magic. We just need to look, listen, and believe that wondrous things are still possible.'

Vonnie Winslow Crist

Acknowledgements

I would like to thank Michael and Emily Eavis for putting on the brilliant Glastonbury Festival. If I ever get lucky enough to go again, it's definitely on my bucket list. My life needed a shake-up, and I have to admit Glastonbury certainly delivered.

Big appreciation to my incredible mum, who has listened to every boring edit of this book and feigned impressive interest throughout.

Max and Millie, for allowing me to be myself and never once eye rolling (okay, maybe a few times) at all my embarrassing behaviour as I embraced my true self. This 'real me' regrettably loves nothing more than to dance badly and sing loudly, with scant regard for tune, as she drives around the Westcountry in her Mini.

I am beyond grateful to Nano Ponce for his help with getting this project from a scrappy collection of ideas into a coherent book. He generously allowed me to trial his incredible writing programme (The Writer's Wand), and I look forward to repaying him for his investment by the end of 2025 latest. Book royalties would be super helpful!

I would like to thank my editor Karen Sanders for her eternal patience. I have delayed getting this book to her on two occasions. Big apologies!

Heartfelt thanks to Ann Skinner for creating the artwork and giving young Helga a new life as she skips, in doodle form, through the pages.

An award must go to Nick for being there throughout this long and often tedious journey, and serving the full thirty-five years. There will be a medal ceremony!

Thanks to all my wonderful girl friends for their support, particularly Gayner Andrews, Serena Fitzgerald, Claire Tarr, Tracey Tate Walker, Mandy Pitts, Nicola Clarke, Anna Pittard, Anna Deeks, Helen Comer, and so many others (I could go on for days).

Thanks to Andrew, Nicola, and all the wonderful therapists in this book. If it didn't work, I can guarantee, 'It's not you, it's me.' The same goes for all the techniques. There are so many reasons things didn't click for me, but mainly because I just wasn't finished with all the learning.

A massive thanks to Helen and Rita Arpino and all of Maria's family for introducing me to this wonderful woman.

Thanks to the universe for giving me not only the challenges but the ability to get through them. It's been one hell of a ride!

Preface

This is a version of my story. I could have written it in so many different ways, depending on my mood, the year, month, week, or even day I chose to sit down and write it. There have been many versions of this story, and none are quite the same. Not because I have lacked honesty, but because the way I see my story is forever changing. In any given moment, I might notice something new, and my story naturally evolves. I can't seem to pin the tail on this particular donkey.

I wrote my memoir, 'Don't Panic,' over two years, and as each month has passed, my relationship with the story has altered. I keep taking new leaps and having new breakthroughs.

Editing has been a nightmare. I desperately want to capture my voice at the time the words first tumbled onto the page, but the pesky shouts of my current perspective keep threatening to overpower. It's been a challenge. All I can promise is that my words were absolutely true at the point they left my pen.

I have intentionally left out names of characters, unless it is to wholeheartedly thank them, and that, they will have to take on the chin. I am more than aware that other characters in this book would have quite a different voice. They have the option to write their own memoir. This is mine. I write this in the hope that someone out there will discover something in my words that they find useful. Maybe simply an internal nudge, a curiosity to look at their challenges from a fresh perspective. If that curiosity leads them to toss my book aside and step out into the world to speak their truth, blue baby gives a small whoop. It's more than we could ever have hoped for.

Introduction

'Perhaps this is what I'm seeking too; the ability to step into the
world's flux, to travel with it rather than rasping against it, let my own
form dance across it.'
Katherine May, *Enchantment*

I'm wearing a pair of spectacles. I have another pair on my head and a third on my desk. I am forever reaching for my glasses to help me see things more clearly. It is also a metaphor for my life with anxiety and panic; a much-maligned duo that have been my trusty companions for decades. How I see them has depended on the particular lenses I was wearing on any given day. For years, it has been the darkest of shades. Think Magenta Devine in the eighties, and ones that needed a seriously good clean. Unsurprisingly, through them, things have looked rather murky and confusing. I was yet to discover that other pairs were just within my grasp.

Today, I'm wearing jaunty pink glasses that are clean and exactly the right strength for me. I can see clearly now, but as the song attests, the rain needed to come first.

The particular obstacles in my way were a tense childhood, endless house moves, an inability to put down roots, and a penchant for the unhealthy, from trying to please the wrong crowd, over-imbibing on alcohol, beating myself up on a daily basis, ingesting a diet that barely resembled food, and surviving on a chronic lack of sleep.

This all culminated in a shattering drugs trip at Glastonbury Music Festival in 1990 that saw me enter as one person and leave as someone completely different. I know now that I do this in a less dramatic fashion every day of my life. It's always a school day as they say, but on this one occasion I was forced to sit up and take note.

At twenty-one years old, the Helga who shuffled out of Glastonbury was unrecognisable from the one who had bounced in a few days earlier. This new Helga was riddled with fear and drowning under relentless waves of panic.

Not a good thing, we might all agree. I desperately wanted to get back to the person I was before I popped the pills that catapulted me into this scary new reality. Alas, though, there is no going back in life. This is not all bad news, as it turns out.

The urge to go back was maybe me being too scared to explore a new world opening up to me. I attempted a similar U-turn at my birth. I deeply wanted security and the comfort of the known, even if the known was a toxic concoction of things that didn't serve me well. So, what did I do? I tried to stay put in limbo land. I was pushed into a new existence but panicked and refused to move on. Much like my border collie on a trip to the vets, I hunkered down, refusing to move, having to be dragged along kicking and screaming, or in her case barking, reluctant to step into the something yet to be discovered.

On a deeper level, I knew I was going to have to move forward. Refusing to budge from my comfort zone, one blighted by agoraphobia, was unwise and not actually comfortable at all. Far from it. Blindly banging my head and scraping my fingernails against the closed door to my past in an attempt to retrieve some old version of myself turned out to be remarkably unhelpful also. All I did was leave long scratch marks on a permanently deceased chapter of my life.

So, there I was, at twenty-one, stuck between two worlds and afraid to move forward. Home became my place of safety, and I clung to it like a life raft. The thing is, it's not only impractical to stay at home for the rest of your life, but also, in between all the fear, remarkably boring. I wanted to step out into the world, but I was just too afraid. It all looked so dark and sinister. 'That'll be the shades', I hear you cry.

Ever resourceful, with ADHD superpowers, I invented a way to move forward that felt safe. I created a rule (the X-rule) that as long as I was a certain distance from my home, I would be free from panic. This was an arbitrary rule that I told myself and chose to believe because it suited me.

I could just as easily have said, 'providing I am eating a cheese and pickle sandwich, I will be fine,' but we will come back to the placebo effect and other wonderful tricks of the mind later. The distance was variable and could be anything from a mile to around 100 miles from my home. This was genius on some level, as within that 'safe zone,' my panic attacks all but disappeared, the shades came off, and I could live a fairly normal existence. This was okay for a few weeks or even months. It was one hell of a relief at the start. Over time, though, I started remembering my life free from travel restrictions and hankered to experience it again. Thinking my only happy life was back in the past meant I had to rely on time travel to transport me to the moment before I swallowed the drugs and grab them from my sweaty palms to prevent the unleashing of the scary out-of-body/near-death experience that followed. The fact that this was impossible was a major fly in the ointment. I can't tell you how it irked me that it wasn't an option.

So, I have spent much of the last thirty-five years devising cunning plans (call it overthinking) to get me back to my pre-Glastonbury self. Talk about rose-tinted glasses. I conveniently forget that this young version of me was the one who accumulated all the stress that made me go pop at Glastonbury in the first place. To show you how it all fits together, here is a handy summary.

A brief history in time

1969: Born blue – surely a sign of superhero powers and not merely that I had severe oxygen deprivation (you'll find this 'blue baby' reference throughout the book. It represents my soul on a mission!)

1969 – 1980: Move from Holland to England – a tricky transition, changing primary schools three times, a near drowning, a close call with a fast-moving train, undiagnosed ADHD, high-stress home life. Definitely not living my best life at this time

1980 -1987: Moving schools twice, finding drugs, alcohol, self-harm, and bulimia, another two near drownings, discovering the power of people pleasing, and making a hash of it despite giving it my best shot

1987: Getting my own flat in the Royal Crescent, Bath, at the tender age of eighteen. What could go wrong?

1987 – 1990: The university years of more drugs, alcohol, and bulimia, but thankfully, a ditching of the self-harm. Still people-pleasing for England and eternally confused by the rules of that particular game.

1990: Exams taken from a hospital bed, big drug trip at Glastonbury, and 'Pop goes the Weasel', or in this case, young Helga.

Back to the intro...

These last three decades have been me trying to dip my toe outside of my self-created safe zone and rejoin the rest of the world. In this quest, I have turned to, amongst other helpful souls, the author Douglas Adams for help.

One of the best things about younger me, aside from all that reckless behaviour and iffy decision-making, was my intense passion for reading. Whilst trying to live up to whatever wild version of myself I thought society expected from me, all I actually wanted to do was curl up and read a good book. One of my favourites had to be *The Hitchhiker's Guide to the Galaxy*. Now, *that* was a world I wanted to inhabit. This is the point where I can't help but feel the urge to say, 'Be careful what you wish for, Helga.'

My drug trip at Glastonbury felt like it launched me, unwittingly, into an unknown galaxy, and I was as unprepared for this as Arthur Dent when he heard earth was to be destroyed in approximately twelve minutes. The only difference being, Douglas Adams helpfully handed his character Arthur, the invaluable *Hitchhiker's Guide to the Galaxy,* with the words 'Don't Panic' emblazoned across its front cover. Handy for Arthur, but less so for me with no guide to help me traverse the unknown.

What I did have was Douglas Adams' theory that the answer to life, the universe, and everything was (sic) 42, and with little in the way of options, I decided, tongue-in-cheek, to test just that.

It's no coincidence to me that Arthur Dent's spaceship was named the Heart of Gold—authenticity and love play an interesting part in my recovery—nor that it was equipped with an 'improbability drive' to manipulate the probability that Arthur could achieve the seemingly impossible. That's precisely what I needed, and I have come to discover that we all have this drive built in as part of our human factory settings. We can all achieve seemingly impossible things, provided we point ourselves in roughly the right direction. I have achieved a calm life, free from unmanageable fear. Daily, I'm doing new things that were, only a few short years ago, seemingly impossible. I hope this book points you in roughly the right direction too.

This is the tale of my travels through the forty-two different treatments I trialled to banish anxiety and panic from my life forever. To blast them into hyperspace. Time will tell how well that went. Along the way, I even wrote my own nifty guide called, *Don't Panic*. The very book you hold in your hands today. How cool is that?

Notes

Chapter 1 – Meditation

I currently meditate. Not very well and not often enough—a recurring theme for all my attempts at enlightenment—but I freely admit it helps.

I start most days plugged into the Calm app, listening to The Daily Trip—I just love the humanness of this 'Jeff' man —staring through my skylight at the gulls overhead and trying to take a few deliberate, slow breaths. More often than not, I flick through two or three different short morning meditations, giving my body some calm before I launch into the new day.

Then it's strong coffee and possibly the 'real' meditation for me—a dog walk in the Devon lanes. Twenty minutes into any walk, the need for me to DO anything evaporates as nature takes over, stress unravels, and the chatterbox in my head takes some much-needed time out.

Call me a kid, but I always try to catch a falling leaf at least once a year. It's way harder than you think and impossible to do unless you give it your fullest attention. I've been trying for months. On each attempt, I can't help smiling as I frantically run from tree to tree, hoping with every fibre of my being that I'm not being watched by the neighbours.

Note to self: stop people-pleasing, but hey, I can only take one step at a time.

These days, I'm finding it easier to experience my thoughts without getting in deep and wrestling pointlessly with the many uncomfortable ones. Clearly, I'm far from accomplished at this, but the word choice seems to pop up more often, and I question, 'Is this helpful?' The answer is usually a resounding no, and the chatter often mysteriously vanishes.

My go-to meditation image is sitting on a riverbank with my thoughts flowing past in the river below. I see them but resist the need to dive in for a swim. Imagining this helps me to step back a little and engage less messily with the tricky ones.

Rewind to a certain festival in Glastonbury 1990, and I had an experience that many lifetime meditators might consider to be quite the result. In fact, only last week, someone was waxing lyrical about the 'opportunity' of it all. I had a full-blown out-of-body experience, with my conscious (open to debate) self, floating high in the sky and looking down at my student body, lying spread-eagled in a field below.

Zen, some might imagine? A beautiful moment when my young spirit was freed from the shackles of its body to explore the wider spiritual plane?

In my reality, it was like driving the wrong way down the motorway with a juggernaut heading towards me at breakneck speed. No pleasure for me in that particular dabble into the spiritual realm.

It took over twenty-five years (and another dice with near death) before I was willing to see that meditation might have some genuine merits.

My first few tries at group meditations back in the early 1990s were rather disastrous. It scared the living daylights out of me. My anxious thinking ran riot. I sprinted out of my first session with major heart palpitations. Sorry to all the people trying to disconnect from the noisy world on that occasion. Although I guess it was a great opportunity for a bit of equanimity.

In the end, even the mere idea of relaxing deeply became linked to that experience at Glastonbury and the deep-seated fear that I might lose control again. Being anything other than hyper-vigilant seemed reckless.

I remember reading this quote from Katherine May in her book *Enchantment* that voices this feeling so precisely for me:

'Danger, when it is always imminent, does harm. It doesn't need to actually arrive. You exhaust yourself in the act of forever looking over your shoulder. Your body readies itself to fight and never quite discharges that chemical cocktail. You channel it instead into anger and self-pity and anxiety and hopelessness. You divert it into work. But really, what you do, with every fibre of your being, is watch. You are incessantly, exhaustingly alert. You don't dare ever let up in case the danger takes advantage of your inattention.'

I don't think it takes Einstein to see where this was heading. The learning I took from my Glastonbury trip was that in any situation where I perceived that I lacked rigorous control, anxious thoughts emerged. Warning bells should start ringing at this point. Wherever I looked, I was not in control. A train was unsafe unless I was driving, a pilot's licence was needed to go on a plane, keys were needed to go into any building lest I should get locked in. You can see how an innocent misunderstanding of how to keep myself safe resulted in chaos in my life. This chaos lasted a very long time.

From the day of the festival onwards, my sanity seemed to unravel at quite the pace. Initially, I panicked on the tube, then the bus, before viewing London, not just its transport system, as the problem.

When London became too overwhelming for me, I decided to do the only sane thing and chose the 'safety' of my family home in Wiltshire, which I had quit for legitimate reasons years earlier. This was the first of many errors. You may not be surprised how that one worked out.

I fell apart.

Slowly but surely, I avoided more and more things in my life, seeing danger in anything I didn't think I could control. Boy, was I clutching at those control straws frantically, yet failing to pick up a single one. Going from one bad idea to another, this was when I had the genius idea to bring in the X-rule. I stranded myself first in the Westcountry, then in the county of Devon, shrinking to Exeter and eventually the confines of a three-bedroom mid-terrace in the centre of the city. The start of my very own thirty-year lockdown.

Going back to Glastonbury, clearly, how much of that story is real and how much is a complete hallucinogenic fantasy is also debatable. There were many things about Glastonbury that messed with my sense of reality. It was nearly twenty-five years later, after a drunken late-night conversation at a party, that I found out that cars really did drive over the roof of the pyramid stage at Glastonbury '90 Festival, and that this, at least, was not just a part of my drugs experience. Michael Eavis, you have a lot to answer for!

The bottom line was that meditation, when I first tried it in the early 1990s as a cure for my anxiety, didn't deliver, and that was entirely due to user error.

The spiritual path became an absolute no-no for my younger self. The God-word terrified me, and everything vaguely outside of the everyday norm was flaky and potentially dangerous. The walls of my reality had crumbled once, and I was beyond scared that it could happen again.

Yet anxiety treatments in the 1990s were far from mainstream, and the treatments regularly involved dabbling in the unusual and often untested. Keeping anxiety as my dirty secret often left me an open goal for the purple-cloaked, unscrupulous anxiety mentors laser-focused on my bank balance—the only thing guaranteed to reduce under their tutelage.

Meditation, my absolute daily essential today, proved to be 'too scary' to embrace in the nineties.

I would have to find something else. Where to look next? Well, reflexology seemed a fairly unintimidating bet.

Chapter 2 – Reflexology

I tried reflexology a bit in the early 1990s and returned to it often as a 'safe bet' treatment. Admittedly, it took some getting used to, and the insanity of voluntarily allowing someone to tickle my feet was initially a kind of paid-for torture until I managed to relax and let go— note to self: there is a clue here. It calmed me down without feeling invasive. There was no danger of it messing with my mind, and it felt safe. This ticked a lot of boxes for my freaked-out younger self.

To further extol its virtues, reflexology was also my first foray into an entrepreneurial life.

On one of my father's many business trips across Europe, he met a man who crafted incredible things out of wood, including intricately carved chess sets, wooden bowls, and surprisingly, wooden reflexology foot massagers.

They were genuinely brilliant. A few minutes of teasing my feet across the wooden rollers welcomed more calm into my chaotic little life than a barrel full of my former go-to-of-choice, chilled Sauvignon Blanc. More surprising still was that my Daily Mail-reading father, who considered Marmite to be a bit 'out there,' should then decide to create a business venture selling the massagers in the UK.

To cut a long story short, it didn't work out for him, advertising his product to the unenlightened readers of his favourite rag, but it did leave a stockpile of wooden massagers that he passed to me at cost price. I seized the opportunity.

I rocked up at every village hall and reasonably sized fete this side of Wiltshire—I was obviously having a good phase with the X-rule—to show the people of the Westcountry what they had unknowingly been missing for the whole of their lives. I was positively evangelical as I coerced the elderly of Devon to rest their weary limbs on my sales chair extraordinaire, pop off their shoes and socks, and transport themselves to the place of bliss that I too had experienced. And it worked. Once you had felt the effects, rather than skip past an advert in The Mail, people were walking away with often two or three, to give as presents to loved ones, friends, or the favourite aunt that's impossible to buy for.

I sold the lot, made myself a nice stack of notes, and rather than re-invest them and develop something that could have turned out to be a nice little business, I spent the lot on testing out the next seriously expensive attempt to cure my mental distress. This was when a man in a pub told me about Feng Shui.

Notes

Chapter 3 – Feng Shui

It is a recurring pattern of my life that, being born an optimist, I bound into new opportunities with the unbridled zeal of a hyped-up Labrador puppy. It is within moments of trying something new that I am certain, without any doubt, that whatever wonder is being revealed to me in that moment will certainly be the absolute, guaranteed answer to my problems. Many thousands of pounds later, I have a hunch that may not be true, but for now, let's get back to the story.

I don't remember where I first heard about Feng Shui. Maybe I read an article in The Guardian as I waited for one of my many doctor's appointments. Maybe I really did chat to a man in a pub about it. Who knows, but with scant facts at my disposal, I was beyond certain that reorganising my home was the answer to not only revamping my literal front room, but more importantly, the mental front room of my brain.

So, with my whole house needing a rearrange, the most cost-effective approach seemed to be to buy a book. I bought a comprehensive guide to

Feng Shui. A thick tome that offered solutions to all areas of my home. The thing was, it was all a bit complicated for me. Overwhelmed and in desperate need of a quick fix, in a phase where the X-rule was defining X as no further than a couple of depressing miles, I decided to take my stash of recently-earned cash and find someone to help me. Nothing could dissuade me from Feng Shui being the answer to my problems, so no price was too high to pay for getting my freedom back. I surmised that when I was of sound mind and able to work in a 'proper' job again, I would reap the rewards and quickly be able to replenish my cash.

They must have seen me coming.

A quick search of the brand-new internet found me two wonderful saleswomen offering Feng Shui for the cut price of £500 a pop. If I flinched at the price tag initially, after a comforting brew of chamomile infused with who knows what, I was persuaded that it would be sheer insanity not to invest in myself, resolve my inner conflict, and go on to lead a happy and fulfilled life. The problem was, £500 never quite seemed to do it. For the first £500, my house was tested and found to be severely lacking. I'm not talking about the mere rearrangement of the furniture or the purchase of a leafy houseplant. No, I simply had to move as the combination of the road with the position of a distant river all culminated in me being in enormous peril if I stayed put. This, may I say, is not great news to deliver to a sufferer of deep-rooted anxiety.

So began the many estate agent viewings, accompanied by two canny 'feng shui masters.' Each trip another £500. How they must have enjoyed their days out, of which there were so very many. I'm sure I must appear in the memoirs of at least one Devon estate agent as I consulted my purple-clad gurus, who shook their heads at the proximity to water, the angle of the sun, the dominance of a doorway, and the angle of the stairs, to name but a few. Gardens were too sunny or not sunny enough, with the sun rising incorrectly or seemingly not at all. I can't remember whether it was the estate agents or my long-suffering partner who convinced me, many thousands of pounds and much heart-wrenching later, that these women didn't have my home serenity at the core of their decision-making. I didn't move with their help, and sadly, the whole episode brought my X-factor right back to home, and I fell into a depression that lasted many months. One could say, undoubtedly my fault for not having made an assisted move. So, where next, you might ask? It was, surprisingly, The Samaritans.

Notes

Chapter 4 – The Samaritans

This will be brief, but I have to thank the Samaritans for picking up the phone at night and talking me down from some of my most horrific panic attacks. I was living on my own at the time, and however bad my panic surged during the day, the nighttime took on a momentum of its own, and I would learn to dread the arrival of dusk. Dusk marked the arrival of the long, fearful nights where anything that terrified me during the day ramped to unbearable intensity as darkness fell. I thank the Samaritans who talked to me when I truly feared I might permanently lose my mind. Now my sanity has fully resumed, I will repay that kindness and volunteer myself.

There were times when I was right on the edge, and only the kind and calm voice of another human prevented me from losing myself completely into the abyss.

So, thank you Samaritans, and on to more chipper subjects. My next throw of the dice led me to homoeopathy and the meeting of a definite mentor in my life. A marvellous man called Michael.

Chapter 5 – Homeopathy

I don't remember the exact path that led me to Michael, but I was in a pretty sorry state when I arrived. His office was upstairs in an old building that brought on the following fears before I even sat down on his comfy office chair: fear of the entrance door locking and me being stuck forever in a building in a quiet street in Exeter. Fear that I would get lost on my way to his office and be, again, forever stuck. Fear that I would fall down the very steep stairs that led to his office in my desperate panic-laden rush to leave, and then when I finally reached his office, fear I would get locked in—he kindly let me keep the door open—and fear that I would embarrass myself with all my phobias, but that particular cat was already well and truly out of its metaphorical bag.

With all of this taken into consideration, you can imagine how I presented myself to him on that day. Yet, despite the most intense desire to run for safety, I took the brave step of staying in my chair and telling him a bit about my life.

The first thing to mention about this treatment is that, at this point in my life, I had a profound fear of death. Probably down to that rather spooky out-of-body experience. I couldn't even look at an undertaker's if I drove past. Against every sensible piece of advice contained in the highway code, I always turned my head and looked the other way. Given the option, I would drive miles out of my way to avoid any death-related scenery. What I was unaware of before making my appointment with Michael was that in addition to being a homeopath, he was also an end-of-life coach, so pretty much every book on his shelf had death in the title. My already terrified self simply didn't know where to look.

Now, as I write this, I realise I'm actually describing his second office that I visited many years later, but this leads me to an unrelated important point.

(Did I mention I have ADHD?)

Memory is surprisingly unreliable, and memories have a knack of jumping around in time and space. It has been a fairly recent revelation to me that my memories are actually stories I tell myself and are far from watertight. Too many times recently, 'cast-iron' memories have been challenged and crumbled under scrutiny. Bottom line, though, it doesn't matter which version of Michael I'm remembering. What I do know is that there was something uniquely calming about simply being in the presence of this man, despite all the death books.

I could tell him anything from my *The Hitchhiker's Guide to the Galaxy* theories about the Total Perspective Vortex, to my crippling and pervasive fear of death, which only shifted when faced with another near-death experience in 2016. In fact, he barely blinked at any of the extensive fears and insecurities that were plaguing my young mind and preventing me from finding any peace. He made me feel human, and despite all the things I revealed from my Mary Poppins bag of terrors, he never looked visibly alarmed, although he may have been frantically clutching the panic button underneath his desk. Who knows? Anyhoo, he made me feel there was hope and things were definitely going to get better. Priceless!

Much like all the topics in this book, I know very little about homeopathy. I have read a few books, and it seems that the amount of any substance in the remedy is so minuscule that sceptics wonder how it can have any effect at all.

All I know is that Michael gave me a remedy that lifted anxiety right out of my body. My anxiety had its own out-of-body experience, and I cannot tell you how mightily relieved I was. I remember sitting on my sofa at home, preparing to take the pill. Having had my bad drugs experience, taking another pill felt risky, thoughts of Laurel and Hardy saying, 'Well, that's another nice mess you got me into,' kept bobbing about in my mind.

However, feeling utterly broken and without a great deal to lose, I walked to a small car park by the side of my house, sat on a wall, took the pill, and waited nervously for something to happen.

What happened, though, on this occasion, was incredibly good. A phenomenal release. It was like all the fear and negative emotions whooshed out of my body. It didn't last, sadly, but that much-needed brief reprieve from fear gave me the chink of light I needed to carry on.

We tried many times after to get that same release with various remedies, and it never happened again, but I can cite that occasion as an absolute turning point in my journey to recovering my sanity.

The march towards a longer-term solution went on. Taking me to, oh my goodness, I can't quite express the excitement I feel about talking about this one. The one and only magical Maria. An angel in human form. One of the best people I have ever met.

Chapter 6 – Magical Maria and The Serene Space

What you may note is that I'm not true to any kind of accurate timeline in these ramblings. I genuinely don't believe it matters. Sometimes, the order of life events is key, and other times, I'm happy to pop in a story totally out of context because I want to tell you about it. Let me introduce you to the concept of 'The Serene Space.'

Firstly, I want to let you know that I appreciate that it's a privileged indulgence to have a room to call completely mine. I don't have one currently and have very often not lived with such luxury. However, for one wonderful phase of my life, I had The Serene Space. A room of my own.

I have to thank a truly incredible human called Maria, an angel now weaving her magic in another realm, for this. Maria was a reflexologist I visited to help myself regain a little calm at a particularly difficult time on my journey.

Little did I know the incredible, life-altering person I was going to meet. Maria was petite, a little older than me, and of Italian heritage. I say this so her family might recognise her if they ever read this book (hello, Rita, if you are) and realise what an incredible difference she made to me.

Note to self: Perhaps it would be easier to write to them.

Back to Maria. I met her at her office. This brought on the full array of usual fears. It was upstairs, so faced with locks, small spaces, and meeting someone new. My go-to instinct in her waiting room was to run at speed and escape before this 'therapist' could open her door. Fortunately, I left it a fraction too late, and there stood Maria with her amazing smile.

It still makes me teary when I think about her, as at the time, she was dealing with a terminal diagnosis, and despite knowing this, she chose to expend her precious available energy to help others.

Putting her own pain aside, she was entirely focused and saw with clarity how she might use her gift to help. I remember her asking me about the X-rule for travel and questioning gently where that line might be. Could I have one foot in Devon and another in Dorset—easily done in Lyme Regis—and how might that be? Could my two feet have a completely different experience on any given day? It was the first time I had properly questioned the X-rule in such a simple way.

No, it didn't make sense that one foot would be okay and the other engulfed in panic. So, she gently probed where my imaginary line lay. Was it something I could physically draw on the ground? If I hopped from one side to the other, would it fundamentally alter the way I felt?

It was difficult to answer, and I was puzzled. Yes, I countered, there were absolute lines. Like crossing the channel. So, she asked again, was the beach in Dover okay and a toe in the sea water a problem? Let me be clear, she never once made me feel foolish, but she did encourage me to probe the validity of the X-rule. It certainly gave my subconscious something to chew on.

At the time, I was living in a house that reflected my broken state. I get the irony, by the way, that it possibly wasn't the Feng Shui that was at fault but the way that it was practised in a wildly unregulated UK. Cupboard doors were hanging off their hinges, locks were broken, door handles hung loosely from their fittings, the heating was sporadic, with over half the radiators not working, fence panels flapped hopelessly in the wind, and mould grew defiantly on the window ledges. In reality, the house was beautiful. I can see that now, as was my life, with my incredible children cascading sunshine into my days, but being surrounded by dysfunction in my home was having a seriously negative impact on my mental state.

Maria saw this immediately and questioned how I felt when I was at home. 'I feel like I'm suffocating. I feel overwhelmed. No matter what I do, I can't make the space beautiful. I feel trapped.'

'Could you create a space of your own?' she questioned. 'A space, no matter how tiny, that can be your perfect sanctuary and 'escape'.'

I told her that no such space exists, yet amidst all my noisy objections, a small idea popped determinedly into my head. That being the repurposing of my husband's beloved cinema room as my Serene Space.

So, the challenge was set. How to convince my film-loving partner that not only should he dismantle his man-space to make way for mine, but he should also get out his paintbrushes and rollers to redecorate it to create my perfect blank canvas. All credit to him, and the fact that we also had a gigantic projector upstairs in our lounge, he did help me to create my perfect space, putting up curtains, hanging pictures, and painting over years of mould.

I cannot begin to explain the sheer joy I experienced putting this room together. From moving to my first flat in The Royal Crescent—£22 a week with an eccentric landlord who used to bring us bags of weed and would often 'forget' to collect the rent—to my room at university, and every other house since, I have loved creating a beautiful space.

I positively zing with energy when I'm making a space my own, choosing photos, books, bed coverings, ornaments that all have meaning and make me feel truly at home. Wherever I looked, the Serene Space was filled with beauty, and it screamed out such a clear desire to be free, from the choice of art on the walls to the books overflowing from my oversized bookshelves; I am a self-confessed book addict. The Serene Space was my dream space. My life free from the pressures and judgements of the outside world. A space where I could shut the door and be my frenetic self from blasting out the Stone Roses to freewriting my journal, to dancing without a jot of coordination, to eating bowls of liquorice torpedoes at midnight.

Those four walls were my freedom, my deep sigh, my letting go of all tension. A feeling many get when they go on holiday. So, the Serene Space was my escape, my Narnia, but way warmer with my trusty fan heater and Paul Oakenfold helping to create a warming Ibiza vibe.

It enabled me to enter another world, and I was so busy dancing and singing at the top of my voice that I missed the distant rumble of something shifting in my universe. A crack was appearing in my distorted world view, and things were beginning to shift in a good way.

It is not lost on me—'lost' being an interesting choice of word and one of my most deep-seated fears—and worthy of a mention that my anxieties have been attached to things I love in a way that clearly defies coincidence. It has certainly been an effective way of grabbing my attention.

Had anxiety prevented me from cleaning out my car, doing the laundry, or filing my tax return, I might not have had the impetus to seek the forty-two different ways to overcome these obstacles in my life, but focusing my fears on boats, planes, holidays, and any chance of working abroad for an overseas aid charity, it was clear I was not going to get through life without cutting back the fast growing thicket of fears that threatened to engulf my precious existence. Who knew that when I understood more and made a few decisive cuts, the thicket would start to shrink back all on its own?

But back in the noughties, I didn't know any of this and continued blindly on my impossibly hard quest to remove anxiety completely from my life. I did, at this time, not ponder the fact that anxiety might merely be an emotion, much like joy or excitement, and it was as much a part of my human experience as the much sought-after happiness. And that, far from focusing my attention on removing it, I might perhaps consider looking a little deeper into what it might be attempting to alert me to. No, all that would require a level of bravery I didn't believe I possessed. I went out of my way NOT to look at my anxiety at all. I just wanted it gone.

It was so unbearably scary, and dealing with it required resilience that the thirty-something version of me wasn't prepared for. I simply wanted a quick fix, so off I travelled in search of this, with the next destination to present itself to me being tapping or Emotional Freedom Technique (EFT).

Notes

Chapter 7 – Emotional Freedom Technique

I heard about tapping from a friend, and not the sort of friend you would expect to offer any solution that was not clear-cut, black and white, and solidly based on science. This was my straight-talking friend. Everyone should have one.

I am fortunate to have many friends, and this particular one was one of my most reliable, but very much in a 'pub and a pint' kind of way.

So, for this friend to tell me her school buddy, who had been at absolute rock bottom with depression, had taken up tapping and was now living the Dolce Vita was beyond intriguing.

I couldn't get on the internet fast enough to find me a practitioner.

This scenario may be becoming familiar to you now.

I get an idea, find the first person whose name pops up and I like the sound of for some reason, hand over a pile of cash, and anticipate that within a short while, my long-standing difficulties with anxiety will be magically resolved.

I'm very much a pint half-full kind of girl—even with anxiety.

Having never heard of EFT, I found a reasonably local person, had a brief chat on the phone, and booked myself an appointment.

This woman was firmly in the camp that believed, without the slightest element of doubt, that she could speedily eliminate my anxiety forever. Within less than three sessions, I believe she claimed. She was unflinching in her certainty.

I was sold, as I am sure you can imagine. It was the hot summer of 1996.

If you know the *Three Lions* song from Euro '96, you'll know the words, '*thirty years of hurt, never stopped me dreaming*'.

I was positively punching the air, so excited to know that before the month was out, the anxiety I felt was ruining my life would finally be kicked out.

I started to think about all the things I would be able to do again.

This woman was certain. She had a magic method. I had found it at last.

Now, I see things differently.

Anxiety is a normal, healthy functioning part of my humanness, and she was no more capable of eliminating my anxiety than she was of stopping me from laughing, crying, or expressing any other of my normal, human emotions. I guess what she intended was to bring down my anxiety to a lower level, so it wouldn't have such a profound effect on my life. That's not what she promised, though. She promised a complete elimination.

Something that occurs to me now and is indirectly an apology to many of the forty-two practitioners who worked with me over the years is that if I had NOT held the expectation that my anxiety would be eliminated, I might not have been so hyper-vigilant, scanning myself for the merest hint of a heart flutter, sweat to the palm, or dry mouth after any therapy.

This would, in turn, have stopped me from wrongly concluding that every therapy had failed the minute I felt almost any sensation in my body, which I then slapped with the label 'anxiety.'

But I wanted it all gone and hunted for anxiety in my body. This was the only thing I applied myself to methodically on my quest, and not surprisingly, this focus created anxious symptoms. I was terrified those anxious symptoms would then escalate into a full-blown panic attack, and this intensified my symptoms even more. I began to fear the fear feelings that came before a panic attack. I would run to the safety well before any attack came on.

Had I done a better experiment on my anxiety, with a control to see if running really was the answer, I might have found the road to recovery more quickly. But hey, I'm an artist, not a scientist! I didn't clock this and continued thinking in my rather skewed way.

It would be many years before I realised my own misguided thoughts were creating my anxiety, not the million and one external situations I blamed it on. I was totally okay, but for the thought that I was not. There is a great TED talk by Kelly McGonigal on how to make stress your friend—I love her 'biology of courage' concept.

A classic example of this was my unwillingness to get into a car with anyone other than my nearest and dearest. If I was going anywhere, I always needed to drive. I also had to physically have the car keys on me, so the car could not be moved, leaving me 'stranded.' If I was going out to a café, I would drive, have my car keys in my pocket, regularly check that they were there, obsessed that if I couldn't escape at the exact moment I wanted to, I would have a meltdown.

If all the above applied, I could happily sit in that cafe for three hours or more and not have a panic attack. However, if I thought I had lost my keys or a friend was in control of the car, anxious feelings would surge, and I would need to run. Control was everything.

Letting go of this need for control over my travel has been a very recent thing. Now I think, why couldn't I have called a taxi? I know why, though. It was because I needed to know I could leave the second I wanted to. Any delay could result in anxiety building to an uncomfortable level, and that was quick for me.

It's one of the reasons I couldn't go on public transport. I was scared of the gaps in the timetables. When I arrived at a destination, there might be a thirty-minute wait for the next bus home, and even if I didn't want to go home, I would start thinking about feeling 'stuck.' Just thinking that would bring on my anxious symptoms. If I had a cast-iron way of getting home quickly, I wouldn't need to escape, and my anxiety would settle.

When I did find myself stuck and had no choice but to deal with it, the way I used to cope was to imagine a variety of escape methods that would get me home safely.

I would tell myself stories about how I could get away, knowing I wasn't going to do any of them, but to give me options. I would focus all my energy on thinking about escape whilst trying desperately to push the panic thoughts aside. This often worked to some extent, but it exhausted me.

It didn't occur to me that my running away strategy wasn't doing anything at all. It was just a habit with a story attached. I believed it reduced my panic, and because I considered it to be true, it worked. I might as well have said, 'liquorice reduces panic' and eaten a sherbet Dip-Dab. I'm surprised someone didn't charge me £500 to chew on a liquorice stick and jog on the spot. I probably would have handed over the money as long as they'd given it a fancy therapy name, maybe 'the root technique' or something.

What was a jaw-dropping revelation to me was that other so-called 'normal' people, including me before the drug trip, often had the same physical sensations I hated but hadn't had the thought to panic about them. Whaaaaat? They had the same feelings but didn't care? Yup! That appears to be true.

Someone asked me once, 'What do you stand to gain from your anxiety?' which didn't elicit the most positive of responses, but as with all difficult questions, it made me think. I have a fairly strong hunch about it now, but that's for later.

Back to the EFT. So, I arrived at this woman's house, and she seemed nice. Super confident in her method, and I truly believed I had found The One.

She said it would only take a few weeks. Hallelujah!

I spent week after week at this woman's house, learning how to tap. I tapped at home, but not as much as I should have, and my initial supreme confidence that 'this is it' started to wobble. This was very depressing because I had, again, invested heavily financially and emotionally in this being the answer.

I was also beginning to wind up my practitioner, and she made a bold promise that I could have endless free sessions, after having paid for fifteen without success, until we cracked this problem.

She was getting a bit like a driving instructor with first time test passes. I was ruining her statistics. EVERYONE got better within a few weeks!

Not being a keen taker in life, I offered to help her in other non-monetary ways, which unleashed a beast in her, and from then on, nothing I ever did met her exacting standards.

Things began to get tense. I got more anxious, not less. She suggested I lock myself in the loo at her house and tap myself calm. I did eventually agree to do this, but I tapped myself into an absolute frenzy and burst out of the toilet with my heart banging out of my chest.

She assured me this was great progress. My doubts grew.

And so it went on until it all became rather excruciating. She couldn't bear that I wasn't one of her miracle stories, and I couldn't bear her over-controlling ways.

We decided to part company.

I was not cured.

Notes

Chapter 8 – Hypnotherapy

Onwards and upwards on my quest. So, all I desired at that moment in my life was instant gratification. I know. Eye roll moment. I'm the classic hare, and as we all know, it's the tortoise that wins the race. I like things to happen quickly. Very quickly. Whether it's getting to a healthy weight or training for a marathon, whatever needs to be done, I want to be there yesterday with minimal effort. As you can imagine, this has not served me enormously well in life. As soon as a long lead-in time is required—I certainly didn't see thirty-five years looming on the horizon to solve this particular conundrum—I quit unless there is no other alternative available to me. When faced with ZERO choice—whether it's a panic attack, running a restaurant after I have signed the lease, or staying in my seat once the plane has taken off—I crack on and deal with it remarkably well, but will take the easier option if it presents itself to me. Who wouldn't?

This quirk of my personality, therefore, made hypnotherapy most appealing to me. Often, it was said, in as little as one pricy session, I could be entirely free of anxiety and skip off to lead a 'normal' life.

It was like catnip to a greedy pussycat. Irresistible.

There were many different attempts with this one. Each time a session didn't deliver, bearing in mind I was striving for the impossible—complete elimination of anxiety, which is not actually achievable—I would be lured, much like my scratch card addiction, into believing that the next session would be 'the one.'

When things didn't go to plan, it wasn't just me who was disappointed.

One hypnotherapist, who lived in the middle of nowhere, the only approach down the narrowest imaginable single-track lane—my anxiety used to flare just at the thought of going there—concluded rather too swiftly that I was possessed, and I would need some sort of exorcism to remove the demons that were plaguing me.

If you bear in mind that I won't even watch *The Goonies* because it's a bit too scary and am definitely scarred by teenage horror nights of the past, you can imagine what that diagnosis did to my anxious little mind. I was totally freaked out. The last thing you want to hear when you have anxiety is that there is indeed something wrong with you, probably something unfixable, and that society may be forced to throw away the key. If anyone reading this is having any such harsh thoughts, let me reassure you that anxiety is normal, you can totally calm it down to acceptable levels, and you may even come to appreciate (you will have to bear with me on this one) the important role it might play in guiding you to where you should be in your life.

Anyway, after reporting the therapist for her dubious approach to some even more dubious 'regulator' of the industry and receiving a letter back that she had been rapped on the knuckles but would continue to offer her specific brand of hypnotherapy to other unsuspecting and vulnerable people, I decided I would cast hypnotherapy aside forever and seek an alternative cure.

Watching a famous stage hypnotist on daytime TV a year later and getting the itch again—I saw a woman, terrified of heights, walk across a sickeningly high bridge—I determined to see if the celeb himself could help me.

The person I found claimed to be an assistant of the famous hypnotist and had trained with him and learned all the same skills. He was charging a gazillion pounds per hour, and I needed to make my way to Wimbledon; a horrifying thought. He claimed it would take one session. It would definitely work. With the true level of optimism that I believe only I possess, I persuaded my jaded husband to not only part with the sizeable amount of cash required, but to drive a quaking me up to

London for the treatment of all treatments. The one that would, without a doubt in the world, one hundred percent work.

I arrived at a very dismal-looking small office, knocked on the locked door, and entered the tiny reception to be shown to a room where a laid-back man was sprawled in his chair, his receptionist shouting back at him, 'I'm just off for lunch,' as she left, locking the front door and my only exit out.

Panic surging immediately, I told him I couldn't bear to be locked in and could we please unlock the door, or at least put the key in it so I had a way out. He told me this was the perfect scenario to begin our treatment, so he carried out a number of different exercises (which I have tried again since with more success) on me there and then, sure to banish my anxiety forever.

I have to say, far from calming me down, I was internally climbing the walls, and it took every ounce of my self-control—mastered after years of masking anxiety—not to run screaming to the front door and plead to be let out, which in fairness, he said he wouldn't do anyway.

This went on for an hour. I was traumatised. His receptionist came back after enjoying a delicious sandwich in a nearby eatery, and I handed over the cash, making a mad dash to my husband in his waiting car and begging him to drive at breakneck speed back to the safety of the Westcountry.

Before I left, the hypnotherapist dropped this final little nugget with me. If I, in any way, doubted any element of the treatment I had just experienced, it would not work, and it would be entirely my fault for not having followed his precise instructions. This was a stroke of genius on his part.

On the way back in the car, my partner asked me how it went.

'Oh, great,' I said, not wanting to bring about his prognosis of doom for those who doubt. 'Wow. That's great. So, do you think this is the one that is going to make all the difference?'

'Absolutely,' I replied, and I carried on this little charade for about two months before I caved in and admitted it hadn't made the slightest bit of difference. If anything, it had totally knocked my confidence.

Years later, I had another go with a friend, and it was an altogether more positive experience, although I do wish she hadn't mentioned Generalised Anxiety Disorder, as that certainly got the wonky thoughts free-flowing. Anyway, she was kind and calm, and the treatment certainly made me more relaxed. I was still, at this point, under the misapprehension that I wanted my anxiety to go entirely, so even the slightest rise in heart rate would be slapped with an anxiety label by me, meaning the treatment was quickly dismissed as yet another failed attempt. At the time, any tiny sign that I could interpret as anxiety set me down a thought rabbit hole, and I could get terribly lost.

In effect, whatever that first little feeling was, normally sweaty palms, it was the trigger to press play on 'The Panic Attack is Coming' movie that I had written, produced, and directed in my mind. An avalanche of anxious thoughts followed, and not surprisingly, I moved closer to the point of a panic attack every time I watched it. Interestingly, I have not had that many full-blown panic attacks at all in life. I've felt intensely fearful, but like any good movie, I got caught up in the story and didn't realise I was helpfully suspending my disbelief rather than critically challenging the contents of my film. I now see the 'Panic Attack is Coming' trailer and take zero notice. It was a B-movie at best.

What I have learned since, call it a top tip, is that if I notice that first little niggling indicator and look it square in the eye as opposed to looking fearfully away, I usually see it's nothing more than a pretty neutral feeling, much like the funny sensation you get before you sneeze. A nudge that something may be about to happen. Not something catastrophic, just a little indicator that I might be rushing around too much and not breathing properly. Many of my early indicators, such as feeling like I'm in a dream, racing heart, and sweaty palms, are signs that I'm breathing shallowly, and a few deep breaths can give my hard-working body a top-up of much-needed oxygen, enabling me to relax. Without fail, those pre-anxious feelings dissipate.

Obviously, historically, any such small sign or physical symptom would make me breathe even more shallowly, flooding my brain with doom scenarios like the old favourite where I lose my mind whilst wailing loudly, drawing enough attention to me to ensure I embarrass myself to an untimely death (hmm – never seen that on a death certificate). This was how my thought process ran.

I write this not to be facetious. Those feelings were absolutely real to me at the time. I am rather curious now about the thoughts that lay behind those feelings, but I do want to shed some light on the effect that this labelling had on my overall anxiety levels. It makes me think of a cartoon mad professor, randomly taking samples of experiences in little specimen bottles and sticking incorrect labels on them in the lab, but I digress...

If I feel a small increase in heart rate and choose to label it 'excited about going out,' or 'rush of love for my children,' or quite possibly due to my love of eating rich food, 'indigestion,' I don't immediately spiral into panic. During the many decades of severe anxiety, I was exceptionally slap-happy and plastered 'severe danger' warnings on even the slightest adrenaline-based sensation. This enabled my exceptionally well-rehearsed disaster planning strategy to kick in with immediate effect, namely running away at speed and hiding in the nearest safe space, ideally under a duvet.

It got to the point that I couldn't drink coffee anywhere other than in places I deemed safe by my X-rule (with X varying depending on my overall stress levels). Caffeine creates in me feelings that are similar to anxiety. My heart can race, my thoughts can get distorted if I have too much, and all in all, the speeded-up feelings that I'm perfectly happy to accept when attributed to coffee are the exact same feelings that plunge me into terror if I incorrectly label them as the start of an anxiety attack. How can the same physical feelings be both truly dreadful and completely acceptable depending on my labelling? This is most curious.

At my anxious peak, if I had a coffee in an area I wasn't comfortable in, I was unable to be 100% sure if it was the coffee that was making me feel that way or the location, so I felt I had to stop drinking it altogether. I became scared to drink coffee away from home.

This tells me two things. One, coffee probably isn't that great for me personally, but more importantly, I'm totally fine with those early-stage feelings if I can find a pleasant enough label to confidently attach to them, like it's the caffeine that's making my heart race, NOT anxiety. This can't help but bring me to the conclusion that my feelings might actually be pretty safe. Could the problem be as simple as the meaning I attribute to those much-maligned physical symptoms? If it's coffee, love, excitement, or even 'good' anticipation, I feel absolutely fine.

The problems only stack up if I can't find an 'acceptable' label quickly enough. I look around for an external cause for the sensation, find nothing concrete, anticipate a panic attack, and then all hell breaks loose in my body as I try to hold back the tsunami of panic, not noticing that it was me who plugged in the thought wave machine.

This explains why the X-rule was initially so effective. It was a lovely, clear label for what would be okay for me and what would not.

If I had the start of anxious feelings in my 'safe' zones, I would swiftly tell myself to ignore them and I would be fine. Lo and behold, I always was.

If I was outside the 'safe' zone, I would be on red alert for potential problems, constantly body scanning for early signs of anxiety. The fear that I might panic would cause me inadvertently to hold my breath, and the lack of oxygen would make me feel light-headed. This was interpreted as the dreaded 'dream-state' that would scare me silly that I was losing my mind and hallucinating again. Big surge of adrenaline, panic movie played in my head, and I ran to escape. That took enough time for my panic to go down, and I attributed the reduced physical feelings to the fact that I was successfully back in the safe zone. If I had stayed put, the feelings would have decreased too. The trouble was, I would then have checked for panic again, and the loop would have been triggered again. At the time, I didn't see any of this.

I'm typing this sitting at Agatha Christie's desk in the suite she spent her honeymoon in at The Grand Hotel in Torquay. The reason I mention this is that I stayed there ten years ago and had the most profound panic attacks of my life. It was twenty-five miles from my home, and I can remember trying to take my children on holiday and feeling unable to travel any distance at all. I chose this hotel as it had a fancy suite, and the children got excited about that rather than focusing on the fact that we were still pretty much in our own neighbourhood. I remember lying in bed, unable to sleep, with waves of panic cascading over me from the sheer perceived distance from home and safety. Feeling these intense feelings and having no choice but to go through them was harsh and exhausting, but also, interestingly, provided another chink of light. I saw that I could emerge on the other side of a panic attack and survive. With the children tucked up in bed and unable to drive due to using alcohol as a coping strategy, I couldn't run this time. I had to ride it out. I had to look the panic attack in the eye. It was interestingly not quite as bad as I had imagined.

Having experienced raised levels of anxiety for many years, what I lost over time was the energy and confidence to battle with it, to do that brave thing and take panic on. Maybe battle is the wrong term anyway. It certainly felt like a battle. I wish I could have just accepted those early signs and not responded, but I innocently picked up bad habits, things I thought helped, but which made everything many times worse.

I was operating from some incorrect underlying core beliefs, and this meant that no amount of seemingly clever thinking on my part—and I tried very hard—would ever result in me arriving at the right conclusion.

I give you a few of my many wonky thoughts.

Wonky Thought 1: If I am X distance from home, I will not have a panic attack.

- **Assumption**: It is the distance from home that is affecting my anxiety.

- **Niggling inconsistency I ignore**: X changes all the time, so how can a specific distance be the issue? Where is the line? Can I really be one foot in and one foot out of my comfort zone?

- **Scientific(ish) fact**: Humans love a habit, and if you do a behaviour repeatedly, it becomes second nature. That includes running away to 'fix' anxiety.

Wonky Thought 2: Running back to safety reduces my anxious feelings.

- **Assumption**: As I am running away from a situation, the anxious feelings start to recede, so it must be the 'escape' from the place that is getting rid of my anxiety. Therefore, the place must be the cause of my anxious feelings. Advice to self: Avoid more places.

- **Niggling inconsistency I ignore:** Might those feelings not recede anyway, as anxiety is energy, and it cannot be sustained at its full intensity? Have I tested staying put? How can the places that caused my anxiety vary? For example, one day Lyme Regis is fine, the next it's making me physically sick.

- **Scientific(ish) fact**: Anxiety comes in waves, and when it has peaked, it comes down again. Always. Any other conclusion is like trying to argue against gravity. This begs the question, is running away really what is improving my anxiety, or is running away expending a bit of energy, and more importantly, giving anxiety the time it needs to recede? You guessed it. Staying put —and running on the spot—also works. As does having an ice cream and wholeheartedly focusing on how it tastes, thereby focusing on the moment rather than disaster planning. I would go for the ice cream option every time.

Wonky thought 3 (thought 2 expanded): Certain places and 'things' cause my anxiety.

- **Assumption**: When I am on a train, in a supermarket, or on a plane, my anxiety levels rise, therefore, those situations cause my anxiety.

- **Niggling inconsistency I ignore**: I have all those same feelings when I think about any of the above, even when I'm sitting in the comfort of my living room. This is an indisputable fact. This forces me to question how those things can be causing me to feel anxious if I can feel equally as anxious even thinking about them at home. It is my thoughts that create the anxiety. If I was in a deep sleep and I was put on a train without ever knowing about it (please don't do this), my body would not create an anxious response. Therefore, it cannot be the train that causes my anxiety; it must be my thinking.

- **Scientific(ish) fact:** Every thought we experience creates a chemical reaction in the brain, which then triggers an emotion. There is much useful science you can read on this topic. It was never the planes, trains, and automobiles that were causing my anxious reaction, even though it felt that way. It was only ever my thoughts, often quietly triggered by a forgotten memory. This explained why the things that caused my anxiety were forever changing, increasing or decreasing depending on my stress levels. I have to confess, all of this is still a bit hard to get my head around too, so I'm off for a coffee!

Ultimately, I don't want you to lose the will to read, so I will leave it there, but you get my drift. It is definitely worth checking in with some of your 'absolute certain beliefs' and asking yourself, is that really true? What is the evidence to support that belief? Have a dig. I was amazed at how many things surrounding my anxious beliefs crumbled to dust under a bit of closer scrutiny. Crumbling to dust or falling away is the most joyous outcome of doing a bit of inner probing. Certain anxious thoughts don't stack up to serious examination, and once you see something for what it really is, it's impossible to hold on to that anxious belief. I super recommend giving it a go!

A little example…

Scenario: You're driving along a road at dusk, and you see something lying in the road, moving about in a worrying way.

If you're me, you immediately get panicky feelings because it looks like an injured animal, probably a deer, has strayed into the road and has been hit by a speeding car. As I approach the 'animal,' my anxiety builds, and I start thinking about what I will do next. Will I be able to cope seeing the injuries? How will I get the deer into my car to see a vet? I'm anxious just typing this, even though I'm sitting at my dining table. So, I get to the scene of the 'accident,' and I discover it's actually a sack of earth that has fallen off the back of a lorry and the hessian sacking is flapping about in the wind.

Can I seriously continue feeling anxious about this now? No. It just isn't possible because I have seen it for what it really is—a sack of earth—and I cannot 'buy' into the anxiety story anymore. In such situations, without me doing a single thing, the anxiety disappears. This, surprisingly, and joyfully, also happens when I get curious about my thinking in other situations. Once the penny drops and I catch a thought of the wonky variety, it makes zero sense to press play on the panic movie in my mind.

I simply can't muster up the energy to do it. It makes no sense. So, I have a cuppa and wait for the dodgy thought/feeling to pass, which it always does.

Weirdly, I also do this 'bring it on' thing, whereby I ask my body to turn up my anxious feelings to their max. For whatever reason, this seems to take my feelings down rather than increase them. I think it's because it makes me feel brave and is the extreme opposite of running away. It's a bit like entering a jalapeno-eating competition. I'm drawn to it. Intrigued to see how bad it could be.

By facing my fear rather than looking away, I usually find there's nothing much there, and my anxiety recedes. The worst thing I can do is try to escape from my anxious thoughts because it allows my super creative mind to blow up the thoughts so they are so much bigger than any reality, and you can imagine what follows.

I remember someone telling me about this technique and me thinking, 'Have you lost your actual mind?'

Why would I want to increase the very feelings that terrify me? It's strange how looking something squarely in the eye, though, does enable you to see it for what it is. It works. It's hard, and sometimes, I simply can't face doing it, but it does break down my wonky thoughts that have no substance behind them.

Overall, I recommend having a spring clean of your thoughts and beliefs and checking if they are still serving you well. All systems need a tidy up, whether it's your inbox at work, the gear in your loft gathering dust, or wonky thoughts feeding your over-alert brain. I had a huge load of beliefs that looked super water-tight on initial examination but fell apart quicker than cheap flat-pack furniture under more rigorous testing. If I had to review the quality of my anxious thinking, I would give it 0 stars out of five in a review. It looked good enough for me to buy into at the time, but it was poor quality. I should have demanded a refund, and I certainly wouldn't buy into any of it now.

So, here I am, typing at Agatha's desk, drinking coffee with no fear of the caffeine rush and wanting to give my younger self a big squeeze and tell her in ten years, she will be fine and writing a tome to hopefully help others. Boy, would she have loved to hear that!

Finally, back to the hypnotherapy. I have revisited it in recent years, and it has massively helped to have a spring clean of my subconscious and check out some of the false facts that I've stacked up there from my past. We pick up information from so many different sources when we're growing up. Much of it is nonsense, and we don't realise how it can impact on our current feelings.

Pick carefully if you do go down this route. A fabulous hypnotherapist from Plymouth helped me enormously to clear out some of my baggage. Thankfully, she was not cloaked head to foot in purple—although, it was on Zoom, and who knows what happens beyond the screen—didn't exorcise any demons or charge me £800 an hour. I have definitely learned over the years that it is often not the techniques but the practitioners. They weave the magic. The vehicle they use for it can be incidental.

Notes

Chapter 9 – Don't 'Feel the Fear' - Feel the Curiosity

If at any point over the past thirty years you wanted to wind me up, it would be by telling me to feel the fear and do it anyway.

My husband won't mind me saying that he is terrified of birds. A bird flew into our kitchen in one of the rented houses we lived in many years ago, and he went absolutely wild. He flailed around, hyperventilated, and bashed into things in a blind panic to get out of the room. I totally understood this, and it was accepted that he simply didn't like birds. Perfectly normal. Nothing to talk about here.

This same man, who definitely knew fear, who I had seen appear to lose his mind with panic, would still tell me to 'man up' and 'feel the fear' when it came to anxiety. When things flared up badly and I believed I couldn't go even a few miles from home, he would helpfully roll out that Nike slogan and tell me to 'Just do it.' It didn't help. I think I now know why.

Telling someone they are not afraid of something when they feel all the physical symptoms of fear is utterly ridiculous and not at all helpful. I believe now that my anxious feelings are very much linked to my self-esteem, so having your feelings negated by another person and being told that what you feel is not true or valid exacerbates the feeling of not being good enough.

I fully understand this is likely NOT the intention of any well-balanced person when they are cajoling an anxious person to try something that terrifies them. I'm sure they truly believe the anxious person may be that lucky one in a hundred person whose anxiety crumbles when they are pushed into facing their fears.

For me and many other sensitive souls pushed hard by another well-meaning person when feeling not yet ready, it is anything but the way forward. Gently encouraged? Now that's another thing altogether.

Much like my husband would not appreciate being pushed into an aviary, my anxious feelings, brought on by not feeling good enough, did not delight in being told just to get on with it.

The majority of people whose anxious feelings regularly run amok can already see their fears are not logical, but logic goes out of the window when those intense physical symptoms rear their ugly heads.

However, within this 'feel the fear' method, there is something extremely beneficial that can be experienced when this method is applied in a different way.

When the person with anxiety applies curiosity and experimentation to their anxiety, on their own terms, in their own time, when they feel ready to step out (am I stressing this enough?), then, and only then, interesting things can happen.

One could argue I was very lucky in that my anxiety was so all-encompassing that finding situations that prompted me to launch into full-blown anxiety were many and varied, making experimentation simple and lower in risk.

For those whose fear is flying, it's a bold step to get on the plane, and I understand why 'testing out' what I'm going to talk about next could be much trickier.

For me, I could feel anxious being in a crowd, driving down a narrow lane near my home, in a lift, locking a toilet door. You name it, I would potentially have an anxious response to the situation.

Any number of things in my 'safe' local area could bring on panic and the associated physical symptoms that terrified me.

I remember feeling fine whilst shopping with my children when my daughter innocently mentioned that the shop entrance was getting congested. Just her saying that prompted me to scan my body for anxiety, and in doing so, launched me into shallow, panicky breathing. Lo and behold, my anxious response fully kicked in. I remember running out of the shop in tears, thinking, 'Why did she have to say that?' as if her innocent remark had been the cause of my panic attack.

Closer to the truth was that I was deeply fearful of having a panic attack, so much so that I couldn't allow myself to even think about it for a moment.

I would work so hard to push away thoughts of anxiety and resist all the feelings, that all the resisting just made my feelings stronger and last longer.

I'm not sure who said, 'What you resist persists,' but it is certainly true for my anxiety.

I was constantly saying to myself, 'don't think about anxiety,' and I would, of course, then think about it more, fuelling the unwanted feelings and making everything worse. It was one of my least helpful thought loops.

The 'feel the fear and do it anyway' approach was constantly being forced on me by well-meaning people and did nothing to improve my anxiety.

What did work for me was the 'dip your toe into fear, hesitantly welcome it in at your own pace, have a few little peeks followed by bigger ones until you are brave enough to push through some of the barriers and come out the other side' approach. A bit long-winded, I know.

In real-life terms, this is what it would look like to me:

Walking the Horseshoe

A classic example of the 'dip the toe' approach was my desire to do this beautiful circular walk near my home called The Horseshoe.

I was genuinely scared to be more than a certain distance from home for fear I would have a panic attack. I was also terrified of getting lost, even with a maps app on my phone. Despite this, I very much wanted to go on this particular five-mile walk near my house.

It was a circular route and there was very little chance of me getting lost, but I had never completed it before. I didn't know what the route looked like. I wouldn't know for certain when I had reached halfway, and so I wouldn't know which way to run if I panicked. All these things scared me a lot.

I had been feeling the itch to do this walk for months.

I was a lot happier overall—could it be all that positive self-chat was making a difference? My confidence was growing, and I very much wanted to have another go at overcoming my anxiety.

In the run-up to this 'big walk,' I started experimenting with my anxiety. On occasions when life forced me to face an anxious situation, something unanticipated, I played with a technique where I would say to myself, 'bring it on, anxiety,' and, 'do your absolute worst,' rather than my habitual, rather futile attempts to resist anxiety, push it back hard, and run for safety.

I did this quite a few times, and strangely, rather than making my anxiety get worse, it receded fairly swiftly. The added bonus was that, as a result, I felt elated and a big chunk more resilient.

This made me curious.

I decided to do the walk on the spur of the moment one day and made my way to the start, a beautiful but overgrown Devon track that had both been calling me and repelling me in equal measures for months.

I felt the usual surge of physical symptoms rise, but I welcomed them as best as I could, practised some deep breathing, and decided to carry on.

I considered my physical symptoms and wondered if there was any possibility I was excited to do this. Weirdly, when I called the feelings 'excitement,' they seemed to calm down, and I even managed a smile for a moment as my curiosity was piqued as to what the outcome might be.

This was a fairly safe experiment for me. Whatever happened, I was only a few miles away from home, but the anxiety felt very real to me. As I progressed on the walk, I anxiously checked my phone for the distance from home and to see where I was on the walk.

I walked along the unfamiliar path and kept feeling the physical symptoms rising, and then I would try and welcome them, saying things like, 'all feelings welcome,' which again calmed things down. I know, this is sounding weirder than positive chanting into the bathroom mirror, but bear with me.

It seemed, if I didn't fight the feelings and invited them along for the walk, they didn't have the same power to overwhelm me that they had when I peeked at them in fear and avoided acknowledging them at any cost.

So, I continued my walk along a very quiet lane and got to 'the point of no return.' It was nearer to home to keep going than to turn back. I was now fully committed.

I tentatively walked on, reminding myself to look at the beautiful scenery and try to enjoy the nature that always lifted my spirits. I kept saying, 'all feelings welcome' to myself and found something interesting happened.

I started to enjoy the walk. Like, REALLY enjoy the walk. I was on my own in the middle of the countryside. I had not asked someone to help me, I didn't have anyone on standby to pick me up or do any other safety techniques to make it easier, and I felt like I had literally walked through the barrier of my fear.

It felt incredible!

I don't know if you remember the first time, as a kid, when you did something truly scary. You looked at it and it seemed impossible, but then you just trusted and let go, and you found yourself doing it, whether it was riding a bike or learning to swim. You pushed through an invisible boundary. That was how it was for me.

And once I had done it the first time, I was desperate to do it again. I had felt the fear and done it anyway, but on my own terms, because I felt it was right for me and with respect for myself, rather than the endless inner dialogue telling me I would be a loser if I didn't succeed. No pushing from anyone else, and the result was fantastic.

It was easier for me, as I had small challenges I could work through before tackling the bigger ones, but that feeling of pushing through the barrier and experiencing fear disintegrating was truly exhilarating. Talk about a dopamine hit! I couldn't stop grinning!

I was like a kid going down a big slide for the first time. Once I had overcome my fear and let go, I wanted to do it again and again. This was the start of something…

Notes

Chapter 10 – Aromatherapy

This is an odd one. Aromatherapy would seem like a fairly safe option for anyone looking for some relief from anxiety, and I'm sure it is.

The trouble was that I picked this particular therapy at a time when I was spiralling out of control and struggling to leave the house, had chronic insomnia, couldn't eat due to feeling constantly sick with stress, and was generally in a pretty bad place.

I don't want to dwell on this, but I do want to point out a strange observation. Despite the fact that I was in a genuinely horrible place, my survival instinct wanted me to stay there. Better the devil you know. Being permanently stressed had bizarrely become my hideously uncomfortable comfort zone in that I had become so used to the tense feelings that anything that changed those feelings, for better or worse, was something to be frightened of. Bizarre!

Change of any kind to my fragile state of mind made me even more tense.

I didn't know this at the time, though, so when I turned up for a gentle massage and experienced a floaty, calm feeling from the effect of the oils on my stressed-out body, I completely freaked out. This long-forgotten relaxation feeling terrified me more than being anxious itself.

What was this weird feeling, and would it be dangerous? It felt totally unreal, as I had been holding on to my tension so tightly that I'd forgotten what a relaxed body felt like, and my brain needed a label, so I slapped on 'drugs flashback.'

No sooner had the therapist lit the candles, smothered me in a delicious blend of lavender and geranium and allowed the gentle whale music to envelop me, than I was up off that massage couch, frantically getting dressed and crying that I would NEVER get over my anxiety.

What I needed to get my head around was that just because something felt different, it didn't mean it had to be scary. I got so used to feeling scared and uncomfortable that any change tipped me off balance. I was so terrified of things being different, and how my imaginative mind might interpret that, that clinging on to the familiar felt safer than experiencing something new, even if the familiar was constant stress.

I have since learned that just because I think something, that doesn't mean it's true. When my brain is telling me some pretty dodgy facts— like having a massage is potentially lethal—it has the knack of doing this in such a fabulously authoritative voice that, even now, I sometimes forget to question it.

So, did aromatherapy help me in the mid-1990s? No, sadly, it did not, and I'm sure I told anyone who was willing to listen the truly awful effect it had on me.

Does it help me now?

Absolutely!

I love nothing more than a lavender bath or the scent of a carefully selected blend of essential oils diffusing in my home. The truth is, like so many of my other therapy experiences, it wasn't the therapy that was the issue, more my thoughts and expectations around the treatment.

The joy of this little nugget is that, as my thoughts and expectations were created by me, it will come as no surprise to you that I was the person best placed to do something about them, but more on this later.

Let me plant that seed with you for now.

Notes

Chapter 11 – Shiatsu

During this time in my twenties, I fluctuated between feeling awful and doing fairly well. If you had asked me a few years ago what the past few decades had been like for me, I would have told you, depending on the mood you caught me in, that life had been a struggle, and I had been battling anxiety over the decades.

To some extent, this is true.

I have found it extremely hard at times, but there have also been brilliant times.

I have set up cafes and restaurants, had countless interesting jobs, brought up two amazing children, and provided a home for a little brood of rescue animals.

Clearly, it has not been a complete disaster.

The trouble is, if I'm not careful, I can tell myself it has all been one big battle. I've struggled with anxiety SOME OF THE TIME, and yes, it does often feel like an exhausting, never-ending struggle, but that cannot be true and probably means I'm just feeling a little low and having wonky thoughts.

I think clever science-ey people would call this the negativity bias.

I can have a panic episode lasting two hours—which feels hellish, I know—in a day and believe this to be my total experience, when in fact, I had twenty-two other hours when I was not panicking and getting on with my day, but my brain didn't stop to have a party to celebrate this.

I recommend you start noticing if the stories you're telling yourself are true. I know when I say I have had an awful day, it usually means a difficult few hours. I now call myself out on this stuff if I can, but those pesky thoughts can be a tad sneaky.

Anyway, back to Shiatsu. My twenties, and my quest to find the definitive solution to my big life problem. I came across Shiatsu as a result of a failed attempt to train as a yoga teacher. Having never studied yoga, I decided, in an attempt to 'quick fix' my life, to do an intensive weekend retreat course in yoga to qualify as a yoga teacher. The writing was probably on the wall for this one, as I was fairly overweight at the time, totally inflexible, seriously unfit, and too anxious (I thought) to be in the remote part of Devon where the course was based. However, the ever-patient teacher was also a Shiatsu practitioner, and what I did get out of signing up for this wildly inappropriate training was a series of Shiatsu sessions.

I don't know what he did to balance my chakras, but I do know he was patient and kind, and spending time in his calm energy had a hugely beneficial effect on me. The sessions were only about fifteen miles from my home, which on day one, seemed almost entirely insurmountable as I lay on his floor having my treatment with waves of anxiety rolling over me, but it soon became a highlight of my week. I learned to enjoy the drive there, take in the countryside, and push the X-distance from home a bit further afield.

He told me he was clearing 'stuff' from my chakras. I didn't really get it, but I started to feel a little stronger. It wasn't a cure exactly, but something was shifting.

What anxiety has taught me better than anything else is how to build resilience. I have been so dogged and persistent in my attempt to find this magic cure for my anxiety that I feel like I've left no stone unturned. This determination and resilience to keep going have, coincidentally, also been intensely useful to me as an entrepreneur.

Also, the fact that I *believed* I couldn't go on fancy holidays and breaks with my friends meant I had a little more money to invest in other things like starting my first restaurant and opening my ice cream shop.

As I *felt* I couldn't locate these businesses anywhere other than in my safety bubble around my home, I had to be creative and resourceful in making the businesses work. For example, I felt too anxious to go to London trade shows for gifts, so I did more online research and found smaller suppliers that perhaps might not have been able to afford to exhibit at the big shows. Every cloud, as they say…

Chapter 12 – Pottery and Other Creative Attempts to 'Live the Dream'

Many of my attempts to overcome anxiety have involved reinventing myself or distracting myself in some significant way. I'm an eternal optimist, and it takes very little encouragement for me to believe I can do something exciting and new. Some people call this ADHD, but I prefer to call it my superpower. Thanks, blue baby.

So, running in parallel with my anxiety has been a deep-seated urge to have more control over my life and be my own boss. It was within weeks of my first trainee management job with Marks & Spencer after graduating, that I discovered the corporate life was not for me. I started searching for the perfect business where I could earn money by being creative, authentic, and spending big chunks of time outside. I'm still trying to achieve this.

If you need a break from all this and want a laugh, let me attach my CV. I won't actually do this, but if I did, it would be a tome covering the over 100 different jobs I have had in my life.

Interestingly, I wrote a multi-page list of what I wanted from life when I was 23, which I recently reread, and it was so on the mark that it begs the question, why did I ignore these valuable insights? I clearly knew my destined path when I was in my twenties.

I guess I learned more by taking the scenic route.

Having little money in my early twenties, my perfect business had to be cheap to start and run, be quick to set up, and capable of paying my rent and modest living costs.

Pottery seemed to be the perfect answer. As most of my inspiration for these new businesses came from reading that genre of literature that makes owning a café easier than brushing your teeth in the morning, ideas ranged from living on a houseboat running boat holidays (too expensive), to running a retreat in Cornwall (too far and too expensive) to selling my art on the Portobello Road (too far from home and regrettably lacking the artistic talent).

You can see why it felt like all the stars had aligned when I found a poster for a pottery course plastered to a telegraph pole outside my house. Having clearly forgotten the key lesson from Margot's dabble with pottery in The Good Life—apologies to anyone under the age of fifty or not resident in the UK in the 1970s—I ploughed headlong into researching kilns, pricing up clay, and unpacking my dungarees from the loft, ready to make stunning designer pots that I could sell from a table outside my house.

The course was close to home (tick), cheap to sign up to (tick), and started the following week (big tick). What could possibly go wrong?

What *did* go wrong was that the teacher was a little unusual in that he would phone me constantly and ask me if he could take me to places.

He offered to take me to pubs and clubs and sit in the car whilst I had a great time with my friends. He said he didn't need to be invited. He just wanted to spend time with me. Help me out. His persistence with this idea, which I now see was stalking, was unrelenting. Also, not the perfect antidote to anxiety.

I always said no because it was a terrible idea, and little did he know, I rarely went out anywhere that would require such an unusual lift.

Pottery classes became strained as his desire to re-enact the infamous scene from the film *Ghost* clashed with my desire to make saleable pots to start up my new business. I left the class, and pottery fell by the wayside along with yoga teaching, jewellery-making, writing a best-selling book (the jury is out), and selling the Encyclopaedia Britannica—

again, a positive oasis for drawing out unusual people who can't wait to invite me into their secluded homes.

Was it the cure for my anxiety? Alas, sadly not. Any therapeutic benefits and a big chunk of my self-confidence were crushed by my predatory teacher. Onwards and upwards. There had to be another way.

Chapter 13 – Counselling

I tried counselling during the early 1990s. I had been living in Devon for a few years, my university relationship had ended, and I was now seeing the man who became my husband.

Initially, when I first met my partner, things with my anxiety improved, mainly due to the rush of excitement that accompanies new love, slightly more sophisticated coping techniques, and a creatively impressive ability to subtly avoid and divert plans; I was deeply ashamed of my anxiety at the time.

Over time, as problems in our relationship arose, I found myself coping less and less well, and at a particular low point, a friend suggested counselling.

My counsellor was newly qualified, had major issues with boundaries that she possibly hadn't considered, and the whole experience spiralled my anxiety in a rather negative direction.

For me, dredging my over-stressed mind for long-abandoned negative memories did not bring relief.

No amount of punching cushions, screaming, or other stress-relieving techniques brought even the slightest relief from my anxiety, and fortuitously for my therapist and me, she took a long vacation to Australia, which did us both the world of good.

Regrettably, all that navel-gazing brought big, bad memories up from the past, which I was now left to battle alone.

The result was another breakdown, many months off work, and a growing concern that I was mentally ill and possibly never able to recover.

As an aside, I found the most hilarious letter of resignation that I gave to my boss during this period. He was insanely kind and told me to take a break. Much to his bemusement, I negotiated a pay cut to make myself feel less under pressure, and I rested myself to better health. If I can find that letter, I must include it. It made me belly laugh for hours—I read it during a house move a few years ago.

Feeling mentally battered from my counselling experience, I sought comfort in less challenging places and happened upon colour therapy from a chance comment made by a tactless work colleague, who also ended up emigrating to Australia. The lengths people go…

Chapter 14 – Colour Therapy

My husband was away on a three-month journalism course, and I was home alone—not entirely true as I had the wonderful company of my beautiful Albino hamster, Harris. So, what better way to occupy my leisure time than to repaint my house?

I had been given this incredible book on colour by my aunt, and I had been inspired to paint the house in bold statement colours, including bright yellow throughout my landing and hall. It was a pretty punchy shade of yellow. Think centre of a daffodil or the freshest Sorrento lemon. I loved it! So proud was I of my new yellow hallway, grass green living room, and burnt orange bedroom, that I invited the people from work round for coffee and cake, hoping for a fantastic 'Fika' bonding moment, sharing stories and getting to know each other.

In the 1990s, no one seemed to talk about mental health. Certainly not in a positive way. I was fairly sure my issues with anxiety put me in a group of one in my workplace, and it hadn't occurred to me that, behind brave faces, others might have been struggling too.

I was intensely private about my struggles and only shared them with the very closest of friends. I had a fairly loud persona, with 'excess' worn as a badge of honour, despite underlyingly being unconfident and shy. It horrified me to think people might find out about my 'dirty' anxiety secret, and I over-compensated wildly to cover up feelings of fear and insecurity.

So, when I proudly unveiled the fruits of my decorating endeavours and was met with, 'Well, you are clearly depressed,' from one of the girls in my team, I was mortified. I had never considered that my choices of colour might give away anything about how I was feeling, and I would have had quite a different approach to the colour chart from Dulux if I had known.

I don't actually think I was depressed. Low mood, certainly, and highly anxious, but the experience did make me a bit more curious about colour.

To be honest, I was a bit sad that, despite all my efforts at hospitality, another of my colleagues couldn't get over the fact that I didn't have a cafetiere and, shock horror, only had instant coffee in my cupboard. I was a tea drinker at the time, but I have since learned the errors of my way. I now have three cafetieres and am barista-trained, but I digress again.

The idea that colour is energy and each colour is a wavelength of light travelling at a different speed made sense to me, and it was a whole lot easier than thinking about why my personal relationship was causing me such mental scarring. So, the next few months saw me changing clothes choices from my standard black and finally ditching that hideously limiting concept that black makes you look thinner, opening the floodgates for a whole array of rainbow delights to find a new home in my wardrobe.

I found it hugely fun, and for me, a fairly healthy thing to play around with. I ate rainbow-coloured food, experimented with wearing orange, loved the boldness that stripes convey, and coupled with my love of punk music, felt I rocked the 'Vivienne Westwood meets Lady Gaga' look.

Bizarrely, this phase was also associated with an increase in confidence and a reduction in anxiety, as during that time I presented the weather for a day on *This Morning* and appeared on *Supermarket Sweep*. No mean feat as it involved travelling solo to Liverpool for *This Morning,* and to Nottingham to meet Dale Winton.

Also, the many doors and security needed to get around those studios showed a level of anxiety-handling that I would have given anything for during tougher times in my thirties and late forties. I remember it being extremely hard in places, but I hadn't yet got so worn down with anxiety that I couldn't make the occasional big comeback.

What this does demonstrate to me is how many good patches there are between the challenges. Catch me on a bad day in my early fifties, and I would tell you I'd had chronic anxiety for over thirty years. And yes, I can easily tell myself that if I go on the hunt for examples of tough times. Even just thinking this now, I can feel my mood drop and that familiar feeling of sadness coupled with fear descend.

It is easy to forget, though, the times when I was on my A-game, putting the travel distance aside, even during those difficult times. I can find many pockets of joy when I hunt them out instead of hunting only for the gloomy stories.

I did this exercise, which I recommend to anyone with a spare half an hour. Get a paper and pen, and without giving it any thought, write a list of 100 great experiences. Don't think about it, and if you get stuck, it can be as simple as finding an unopened packet of Polos down the back of the sofa.

Hunt down those good times. I have just had this memory pop in where I decided to bring a full banquet breakfast into work for one of my friends. For those not as food-focused (read obsessed) as me, bringing in a selection of twenty-seven foods from around the world to celebrate her

27th birthday seemed excessive, and they talked about it for years to come. The point is, this time was also around the time I was so low that I couldn't leave the house and was suffering from chronic insomnia.

The office was almost next to my house, and with my attention firmly on my friend's big day, I managed to come in with my breakfast treats. This is one of my favourite memories, and I'm surprised it comes from a period in life I also view as one of my most challenging.

I love this about life. I'm seeing that my whole experience shifts depending on what I'm thinking about. I'm now feeling hungry, happy, and looking forward to my lunch, all because I thought back to Claire's classic birthday.

Notes

Chapter 15 – Gratitude

Where does gratitude fit in?

It's hard to say.

I heard about it first on Radio 4 —so that dates it to somewhere in my late forties—and I can just remember listening to this famous musician being interviewed and him talking about his gratitude practice and how that had completely shifted things in his life. I didn't really get what he was on about.

I couldn't see how writing a list about things he was grateful for could make any real difference. I considered myself to be a grateful person. I noticed and thanked people for their time and effort and appreciated all the good things in life, from the wonders of HP brown sauce to sitcoms of the late seventies. Still, the one thing guaranteed to get me to sleep is a few bars of the opening titles of *To The Manor Born*. I think I tried 'practising gratitude' for a couple of nights and it fell to the wayside, like so many other attempts to get a handle on my life stressors.

Being grateful was instinctive, and I didn't fully grasp why writing it down would make any difference.

Ironically, despite my love of writing, I still don't keep a gratitude journal (although it is a good habit I would love to adopt) but I can now see that, on a basic level, focusing on the things you're grateful for makes you focus on the good things, and by filling your head with more good thoughts, less space is available for negative thoughts.

As I now understand, after years of not having a clue, that my feelings are a direct result of my thoughts, it does make beautiful sense to try and search out the things in my day that uplift me; even something as small as the win of finding out they are now showing repeats of *To The Manor Born* on BBC iPlayer.

Seems I'm now a closet gratitude major-league player. I don't write it down, but I do practice it in my head every day.

My inner voice is forever pointing out that beautiful sunset, an unexpected glimpse of my kids, The Wedding Present's *Everyone Thinks He Looks Daft* blasting out of a workman's van as I walk up to work. Whatever it is that makes me happy, I seem to have a knack for noticing it now.

I'm way better at paying attention to the little things that make me smile too. Obviously, I'm socially aware enough to keep this mostly to myself as I understand bursting with joy can be a little alienating to all but your closest of friends, but that's what gratitude has increasingly made me feel.

And let me tell you, it certainly wasn't my upbringing that encouraged this positive spin on things. I do believe I was born happy-go-lucky, but the main lesson from my early years was to look out for danger, everything that looked safe probably wasn't, and there was lurking danger everywhere.

I have since reflected on my own language and behaviour around my children. I thought my husband was positively irresponsible when he pushed them too high on the swing or dangled them precipitously from his shoulders, but I recognise that my fear detector was clearly stuck on the wrong setting, and whilst I would have made an epic caveman, this fear response was not serving me particularly well as a parent.

I shudder at the number of times I told my children to be careful when doing something entirely routine or warned them of the dangers of everything from putting hairbands around their wrists to the potential choking hazards of eating pretty much anything. I exaggerate, but I can see that my upbringing, where danger was pointed out at every turn, had a serious impact on how I saw the world growing up. It's only now that I can see the benefits of easing up on all the catastrophising that my anxiety had been dining out on for many years.

I now find myself thinking to myself, 'so what?' when catastrophic thoughts pop up, and they still do sometimes. I let myself off the hook by thinking, 'future me will handle it. Future me will know more and be way better equipped to deal with a future problem. Me in the present can just carry on minding my own business.' Worrying about an unknown future problem feels like using a Deliveroo-style service to pre-order my anxiety. No, thank you!

I now find it increasingly difficult to buy into all my previous attempts to control the 'dangerous' outside world too, which is looking much less hazardous and something I have zero control over anyway.

You may question this 'slacker' approach to anxiety, but it has reaped huge rewards, not least that it's now so much quicker for me to get out of the house without needing my phone (so I can contact people), my phone charger (in case my battery dies), my extra phone charger (in case the first one is faulty) etc.

I now just head out, and on the occasions when my battery does give up, although annoying, I realise that no one will die, and I simply deal with it.

Who knew I didn't have to experience every problem at least twice; once when I pictured it in my head, and secondly, if it actually happened?

If you consider that my phone was one of a list of approximately fifteen essential things I needed before I could go anywhere, you can imagine how much quicker it is now to get out of the house, how much lighter my load is—literally and metaphorically—and how much hard cash I've saved in buying spare Kalms, lavender oil, travel bands, and other vital items rarely used but always deemed essential to be in my possession at all times.

Anxiety, for me, was like having multiple problems for the price of one —the worst kind of BOGOF offer, where you don't need what you're 'buying.' I would get an anxious experience in real life, and then get all these free opportunities to relive it in my head as I catastrophised it happening again and again.

My poor, tired body responded perfectly to every crisis—real or imagined—with cortisol and adrenaline flooding my system. This now feels like such a waste in so many ways, not least that I would rather save my precious brain chemicals for when they are needed, rather than constantly putting them through dress rehearsals for a final performance that, in most cases, never materialises.

My younger self had come to learn that merely the thought of having my special anxiety-fixer products on me was enough for me not to need them.

I now see that having my anxiety crutches simply enabled me to replace a catastrophic thought with a reassuring thought that I had a tool to deal with anxiety if it arose. I then felt less need to constantly check if I was anxious, resulting in me not triggering a load of extra anxious feelings. The reverse obviously happened if I lost my bag of tricks.

What I feel sad about is that I still missed the point that it was paying such close attention to my anxiety whilst frantically packing the fifteen essential 'anti-anxiety' items in my bag that created more anxious thinking. Feeling for my Kalms or Rescue drops did nothing but helpfully shift my thinking back to something more reassuring.

It was this yo-yoing between thoughts that was so exhausting. It happened all the time. If I drove to work in my perceived safe zone and thought my car was safely parked in a car park, I was totally fine. If my husband took it without me knowing and it was back by the time I needed it, there would also be zero anxiety.

The problem arose if he told me he was taking the car, as it would trigger an avalanche of anxious thoughts, and I would be unable to stay at work for fear of feeling trapped there. Nothing in my immediate physical environment changed. I couldn't see my car from my work. I didn't need my car. I was unaware if my car was parked up in a parking space or having the trip of a lifetime around the surrounding countryside, but the thought that it might be gone would send me into a tailspin.

My husband gave up asking if he could borrow the car while I was at work.

I clearly see now that I unwittingly pre-ordered anxiety every time I considered going anywhere by focusing on my fear of anxiety and planning ahead for all the things I could do to combat it if it arrived.

Now, I liken it to being scared of a dog and then buying a special dog whistle to call it repeatedly so I can use all the techniques I know to shoo it away again. Exhausting and ultimately pointless.

Now, I get that if I go to a (metaphorical) park, I might very well come across a dog, and it may not be pleasant, but I'm not going to start calling random dogs over to me if that's not something I want. That seems illogical to me now, but it was what I regularly did with anxiety.

'Hey, anxiety, are you there? I don't want you to be, but are you around? Let me check every corner of this place for you, but I hope you don't appear.' It's not the way to go for me anymore.

Anyway, I'm supposed to be talking about gratitude, and I am in an around-the-houses sort of a way. What do they say? 'Where your attention goes, your energy flows.'

I put my attention on the many good things in my life, and that helps me to see a growing number of good things every day. I look to find that elusive silver lining, and I'm happier as a result.

Clearly, if I could have experienced this 'aha' moment years ago, I might have successfully ditched my anxiety issues shortly after they arrived, but I didn't. Life obviously had more to teach me, so my quest to find an anxiety cure went on, bringing me to the door of the mystic yogis.

You will have to ignore the wild time-line swerve.

A Random Aside – The Family 'Baton of Fear'

Anxiety didn't come out of nowhere. Mental health challenges have been a thing in my family for decades. Even glancing back just a couple of generations, I see how fear was passed from parent to child, intense fear-based learnings that became so normal that no one noticed how distorted and out of shape they really were.

Fear was expressed in numerous ways, with the worst affected members of the family entirely unable to see how fear underpinned their drinking, anger, self-loathing, and hatred of the world.

I turned my 'gift' of fear inward, and anxiety was the outcome.

Of all the ugly heirlooms from the past, stashed in my under-stairs cupboards, that well-used baton of fear simply had to go, along with all the stories of inadequacy, the need to toe someone else's line, and the treasured family tradition of stamping on 'impossible' dreams.

If I'm passing anything to my children, it is simply to trust in themselves.

We are 'gifted' with many things in our childhoods that we accept without question. This book has forced me to look more closely at my own gifts or learnings, and to weigh up whether they still serve me today.

There has been a rigorous clear-out.

Good riddance to the 'baton of fear.' It weighed down my father, his father, and his father's father. That's enough generational damage for one family. I give instead the gift of 'too much love.' No doubt, my kids will say that this too is a burden, but not one that will bring them down in any unbearable way, although I appreciate it's still a bit too early to call.

Notes

Chapter 16 – Yoga

I've had many a dabble with yoga, not least the overly optimistic belief that one yoga session in my twenties could set me up as an ideal candidate for yoga teacher training. I have mentioned this experience briefly already, but it's an attempt at anxiety-annihilation that I feel warrants a revisit. Mainly because, bless me, I was so clueless.

Everything about the yoga teacher training was a challenge. Firstly, my zero experience of yoga, then my lack of flexibility from a lifetime of avoiding strenuous exercise. Finally, most crucially, it fell on a Saturday when I was still a heavy drinker, and whilst vehemently against taking drugs, viewed alcohol as fairly innocuous, guaranteeing me a monumental hangover at the start of every yoga weekend. As such, quiet meditative times on my yoga mat were spent trying desperately to control alternating waves of intense anxiety and extreme nausea.

The anxiety, which I truly believed was caused by the lush Devon countryside outside our beautiful but remote yoga studio, was way more likely triggered by a terrible diet, excessive use of alcohol, poor sleep, and a turbulent period in my personal life.

Sticking to my initial theory that my panic related to my distance from home, I failed to address all the genuine issues straining my poor body and focused again purely on the miles.

The countryside *had* to be the cause.

This did make it easier for me to continue with my hedonistic lifestyle, albeit from my house, as changing behaviour habits is hard, and the familiar, no matter how unhelpful, can seem so much safer than breaking out and trying something new.

I stuck out the ten-weekend training course, but at the end of it, I was no closer to helping others through yoga than I was to finding the answer to wormholes in the universe, or why Ford Prefect always carried a towel.

Other attempts at yoga have been more promising, and I now realise I needed to look at other areas of my life like perfectionism and being overly competitive before having another go at yoga, which I can now see is a genuinely beneficial practice. Yoga had all the hallmarks of offering me exactly what my younger self craved. A business opportunity, the chance to be self-employed, and the opportunity to work outside, but the downside was that it would take effort, discipline, and the need to apply myself fully and not just pay a lump of cash and pick up a certificate.

Not the perfect fit for the Queen of Instant Gratification. Onwards I marched, looking for solutions to anxiety, my true self, and a purpose on the way.

I don't know how far I'd travelled down my list of 100 jobs that I've tried in this lifetime, but I was certainly caught up in the addiction of attention from job interviews (weird, I know), fear of failure once I got said 'dream job,' and secret anxiety that I would have to travel for work, which obviously meant I had to resign there and then.

My ego loved the dopamine hit of getting a new job, but my perfectionism meant that I worked so insanely hard for the first few weeks, set the bar so high for myself that I couldn't reach it again, and had to quit before they discovered the truth about the person I really was. Could there be a better time to consider the Japanese art of Kintsugi? I hoped for an answer.

Notes

Chapter 17 – Kintsugi – The Japanese Art of Imperfection

Fear of failure, perfectionism, the addiction to a pat on the head, and my dopamine addiction are all the things that draw me to the concept of Kintsugi.

I'm often so far away from this concept but know that the version of me that is striving to be 'perfect' is the me that has yet again taken the wrong path and is lost in the dark forest of people pleasing.

This is also the same me that is judging myself negatively right now and causing my head to spin (laughs at self)!

As with almost everything on this journey, the things I thought I aced at and that got my ego all revved up have always been the very things that veer me right off my path – forcing anxiety to step in and get me back on track. Until I find a better way of noticing I have taken a wrong turn, anxiety will remain as the emotion that warns me something is off. I guess that is its real job.

As an entrepreneur, overthinking and addiction to busyness were considered my superpowers. When someone suggested I was a control freak, I was lost. How could my top skill also be my downfall? If this was true and all my busy-ness fell away, what would be left? It was my identity. I was scared no one would love me if I wasn't insanely productive at all times. Every time I met up with a friend, their opener would be, 'What are you up to now?' and I thought this was a challenge rather than, as is more likely, their confusion that everything in my life was built on moving sand.

Put far too simply, Kintsugi is the art of making something new from broken pots. The 'failure' of the broken pot is utilised to make something new and beautiful from its imperfections.

When the broken pieces of the pot are creatively joined back together with gold, the cracks become the highlight of the design, something to be celebrated, with the finished piece taking on a new beauty that the previously uniform 'perfect' pot may not have possessed. The pot has transcended from a utilitarian pot to a piece of art. It is not being repaired with the intention of hiding the flaws, but for the so-called flaws to become an intrinsic part of the design. Without the cracks, the piece would not be unique.

Could that be true for me too?

This is an important concept for me to consider as it taps into my well of shame that exists for every failure I have ever experienced. I used to (I still often do) feel failure like harsh physical pain in my body. It winded me like a blow to the stomach. It was this hideous darkness I couldn't bear to look at. I used to push all those feelings away for fear that even looking at how weak and hopeless I was would cripple me with shame.

What a gigantic waste of time and energy.

No matter how much I read about Edison failing endless times before inventing the light bulb, I still couldn't allow myself to fail.

I'm struggling to comfortably type about my 'failures' right now.

So, for me, this concept of Kintsugi is particularly relevant in my life. I have had some rather spectacular 'failures' in my time. Cringing events that used to make me shudder at the mere recollection. For fun and the purpose of helping me learn to live with them a little better, I will list a few of the particularly brutal ones:

Appearing on the children's TV show *Screen Test* in the early 1980s and spending the greatest part of the show spinning around on the chair (why would they give you a fancy chair that could spin around 360 degrees when you were supposed to be concentrating on the film clips) and having no clue about any of the questions I was being asked.

At a time of gender rigidity in the mid-eighties, my ultimate humiliation was when I was asked the name of the 'boy' behind the goal post in *Gregory's Girl* and saying a girl's name, Ivy, which was apparently the funniest thing a person could ever say. I wasn't used to the heavy Scottish accent. When I was forced back to school by my parents, despite begging to be allowed to leave at fourteen and go and get a Youth Training Scheme (YTS), the school playground turned into a torture chamber with 'Ivy' being chanted at every turn. I had to wait four horrific months before the show was aired, knowing what would be coming my way, so you can imagine how much the anxiety built up in that time.

I couldn't watch the programme; even mentioning it would make me feel sick. Watching Clare Grogan in Altered Images on Top of the Pops brought fresh flashbacks (she starred in the film) and even typing it now, I can feel an uncomfortable twinge.

It should have been a golden moment for me. I was picked from my school to appear on a national TV show, and all I came away with was long-lasting shame. Talk about focusing on the negative.

Another cringe-worthy shame moment was making my first ever speech at university in my hope to get nominated as the 'rep' for the new first years coming to Nottingham. I not only didn't get selected but had a massive glass of wine to settle my nerves and made one of those speeches where even the tumbleweed made a sharp exit from the room. My mum was visiting me, and the shame of that event overshadowed my entire evening. Again, I still have an emotional ripple when I think about that speech now. The faces of the crowd...

And so it goes on, from disastrous sexual encounters to humiliations in primary school (my sister announced to the whole of school when I first arrived from Holland that I had fleas and still wet the bed. Untrue and not great for making new friends at a strange school).

Shame when I got things 'wrong' was the perfect fuel for my anxiety. My stress would spiral, my body would suffer, and my anxiety would try and take care of things by getting me out of the way of danger by hiding under the table when I was a kid, and then in my house, or in extreme cases, my bed as I moved into adulthood.

Fair play, anxiety. It got me away from the external stress as quickly as possible in an attempt to turn off the tap of shame.

As time went on, and my shame muscles grew from continual use, I could feel unparalleled shame even if I served a bad coffee in my café, or if we got a bad review on TripAdvisor.

I couldn't rationalise that it was only one person's view or that, if I had made an error, I was only human and could learn from it and move on.

Sadly, these public 'failures' had the ability to bring me down physically as they put huge strain on my body.

I tried harder in all areas of my life to be 'perfect' – and if this wasn't possible would publicly pronounced myself as useless. It didn't feel safe to try things out.

I needed to know I would be good at something before giving it a go. I used to believe myself to be uncompetitive until my then boyfriend pointed out that I was so intensely competitive that I didn't even attempt to compete unless I was fairly sure I would win. Intense pressure.

That I developed an anxiety disorder is now looking a little less unfathomable. Feeling an increasing pressure to be perfect in the very many overwhelming situations I pushed myself into, anxiety became the only tool I felt I had to escape the stress.

Anxiety was the non-negotiable one. When anxiety kicked in, I would drop all the crazy stress-inducing behaviour and go off to recover. It worked, but I have since found better ways of evaluating situations and clipping on my safety harness well before I fall off any high cliffs. I have better in-built methods for keeping me safe, but I can't knock anxiety altogether. It certainly always got my attention and forced me to curb my wildest excesses.

I would do something new, aim for perfection, work way too hard, get close to achieving it, and then run away in an anxious frenzy, scared to look at the outcome in case there was any tiny element that might be considered imperfect. Wow! So much unnecessary pressure. The pressure wasn't just on me though, but also on all the people around me. Eventually, the only way to make things sustainable, was to work for myself. Weirdly, the pressure then fell away as I didn't need to be perfect for myself; I simply feared not meeting other people's expectations.

When I worked for myself, I was brave, competent, and successful. As soon as I was in a partnership, I imploded with stress and self-loathing. My husband and I working together was a disaster for our relationship and my anxiety.

Obviously, working for yourself does bring you into contact with others, and at each of these stress points, pressure would build up as my fear of failure bubbled away under the surface. I'm not saying it was all bad. I had a lot of success in my businesses but I often grappled with the line between doing a good job and selling my soul to perfectionism.

Moving forward, I very much wanted to do things well, but I needed to focus on the why of this. Why did it matter? If the why was strong and in line with my values, working hard made sense to me and didn't cause me stress. If the why was wrong, pressure swiftly built up until I addressed whatever the inconsistency was. This ability to detect my 'why', using my intuition, became a way more useful superpower than the ability to overthink and strive to over-achieve.

How this comes back to Kintsugi is that I am now seeing how all my 'failings' have been valuable components in making me who I am today.

I have learnt unexpected things from the disastrous love affair, or met interesting people in that job from hell, where I embarrassed myself so much that I couldn't visit one of the cities where I worked for many years after.

It doesn't take a genius to see how this all plays into my travel anxiety and my fear of going any distance from home. If I totally screw up, how can I run back to my cave if I'm a two-hour flight away?

The truth is, I'm starting to see the benefit of peeking at my dark side, opening a few windows and shedding light on those parts of me that I thought were too shameful to mention. I don't have to run away.

I love the concept that I am 'in training' rather than succeeding and failing.

If I'm in training to become a traveller and I don't make it on any particular day, it's not a big deal, and I can train harder the next day. It's a continuum of learning, and as with everything in life, I'm seeing that hard boundaries no longer feel true for me. Right and wrong, success or failure, truth or lie; there is too much grey in-between for me to buy into hard and fast rules. I shall settle for being a traveller-in-training and rejoice in accepting my broken experiences, many mentioned in this writing, coming together to create this unique journey that I'm on in my training to be a complete human able to enjoy a full and rich life.

None of my experiences have been wasted or 'wrong.' Many have been challenging, but in those challenges, I have learnt vital things about my resilience and my ability to cope.

I'm proud of myself for coping when the Eurostar broke down in the Channel Tunnel.

At the time, I was hard on myself for feeling so emotionally drained after the event, but even the most Zen monk might have had a moment when the lights went off in the tunnel, with no announcements, and stayed that way for the best part of four hours.

I now think, *hats off to me.* I stayed in my seat and got through a very challenging time. I feel if that happened now, I might be able to relax more, breathe a little more deeply, but I did my best and I got through it. I should give myself way more credit for that. Actually, I would be bloody scared now too.

I'm starting a new and exciting work project that happened as a direct result of my, on paper, failing in another job and leaving. On this occasion, I did not run away but realised my hard work and positive intent were being poured down a metaphorical toilet, and I would be better off using my precious life energy in a more on-purpose enterprise.

Lo and behold, another wonderful opportunity has appeared in my life, and the previous job was the vital stepping stone needed to get me there.

All my broken pieces are finding a new way of being re-purposed. I am a work of Kintsugi in progress!

This is a relatively new one for me, but could I love anything more? I have been held back for my entire life by this misconception that you have to be exceptionally good at something to have a go.

I realise now that this cannot be true. There is no way that every person who has been successful in life was great from the get-go. If that were true, athletes wouldn't train for hours every day, chefs wouldn't work as apprentices in the kitchens of other culinary geniuses, and chess masters wouldn't spend their entire waking hours playing chess.

I'm off to dance badly, whilst singing out of tune and doing a spot of break dancing. I'm not making a video of this or sharing it on my social media. I'm simply going to have a bit of fun. We all know it isn't going to be perfect, but I won't give a hoot!

A Random Aside – COVID

Never has a person had more training for a challenge than me for the arrival of the Covid-19 pandemic in the UK.

I question now why I wasn't pulled into the UK Government's COBRA room on day one. That anxiety would flood the nation when people realised they were trapped in their homes indefinitely hardly comes as a surprise to me. This was something I deeply understood. Catastrophising about being trapped had been my go-to for the past thirty years. I had also learnt quite a few handy tools to cope.

My training for Covid-19 had started in earnest, though, two years earlier, and it was called The Beast from the East.

The Beast from the East was a severe cold weather episode that resulted in widespread snow suddenly descending across the UK. I was working in my small seaside café at the time, and the news was packed to overflowing with stories about the extreme snow that was on its way. It was about nine in the morning. I remember looking out at our external seating area, not a flake in sight, and wondering what all the fuss was about. Less than three hours later, I was cycling home in a full-blown blizzard. A ten-minute journey took nearly an hour.

Now, in theory, I love snow. I live near the sea, and snow is something I rarely see. The kids were at that age where a snowball fight was still the very best way to spend an afternoon, and the buzz from 'snow day' was reaching fever pitch by the time I made it home. It genuinely felt like I had fought my way home, so severe was the snowfall. Everyone was excitedly scouring the loft for my childhood wooden sledge, gloves and scarves excavated from the back of dark and dusty drawers, and I, with a fake smile plastered across my face, was starting to rock internally with Richter-scale nine anxiety.

The chat turned to road closures. My husband and kids went on what turned out to be a near-arctic expedition to retrieve a sledge from my parents' house three miles away and were gone for hours.

Without thinking anything of it, the family came back, chattering excitedly about cars being abandoned, snow drifts as high as the roof, and everything grinding to a complete halt. With only unbridled joy in their hearts, they talked about us being snowed in for days. My anxiety catapulted right off the Richter scale.

Fear and constriction flooded my body. Checking for the accuracy of the information, I joked, 'Surely that's a bit of an exaggeration, peeps.' No, they all affirmed, we really were going to be snowed in for days. I was stuck. Panic was ricocheting around my body. I couldn't stand up. I needed to get out. To escape. The urge to run was overwhelming, but to where?

And more importantly, why?

I wasn't sure why. Normally, all I ever wanted was to be at home. Yet, trapped by the Beast from the East, I had to be free. From what? None of it made sense.

I tried to ask myself, where would I want to go to if the roads were driveable? Nowhere. Yet the panic raged on. I couldn't bear the idea of being trapped.

I had had a similar experience a few years prior, when I realised my passport had run out. Despite the fact that I was incapable of going anywhere, the idea that I couldn't leave the country brought choking panic feelings up in my throat. Don't even get me started on the feeling of being 'stuck on an island.' I had to fight off that fear with all my strength most days, thinking about the fact that the UK was surrounded by sea, and I was incapable of going on a train, plane, or boat to escape would send my panic right through the roof. Even a foggy day could render me panic-riddled.

So, there I was, snowed in at home, and rather than being able to enjoy it, I spent the entirety of what turned out to be roughly three days battling intense panic feelings and unable to enjoy the experience. Old coping techniques came out; drinking alcohol and over-eating in the hope I would fall into a stupor, whereby I might sleep a little at night. The nights were the worst. As soon as the roads were driveable, I tried to cajole the kids into playing with me in the grey and dirty melting snow. Unsurprisingly, they declined. I had completely missed the moment.

So, when I started watching the news about the Covid-19 pandemic in first China, then Italy, I remember feeling sick with anxiety and stating categorically I would die if it were to happen here. I would not be able to cope with being locked in my house. It was my absolute worst nightmare.

And we all know what happened next.

Boris Johnson gave a speech on the news. The shutters came down across the nation. I was locked down. No choice. No wiggle room. I waited for the anxiety to kick in. I waited. And I waited.

Then the most extraordinary thing occurred.

Unlike the Beast from the East, which I knew couldn't last more than a few days, this Covid-19 pandemic had no known end date, and I couldn't escape it or ask for special measures as I 'don't do well with anxiety.' No, I was forced to accept that there was no getting out of it. The only way forward was to go through it (the Bear Hunt comes to mind) just like everyone else. I had to surrender to the idea that I might now have panic attacks for the rest of eternity. I had to accept life as it was. No possibility for me to 'tweak' my circumstances. And as unlikely as this may sound, it flicked a metaphorical switch in my brain, and instead of being flooded with the anticipated panic, I felt remarkably calm.

As the weeks went on, I realised I was primed and ready for this. I had ninja anxiety-coping skills, and I could pass these on to people who were meeting anxiety head-on for the very first time.

Anxiety was everywhere. It was as much of a pandemic as Covid. I was no longer this freak (in my mind) who had anxiety; I was the same as everyone else. Actually, I was doing a touch better than many. Covid taught me that when things get tough for us humans, the fear response kicks in. It's normal. I was no longer the black sheep of the flock. Singled out. The whole flock was suffering with anxiety, and I was able to shepherd them to safer ground.

What a revelation!

I wasn't weak and useless. I was resilient and capable. I was able to cope, even with my marriage challenges. When push came to shove, I proved to myself that, at my core, I was rock solid.

The pandemic was a terrible time. It was heart-breaking to hear the news stories, but the fear that was so new to many was my old friend, and I found that, during Covid, I was able to carve out a new relationship with it.

I went to work at a Covid call centre, served coffee at a vaccination centre, and helped people to get back into work with a job as an advisor on self-employment. I found I could help people who were feeling anxious, depressed, or simply needing some positive motivation.

People commented on my uplifting energy. Something which I believed was impossible for me to cope with (being indefinitely trapped), as with the tear to my carotid artery five years earlier, didn't floor me at all. It offered me the opportunity to see myself in a new, stronger light. An unexpected consequence indeed!

It wasn't a complete hallelujah moment. Not a 'this is finally all over' occasion, but it was another part of piecing back together the puzzle that was 'broken me.' With gold at the ready! Covid-19 was Kintsugi in action!

Notes

Chapter 18 – Reiki

I turned to Reiki immediately after I almost lost my life in my mid-forties.

A tear in the carotid artery up to my brain, accompanied by Horner's syndrome, could easily have ended my life, and the case history for others in this scary position has sadly not been so positive. I'm a walking miracle... again. I am so incredibly grateful.

For the first few days and weeks after leaving hospital, I was too scared to sneeze or cough for fear that the strain on my artery could end all plans I had for my future life. Each day was not a given. It never is, but we don't usually dwell on this. When I awoke on any morning, I quietly celebrated still being on this earth. I wrote a poem every day, just to mark my continued existence, and the writing calmed me down and brought me joy.

With two incredible small children and a bucket list running to many sheets of A4, I knew I had to hunker down and focus on finding treatments that might promote my healing and keep my stress low. This was not easy for a person with a long history of having an over-anxious response to life.

I needed help, and quickly. So many situations would crop up that were incredibly difficult. My lovely children, then aged eight and seven, would crawl into my bed at night when they couldn't sleep, and I would fear that they might wake up to a dead mother. This whole time period was extremely challenging.

You might expect this to trigger massive panic attacks. Weirdly, it had the reverse effect. Prior to this episode, I had been plagued with morbid thoughts ever since my drug episode in my early twenties. I couldn't even drive past a funeral director's without looking the other way, and most bedtimes were tainted with fearful thoughts and the accompanying waves of anxiety that followed them.

All of this stopped when I had to face my own mortality.

Could this teach me something about the nature of fear itself?

It repeatedly comes up in my life that, when I face the things I believe are completely impossible for me to overcome, the act of facing up to them makes the impossible possible.

I was super keen to keep my stress low and reduce the risk to my artery. My sister, herself a Reiki master, convinced me that the answer was to go to see an incredibly experienced Reiki practitioner.

Fifty-something me needs to find this woman —I have tried many times — and offer her my sincerest apology.

Firstly, you have to respect anyone who is happy to treat someone who could potentially pop right off this mortal coil whilst on the therapy couch. Very few were keen, I can tell you. It has the potential to be messy and not great for anyone's reputation.

I loved the fact that she was happy to treat me, and it gave me incredible comfort going to see her every week. She used a whole host of tools I had never heard of, from singing bowls, to gongs, and hands-on healing, all in a concerted attempt to help me.

And I'm still here writing this book, against the odds, which I believe is at least in part down to her treatments. I owe her a genuine debt of gratitude.

What I struggled to do at the time, though, was to put my cynical and poorly-educated-in-all-things-spiritual mind to one side and allow myself to fully benefit from her healing gift.

Given the time again, I would enjoy the vibration of the gong or the hum of the singing bowl rather than fight any beneficial effects with a barrage of negative thoughts, rating it from fairly annoyingly harmless to potentially even accusing her of making me anxious.

I ended the treatment because I claimed she had made me worse. My wonky thinking had gone into overdrive. Her way of treating me was too 'new' for me to cope with.

And surprisingly, depressingly quickly, I moved from an incredible appreciation for my life after this brush with death —seeing colours, nature, and everything around me in this beautiful world in a new and extraordinary light— to slipping back to my old ways of focusing on problems, taking life for granted, and getting all caught up in the rush of the everyday.

Even writing this now, it takes me back to the way I experienced life when I had no immediate guarantee of how long I had left to sample it.

It seems strange to even write that now, as I still have no guarantee of what tomorrow holds, but I'm caught up once more in future planning and have stepped away from the reality where everything slows down and only the truly important things in life like love and family hold any relevance. In that post near-death reality, everything that isn't important falls away completely. It's surprising how little really is important when push comes to shove.

Not working ridiculously long hours in my restaurant had seemed an impossible dream pre-artery tear, yet overnight, I dropped my work, knowing that the restaurant would cope, and my survival was so much more important than my business.

I can only ever see this when my back is right up against the wall, sadly.

I remember little things, like being astounded that I had ever rushed like a woman possessed when trying to get my children to school. It became as clear as day that to rush in that way was utterly pointless, and despite my absolute conviction, it made little difference to the end result. Slow and steady really does win the race. Or at least allows you to get to the finish line.

I need to keep reminding myself of this every day. I am the classic hare, racing around, looking for the speedy answer to everything. Briefly, when I was recovering from my near-stroke, I found myself dropping into the life of the tortoise, and I cannot tell you how much better a place that is for me.

Despite this, true to a pattern that I now see, I slipped back into my old behaviour habits, and with each passing month, the hare in me grew strong again, and my desire to start chasing reared up its misguided head once more.

I began to question the Reiki healer, on why, after so many weeks and months, my anxiety hadn't been 'fixed'?

Having originally been grateful for the healing and being alive, I began to demand (not overtly, but in my head) bigger improvements. I questioned why my panic was not receding quickly enough. I had been having all this healing, and if anything, my ability to travel was getting worse.

I didn't see that having a near-death experience would make the part of my brain responsible for my survival, quite sensibly, go into overdrive, and that safety, at whatever social cost, would be pushed right up the agenda. It seemed my body understood that being alive was far greater a priority than making sure I could attend a friend's birthday party in Barcelona.

So, rather than see any of the above, I concluded that the Reiki was making me worse.

I didn't take note of the fact that I never did the 'homework' she asked of me, work that would have been so useful, such as meditating for a few minutes a day or sitting with my anxiety when it cropped up, rather than running away.

I, without noticing, had slipped comfortably back into victim mode, blaming everything in my external environment for my anxiety and focusing on trying to change that world rather than focusing on what was going on inside me.

I'm pretty sure, with a bit of digging around in my inner experience, I could have found some useful answers. I was being way too noisy in my head, though, to hear any whispers my intuition might have wanted to pass on.

After about a year, and perhaps forgetting I was lucky to be alive and flourishing, I decided to quit Reiki, explaining that it was the Reiki that was making my anxiety worse, and no amount of gentle encouraging to consider whether things were shifting but that I was maybe looking at things from a wonky perspective made any difference to my decision to quit.

I now see so many benefits from the treatments and can hear all the useful advice that this wonderful woman gave me that, at the time, went completely over my head. My ears could only hear things that made sense to me back then.

So, having discarded Reiki, I was even more in need of a 'cure,' as my ability to travel had retracted even more disappointingly close to the tiny radius around my home.

Random aside: The anomaly that I chose to ignore throughout the past thirty years was that if I needed to be X distance from home to be okay in this world, how could this 'home' keep moving? I think we relocated eleven times during my peak of anxious feelings, and without the luxury of choice, my safe home base had to move with me.

Sometimes, this was a challenge, like when I moved from my own house in a beautiful estuary town to my husband's house in a built-up area of Exeter city centre, but I had equal difficulty when I had moved from my house in Exeter city centre to that same leafy suburb only a year earlier, to the extent that I stayed up all night before moving day, determined to call my solicitor at nine o'clock on the dot to pull out of the sale, even though we had exchanged contracts and doing so would have cost me thousands of pounds I didn't have to spare.

Each time I was 'forced' to make a move, my inner resilience would kick in and I would acclimatise to my new home.

Why had I never applied this learning to my travel? The difficulty with travel was that there was always the option not to go, or to turn back at the first hurdle. This did not serve me well. I can see that clearly now.

I can also see that I'm resilient and brave. I have persevered with trying to be free of this anxious way of living, and although with hindsight I can see why many of my best attempts might have failed, I realise this 'failure' is just part of my learning, and to quote Edison, 'I have not failed. I've just found 10,000 ways that don't work.' So, try again I did, and my next venture took me to explore food. No hardship, as this is a subject I truly adore.

Chapter 19 – Healthy Living

Optimal nutrition circa 2004

One thing that is becoming clear to me as I write up my many and varied attempts to become anxiety-free is that I have not, historically, been a great listener. This has made me belly laugh today.

I have taken the advice that is easy and quick to implement, giving rather a wide steer to anything that required repetition and staying the course. I say that, but actually, it's my conscious mind that takes this instant gratification route. My subconscious is more than delighted to doggedly apply rules and lessons I have mislearned over the years.

If the diligence I showed in applying my travel rule could have instead been applied to exercising, avoiding alcohol/sugar, prioritising sleep, or having a regular meditation practice, imagine the possible outcome.

I feel like shouting at the younger version of myself and saying, 'Hey, Helga, you are so nearly there. You are so close to finding the solution, but you're looking in the wrong direction.' For now, let me regale you with a tale about how I met with a brilliant nutritionist, didn't apply any of her advice, and consequently spent money on sessions that brought little relief to my anxious thirty-four-year-old self. Not that the money was wasted, of course. You don't really unlearn things. It has just taken me a few (okay, nearly twenty) years to understand what I was being taught about food. Food affects how I feel. In a big way.

At the point when I went to see the nutritionist, I felt I led a fairly healthy lifestyle. I was vegetarian, a non-smoker, and quite liked walking and dancing wildly in clubs. I was not overweight at this point.

I was asked to write a food diary and felt confident turning up to the session with my list that included pasta (the Mediterranean diet was all the rage in the press at the time), vegetarian meat replacements, bread, fruit, a few vegetables, and rather a lot of coffee and red wine.

This was during the phase when the media particularly loved red wine and extolled the virtues of the French diet, with coffee contributing to your fluid intake and having other benefits.

I was drinking way too much coffee, which was causing heart palpitations—always blamed on anxiety—and stopping me from sleeping. I was permanently drained, had way too much time to think with all the insomnia, and medicated with 'healthy' red wine to switch off from the caffeine.

Far from getting a gold star for my food diary, the nutritionist shook her head repeatedly and asked me to change almost everything I consumed.

She homed in on my sugar intake, talked about gut bacteria and the impact that refined carbohydrates were having on my system. I thought it was a good thing that I always had a nap after eating, but she told me this was my body crashing after too many carbohydrates.

She talked wholegrains, fermented foods, lots of fresh vegetables rather than the mainly fruit diet I preferred, drinking eight to ten glasses of water a day, and cutting my caffeine back to one cup a day maximum because giving up seemed too impossible even for her.

And the alcohol? She did not concur that the fourteen units talked about for women were a daily allowance rather than a weekly one, and one that was almost impossible to stick to on any big night out.

After seeing the nutritionist, I did what I always tended to do. I ate fabulously well for a week, got bored, and decided it was way too hard to make all these dietary changes, drawing the conclusion that no one realistically survives on grains all the time anyway. I am, after all, not a chicken.

If I compared myself to my circle of friends, I was one of the healthier eaters. Most of my friends ate processed meat, drank more than me, smoked, and still took drugs. I was doing well compared to my tribe, so I largely ignored the advice and wrote off the nutritionist as a 'crank,' which is always easier than making big changes for yourself.

It wasn't that I wanted to ignore her, but what she was suggesting was hard, and burying my head in the sand felt easier. My anxiety did not improve as a result.

Now, having had years to look into wellness and healthy living, the changes she suggested seem quite reasonable, and when I implement them, I feel considerably better.

The only time I ate particularly well during the peak anxiety years was my brief time doing yoga teacher training. The wife of the yoga instructor used to prepare these incredible Ayurvedic lunches. There are few occasions in life when I have eaten anything more delicious. I wish I had taken the time to learn how to make them.

The next few years of my life were consumed with running restaurants, trying to push away the feelings of anxiety by drowning myself in work.

Restaurant work is not good for anxiety. It is adrenaline, alcohol, and caffeine fuelled with huge, heavy meals regularly consumed late at night. Food too rich to eat every day became the norm. Watching healthy-looking people eating and drinking in front of me every day made unhealthy habits feel normal. I became more stressed, overweight, couldn't sleep, and drank heavily.

I crowed about drinking twelve double espressos a day to get me through an eighteen-hour shift, as if working excessively was some kind of badge of honour. I was so gung-ho about my health, bantering with customers who dared to advise me against my habits. I remember laughing so much when a friendly regular suggested my espresso habit might actually kill me. Not so funny when I was waiting for a scan at A&E.

I rushed around like an idiot, felt super productive but was really a manic employer, absent mum, and cranky partner. I don't mean that to be critical of my younger self. She was doing what she felt was best for her family from her understanding at the time.

To be fair, my 'psychic' sister warned me ad nauseam that I might pop my clogs at any time, but obviously, I ignored her. Who listens to anyone from Totnes anyway? Obviously, I do now, but this was a few years ago. I allow myself a small chuckle.

Another go – circa 2019

Having toyed with nutrition in 2004, it was a further fifteen years before I had another go at embracing healthy food and exercise. Neither came easily to me. I was definitely that last to be picked for P.E. person at school, and with the exception of the cabbage soup diet which lasted about a day, and a three-month spell avoiding carbs in an attempt to get into a teeny tiny wedding dress bought on eBay for twenty-five pounds, I haven't delved particularly deeply into the world of diet.

It has, in recent years, become impossible to avoid the obvious link between nutrition and physical and mental well-being. Food has a direct effect on my body and how I feel. Before you ditch this book for its ability to only state the obvious, it wasn't obvious to me. Certainly not the extent to which food could potentially make me feel better.

I remember years ago, my psychotherapy counsellor told me to eat potatoes to feel more grounded, and The Bee Man telling me about a 'brain' in my gut, but other than that, whilst I knew some foods were better than others, I didn't realise foods affected people in different ways.

Up until that point, I had focused more on how food would affect my weight rather than how food might affect my brain.

That said, my bookcase does hold two unread books from a Patrick Holford that have gathered dust for years, titled *Optimum Nutrition for the Mind* and *Beat Stress and Fatigue*. This demonstrates, as so often before, that I have hovered close to a solution, had the instinct to buy the book, but not taken the action step needed of actually reading the book and, God forbid, implementing its advice. Rome clearly wasn't built in a day…

Now, in my mid-fifties, I see a clear link between diet and food. I can eat a lovely chunky sandwich at two o'clock and be asleep by twenty past or drink a strong coffee on an empty stomach and, again, find myself nap-ready, rather than primed to take on the task ahead.

It used to frustrate the hell out of me when Bee Man refused to tell me what to eat or not to eat, advising me that my 'microbiome was unique' and I would have to find out for myself through a process of elimination, what was right for me.

What? Just give me the easy answer. I am always impatient for an easy result.

Sadly, I can't tell you what will work for you either, but I can say it is incredible what a difference improving the quality of my food intake has had on my physical symptoms of anxiety. Those symptoms I particularly didn't like; racing heart, sweating palms, lightheadedness, and nerves in my stomach. Sugar is particularly noticeable for bringing these on. Experiment for yourself, but if you take anything from this story, it's that when things have gone badly for me with anxiety, the following things have always been out of balance: food, sleep, exercise, and relaxation.

Always. Without fail.

The joy of this is that each one of these things is entirely within my control.

Find what works for you, but do give your body the very best possible fuel if you are looking for positive changes in your life. This is also a note to self. I have just come off two straight weeks of eating less than brilliantly.

I'm now a big convert to kefir in an attempt to befriend all those lovely gut bacteria I have been bashing with my anxiety. Is it helping? Who knows? It makes me feel good and think worthy thoughts about how healthy I'm being, which, in turn, makes me smile, so I see some benefit at the get-go.

Exercise, again, is something that is now a part of my daily routine. I walk to work when I can to get my big old dose of natural feel-good sunshine and vitamin D, do a free exercise class on YouTube, and have even done a run (only once, as I ached for a week). I also have a swimming membership (gathering dust) that I promise I intend to start using soon.

I am the least likely person to have developed an exercise habit, but I do enjoy my daily movement and miss it if I get caught up in the myth of 'busyness' and stop. There is clearly scope to do more. My GP frowns every time I step on the scales in his surgery, but I'm trying to move in the right direction. Honestly! Baby steps, people.

In the past, I have both envied and feared gym-goers, and whilst I would love to have a beautifully toned exterior, I know I will never put in the work necessary. I think the universe realised fairly early on that I would be a big, fat pain in the derriere given the beautiful physique of Beyoncé Knowles. There is hidden wisdom to the gifts we receive!

What exercise gives me these days is joy. I can't quite believe I'm saying that, but I find it liberating to do an exercise routine online, give it a shot, not chastise myself for being less than perfect, and feel my energy soar as I sing, slightly out of tune and out of breath, to the catchy tunes that accompany Zumba for the over fifty-fives.

Ever since I was rated four out of ten for dance moves by a particularly 'judgy' boyfriend, I held myself back from dancing. No more!

Now, I am unstoppable and boogie along to whatever tune is playing, keeping up sometimes, failing miserably other times, but enjoying my divine right to shake my thang. Give it a go. I can't recommend highly enough banishing pointless insecurity, donning a pair of leg warmers, and letting rip to Tina Turner's *Simply The Best,* or even better, Irene Cara's *Flashdance.* I pray no one ever films me.

Dancing makes me feel good. It's not merely a competition sport. Who knew (actually, every three-year-old knows this) it could be so much fun and make me feel so alive? Everything that makes me feel good is to be embraced. Every last thing.

A quick rant about guilty pleasures and my relationship to them. I have numerous things which I would describe as guilty pleasures, from cheap chocolate to films, certain genres of literature, much pop music, and certain items of comfortable clothing. Basically, anything that doesn't enhance my overall image but which I do truly love gets abandoned on the growing pile of guilty pleasures. There is no such thing as a guilty pleasure. These are my genuine pleasures, but I'm not brave enough to own them. I've been doing this for years, from not owning up to people I have been attracted to because they weren't 'cool' to stopping myself from dancing, singing, and generally doing things that require me to relinquish control and risk looking foolish. I am the ultimate people pleaser, pretending not to be a people pleaser. Confusing? You try being me! From this moment forward, I'm going to own my likes and dislikes and accept that, yes, I do like 1970s punk, but I also own an A-ha single. I don't like violent films, and I would rather watch *Downton Abbey* than *Kill Bill*. I could go on, but this is really just a note to self to make a conscious effort to be more authentic and to be honest about who I am and what I like, and that includes liking myself. It is so blatantly clear to me now that any dissonance between who I say I am and who I really am fuels my anxiety. I feel happiest when what I think, say, and do all line up. I'm working on it!

Go ahead and do yourself a favour. Banish that annoying voice in your head that says you can't do the things that bring you joy. That's not your voice.

For me, it's singing in a key that can only fully be appreciated by myself and the neighbourhood cats, dancing whilst wildly flailing my arms around, and watching kids' movies without anyone under the age of ten to accompany me. It doesn't matter what you do, as long as you love doing it.

Doing more of what I love unleashes my brave spirit and pushes fear into the back seat where it belongs, not behind the wheel, influencing my direction in life. That's my take on it, anyway.

A Random Aside – The Power of Love

There was a lot wrong with the 1980s. Some related to my very poor life choices, but no one can overlook the role shoulder pads, the invention of yuppie culture, and neon legwarmers had to play. What were we thinking?

To counter this, it was an era that was also keen to shout loud about the wonder of love, from George Michael crooning his *Careless Whisper,* to Bonnie Tyler having a *Total Eclipse of the Heart.* Not to forget that three different bands in one year alone released songs titled *The Power of Love.* Frankie Goes to Hollywood, Jennifer Rush, and Huey Lewis and the News.

Caught up in a Victor Frankenstein-esque desire to create the perfect 'Helga-creature' at this time, I no doubt scoffed about love and other such wishy-washy ideas, grimacing every time one of these trite songs pushed The Jesus and Mary Chain from the line-up on *Top of the Pops.*

Jennifer Rush? I had to endure her bleating on about love for five solid weeks, clinging to the number one spot and becoming the biggest selling song of 1985. Groan.

So, it is rather sheepishly now that I choose to name this chapter *The Power of Love,* but it deserves to be here, as nothing has had a bigger impact on my anxious experience than love itself.

I first became aware of the strong power of love through my connection with my various rescue animals. My boyfriend (of the Glastonbury era) used to laugh about a funny thing I did with my teeth when I looked at my dog. It was a kind of strange chipmunk impression brought on by the sheer intensity of the love I felt for my gorgeous border collie pup. Her name was Millie, and we had a soul-level bond. I even named my first child after her (and my son after my budgerigar, Max). I don't recall if I made similar chipmunk faces at my boyfriend, but that's a direction we don't need to go in.

So, it all started with my dog, Millie. I can clearly remember the intense, all-consuming feeling that would come over me when I locked eyes on her. I feel that flood of emotion now, just at the thought of her perfect poochiness. The reason for mentioning this is the all-consuming nature of the feeling. It shoves other feelings right out of the way when it rushes over me.

It seems that when I feel intense love, my thoughts run wildly in a direction that does not leave much space for anxiety. Stir in a good dose of happy hormones: dopamine, serotonin, endorphins, and oxytocin, and all in all, the days look considerably brighter.

Knee-deep in anxiety, I sensed love played a role in how calm I felt, but I carried quite some misunderstanding about the precise nature of its role.

I used to believe that certain people 'made' me anxious or happy. When I was falling out of love with one boyfriend, I would conclude that they were responsible for bringing on my anxiety and whatever new love interest would be credited with curing me, as I felt less anxious in their company. Could this have anything to do with the fact that my entire brain space was being crashed by thoughts of love? There was no voodoo being performed by any one of these characters in my story; it was me all along releasing a whole host of happy hormones whilst plying my brain with relentless gooey love-obsessed thoughts or drumming up an anxious experience by telling myself stress stories that released the 'bad boys' of the hormone gang (cortisol and adrenaline) leaving me feeling panicky.

What I didn't particularly pay attention to was the fact that all kinds of love made me feel better, not just romantic love. Love was the drug, as Brian Ferry attested. It was when I experienced the feeling I called love, whether it was love for nature, love for my best friends, love for my hamster, Otto, or love for my friend's new baby, my anxiety inevitably decreased.

Cuddling my friend's newborn baby was an interesting one. The first time I picked up Hatty, I was overwhelmed by love and felt this incredible connection with the small creature in my arms. I had a knack for getting her off to sleep and would clamour for any opportunity to hang out in her company.

I remember thinking, 'Well, this is weird. Who knew I loved babies?' I even briefly contemplated working with little people until I 'forgot' my three-year-old son at school pick up one day (only momentarily, and in my defence, I was chronically sleep-deprived), leaving him in my daughter's classroom until another mum shouted after me, 'Haven't you forgotten something?' It suggests maybe giving the occasional hug or smile might be a safer bet than fully launching myself into a new childcare career. The point is, I had a lot of love to give.

My boyfriend of the 1990s used to find the intensity of my love feelings 'too much' and regularly looked for the animals in our households to deflect the attention away from him. I would gaze at him, consumed with love, and he would clock me and declare, 'Too much love,' marching me off to another room to hang out with my rabbit. Love you, Billy Bunny!

The point of all this is that the stronger my love grew, the weaker my anxiety response became. I didn't exactly see that as I was struggling, but it was definitely something that was vaguely bobbing about in the back of my mind. It worked in reverse too. The more love was missing from my life and the less free I was to be my true self, the quicker the anxiety would ramp up.

The moment this whole 'love influence' thing really hit home was when I became a mum.

For a start, it was a huge surprise. I was thirty-eight years old and sure that particular ship had long sailed. Years of giving up on contraception with my boyfriend (now husband) had resulted in no near misses. He was 100% certain that he didn't want to have kids, but not certain enough to do the few key things required to ensure that outcome, lucky for me. So we drew the wrong conclusion that the universe was not in favour of us procreating.

When I did get pregnant, peeing on a Clear Blue test in a supermarket toilet, I was ecstatic. It took another nine months for my husband to catch up with my keenness, but for me, it was immediate. My enthusiasm for what lay ahead combined with another dose of feel-good hormones, and my anxiety pretty much disappeared when I got those two pink lines. It was how I knew I was pregnant for the second time a year later. This calm descended over me once again. Now, I'm not claiming everyone with anxiety should rush out and reproduce, but what is worth noting is how waves of love can more than overpower waves of anxiety.

The thinking was forced to change too. There was no space and time to contemplate my anxious thoughts. I was too busy running around after two small people born barely a year apart.

It wasn't the being a mother thing that was the key, though. Yes, it made a huge difference personally, but what I see now is that it was the power of love that had the capacity to make the change. Fear was a strong and overwhelming emotion, but love was more than its match.

I see it in myself when I see an injustice towards anything I love. Any fear in that situation is rapidly shoved aside as my love-fuelled indignation powers up a courage in me that I never knew I possessed. You mess with my kids, and I promise there won't be a meek version of me asking you to desist. I am fierce when protecting those I love. Love gives me courage. Love gives me strength, and it sure gives anxiety a run for its money.

So, that's it on this topic. Love has been a huge part of me changing my relationship with anxiety.

I also don't think I can get away with writing this chapter without mentioning the slightly uncomfortable subject of self-love.

I'm too long in the tooth to be entirely relaxed declaring deep love for myself in public as one woman did a few years ago by marrying herself —the full monty, all white dress, gifts, and a huge party. As I write this, that does actually sound fun, but I digress. It would be disingenuous, though, if I didn't 'fess up to the fact that I have replaced internal hate-speak for myself with many more words of love. I am even known to give myself a quick hug, along with any passing tree if I'm certain no-one is looking at me, by way of encouragement in a tricky situation. I mutter lovely, encouraging words to myself now when I glance in the mirror too (after recovering from the inevitable disappointment that it's not Winona Ryder looking back at me. I have always wanted to look like Winona Ryder since Heathers. In all fairness, I can now look at my fifty-five-year-old self and smile with genuine warmth at least.)

I now give myself the love I so desperately sought over the past decades. Years of unrequited love later, I have come to see that if I want to be encouraged and to feel okay with my choices, looks, outfits, whatever, rather than outsource the comments to a quite unpredictable outside world, I can look to myself to provide the reassurance I seek. Phew! This takes the pressure off all those in my life who I still smother with love, but without the expectation that they will reciprocate with the same intensity.

I even save a few of those chipmunk faces for my good self. It seems to be working wonders!

As Philip Larkin says, in the last line of his poem 'An Arundel Tomb'

'What will survive of us is love'

Notes

Chapter 20 – CBT

Cognitive Behavioural Therapy. The first time I heard about it, I was working at the National Lottery Charities Board in one of those office jobs that makes your teeth itch.

Every fibre of my body screamed 'exit stage left,' but I hung in there for a miraculous three and a half years.

That they didn't show me the door is to their credit, as I spent way too many hours crying about my relationship, recovering from hangovers from nights out that remain a complete blur, phoning psychic helplines to provide some solace from aforementioned relationship crisis, and generally loafing about, engaging in gossip and other less than soul-enhancing experiences.

I was plugged into my CD Walkman, listening to Matthew Sweet and The Counting Crows, when one of my infinitely wiser co-workers mentioned that CBT might be good for my head. I imagine it was the snivelling on the desk next to her that prompted her to intervene with this piece of well-placed advice.

Surprisingly (not), I completely ignored the suggestion and continued to self-medicate until I fell off the next cliff. This was only a few short months later.

Presumably, her comment was lodged somewhere in the recesses of my brain because, when sitting in tears in my doctor's office further down the line and CBT was mentioned as a possible solution, I grabbed the opportunity and pleaded with my GP to see if he could get me bumped up the queue.

Within a few weeks, I was sitting in my first session, truly believing that this, at last, was the answer to my universal cry for help.

I am fascinated by the reasoning that goes into where the NHS chooses to site their therapy sessions.

Mine was in what must have previously been a secure unit, as all the windows had bars on them, and the doors had that heavy feel that is common, I believe, in prisons and recording studios.

This did not bode well.

Ever the optimist, I went anxiously into the room, heart pounding, hands sweating, nausea rising, and a whole host of other familiar yet highly undesirable symptoms running through me, with the therapist rising to greet me and moving to close the 'prison' door. Not on your nelly!

I leapt to the door with an instant adrenaline response best suited to fighting wild beasts or dodging fast-moving cars, bolting from that room too quickly to allow the poor therapist to even say hello.

He then proceeded to tell me in the corridor how we would be shutting that door and that he could give me the perfect techniques to calm me down. Hadn't I heard this before?

I was sure that might have been feasible if his voice hadn't come to me in that distorted way that sound travels under water, and my sight hadn't started to blur, and every link to my rational brain hadn't been utterly severed. I ran and never went back again.

Now, maybe this is a me thing, but is a prison-like building really the best choice for hosting a session aimed at reducing anxiety? Is it just me, or would a room with an open window and a view over a wildflower garden not be better suited for the purpose?

Thinking back, even the pre-assessment for this treatment was weird.

I was sent to an assessment centre to establish how badly I needed the help. I was asked a selection of questions about my childhood that failed to interest the assessor (although they traumatised me), and his eyes only lit up when I mentioned how my sister, in a moment of teenage madness, had held a bread knife to my throat and threatened to use it. That seemed to do the trick, and I got the necessary tick in the box to be eligible for treatment.

In another assessment session, I was asked if I had ever thought about pushing my father down the stairs to hurt him. The answer was a resounding 'no.'

What on earth was going on in psychological assessments during the nineties?

The above were real questions, and the brown paper bag was a genuine solution offered for them.

This is one of the many things that remind me that not everything in the recent past was better than it is today. So much, thank goodness, has improved.

My current GP offers acupuncture rather than paper bags.

So, my experience of CBT is certainly not a helpful reflection of what it can offer.

A friend is currently seeing incredible transformative change as a result of CBT. As ever, it's not the treatment that is the key, but the human delivering it.

Human connection is everything. Big shout-out to all the incredible humans I have met over the years who have shared their energy and wisdom to move me forward in my healing journey.

What's interesting to me now is how I have always been fixated on that 'magic treatment' that might hold the key to unlocking the puzzle of why fear has such a massive hold on me.

I had never thought to think about the person.

So many of the experiences that have not been helpful have been more about the lack of connection with the therapist than anything else.

Why did I not put the same focus on finding people I could connect with, rather than focusing purely on the fix?

I now realise that, almost without exception, the treatments that moved me forward have been with people I've felt a connection with, who allowed me to be completely open.

We have then had real conversations, and I've been able to absorb whatever learning I needed to take from the situation.

The exception was the Reiki.

I wonder if I had become attached to my anxiety in some way and wasn't ready to give up the comfortable familiarity of my anxious feelings. Sounds weird, but we are leaving no stone unturned.

I felt overwhelmed, but that was because the Reiki healer had pushed me well out of my comfort zone, from the sound baths she performed, to the advice on sitting out my fear, using breathing techniques, and learning how to meditate whilst improving my diet.

I can see now I was closer than I had ever been to stepping through the fear and coming out the other side.

Oh, I was so close. Something she told me often, but I panicked and stampeded back to my comfort zone. I could so easily have taken her advice and stepped through my fear. I guess I wasn't quite ready for that.

Chapter 21 – Psychic Doctor

You may have picked up by now that I am more than a little dazzled by the potential for a quick fix to my anxiety.

If anyone dangles that juicy carrot, I'm pretty much willing to sell the telly, my record collection, family heirlooms, and jewellery that might raise a few quid on eBay to get my hands on the miracle cure. I believe there is a saying about fools and cash, but I prefer not to dwell on that one.

My sister is also quite prone to believing in the unbelievable. It's both a blessing and a curse.

So, my sister, who had been very unwell with a benign brain tumour, had been to see an eye-wateringly expensive psychic doctor, who had given her advice that she greatly valued that, to my untrained ears, sounded contrary to her medical diagnosis.

Her enthusiasm for this doctor was so effusive that, despite all previous case history of my sister's advice not being even vaguely helpful, I booked in for a £200 consultation by telephone. This was big bucks for me.

To say that she was not engaged that day is putting it politely. She seemed, at best, highly inconvenienced by my call, which had been booked many weeks ahead, and at worst, positively cross.

I'm not denying her the right to her feelings, but maybe she could have cancelled the session that ended up (with prescribed supplements) costing equivalent to two weeks' wages and postponed it for a day when she was more 'in the zone.'

The upshot of the session was that she prescribed me as not having anxiety but a problem with my lungs.

To some degree, I think she was right in that I feel that after years of anxiety, I had developed a bad habit of shallow breathing, and that deep breathing has, in recent years, been immeasurably useful.

However, there was no reason to believe I had any other lung issues, and the supplements she prescribed at enormous cost made zero difference to my symptoms. What remained of them was disposed of in a recent house move.

You guessed it. Things didn't miraculously shift.

I believed they might this time, but it wasn't too many weeks later that I finally had to admit to feeling pretty much the same, and the focus returned to hunting down my next solution.

There was a pattern to my approach to treatments, and that required further scrutiny.

The pattern being that I was, on the surface, committed and enthusiastic to finding a way out of anxiety, but if I probed a little deeper, I appeared to not listen fully to ANY advice proffered, gave up quickly if I didn't see immediate improvement, and judged myself and others harshly if success wasn't fast and lasting.

I needed to be brave and take a deeper look.

I questioned whether, when embarking on a new treatment, I ever really believed things were going to get better.

Did I allow my logical and critical mind to sabotage my best attempts before they ever got going?

Could my go-to thought possibly have been as harsh as, 'this won't work, and I'm eternally doomed to have a life marred by anxiety'?

I fear this may be a more accurate portrayal of my internal dialogue:

Conscious Me (CM): How exciting. I might get rid of this anxiety. Imagine what I could do. Dreams of holidays, trips away with family, freedom, etc.

Sneaky Unconscious Me (SUM): Yeah, right! That is NEVER EVER going to happen, matey. Not on my watch. Imagine the dangers. Let me tell you a story about this danger and that danger. Scared? I thought so. And I haven't even got started yet.

CM: This will be great. Let's part with lots of cash. This time next year, we will be entirely free from anxiety.

SUM: You are going nowhere, sister. What you need is another scary story to keep you in your cave. Remember that time you (exaggerates wildly and the story bears little resemblance to the reality)...Here, take another scary story, and another one…

My body, in the middle of this, feels the pressure and releases a helpful shot of adrenaline and cortisol, just on the off-chance that I do need to deal with any pressing life or death situations.

CM: I am feeling those horrible feelings. What on earth can this mean?

SUM: You are doomed! Told you so. Job done. Please retreat to safety.

CM: Another failed attempt. Pile on the social conditioning about how useless I am and sink into a depressed rut until my natural optimism bubbles up again and I give it another go.

My body collapses in a stressed-out heap.

So, this isn't exactly science, but it's kind of what feels like might go on.

What would be pretty genius is if I could have had a bit more belief in my ability to handle any fear that came my way.

To be fair, the physical symptoms, which I have mentioned before, aren't physically painful. I know this is an old chestnut, and I have been completely incapable of persuading myself of this in the past, but it might be worth revisiting some of these symptoms now, in the cold light of day, just to see how bad they really were.

Could there have been some mislabelling going on here?

I feel like I need to write a disclaimer at this point. Let me categorically confirm, I am completely clear how intensely annoying it is when people minimise the physical feelings of anxiety. I was the first to say I genuinely believed I couldn't bear my symptoms, and the only viable option was to run, not go out, whatever was necessary to avoid feeling them. The trouble is, I do now see that this was just a story I told myself. This required me to take a long, hard stare at my symptoms.

Sweaty palms

This was always my first anxiety indicator, and the merest hint of a sweaty palm would send my mind racing to establish a meaning. I have a fabulous imagination, so it takes very little for my mind to start catastrophising and creating a neat little plot about what these sweaty palms are alerting me to. Even though there have been way more times when a sweaty palm has been a promising sign that things are looking rather good, my reliable old negative bias locked in, and I clicked play on my internal disaster movie. If I took time to fact check, I might have seen that many a first date kicked off with a sweaty palm. On the rare occasion I've had a sporting success, moist palms featured, not forgetting the amazing gigs, birthday parties, and other things where excitement has been a factor.

This got me curious… Could it be that the difference between me welcoming my feelings and it freaking me out is as simple as how I label things? When I tell myself I'm excited, buzzy feelings flow through me, and I feel energised and uplifted. Call them by a nasty label, and those self-same feelings are vilified and definitely not welcome.

Racing heart

Again, call it anxiety, and I prepared to run for the hills. Call it anticipation of something wonderful occurring—I certainly had a racing heart when I briefly, erroneously, thought I had won the lottery—and I saw this very same feeling as a marker that a good thing might be about to happen too.

And all the others too

When it comes down to it, every one of the feelings I can't bear when I label them anxiety are perfectly fine when they go by a more palatable label.

Now, this has made me question a whole host of other 'facts' I take as being true.

Recently, I was trying to lose weight for health reasons and felt slimmer, my clothes felt looser; all signs were good as the scales were giving me a nice, low reading.

When I realised they weren't working, and I was, in fact, significantly heavier than I had ever imagined, I looked in the mirror and saw things very differently.

Catching myself doing this made my thought process unravel a touch.

How many other times could what I believe affect how I respond to something, and if this is true, can working on my inner dialogue change the outcomes I experience?

This neatly segues me into the next technique that popped up in my search for an answer.

Positive psychology, and let me tell you, I didn't come to that with the necessary open mind that might have aided my success. No, Sir-ee! (said in a 'Doris Day plays Calamity Jane' kind of voice).

Chapter 22 – Positive Psychology

Relentlessly positive people have always made me feel uncomfortable. They just kind of shout too loud. Surely, if something was so good, it would come more easily than standing in front of a mirror, chanting positive things.

Interestingly, though, I haven't classically scrutinised the negative voice shouting at me daily either. The one with the loud hailer that, at any given opportunity, bombards me with derogatory comments about myself, or the numerous times per day I have, historically, told myself things weren't possible, failure was imminent, and it was only a matter of time before everything would surely fall apart.

Now, given a choice, the positive statements have to be more appealing than my constant diatribe of negativity.

Isn't whining about how useless I am way more annoying than me talking about how much I'm looking forward to the day ahead, smiling at strangers, and taking the time to notice all the great things around me every day?

Seemingly not, sadly.

I was walking down the street one morning, and made the mistake of smiling at a man passing me on the pavement. His reaction was to bark at me 'What are YOU smiling about'. A strong response. Instantly I retracted. His aggressive reaction triggered my insecurity, and I worried for the rest of that day that I had turned into one of those smiling goons I associated with dodgy salespeople.

If I'm honest, though, I was shocked and hurt. I immediately changed my behaviour in response to the external response.

But why?

I should have told him exactly why I was smiling and gone on my merry way. Or better still, smiled brighter.

It appears, despite the fact that everyone professes that they want to be happy, and many spend huge amounts of money on material possessions in pursuit of that aim, Western society seems to like nothing less than a truly happy person. One that is fit to burst with joy, as I dared to be on that day.

I guess you're allowed to feel happy on your birthday, when you pass your driving test, and maybe if you succeed at school or work, but ideally, you keep it to within your friend and family group, and whatever you do, don't shout about it to anyone. It's frankly too annoying, and certainly not British!

I'm ashamed to say that one of my children's friends was always saying, 'This is something I'm really good at,' about pretty much any activity we did, whether she could do it or not, and it grated on me.

How sad of me not to encourage and support her positive belief in herself.

I didn't go as far as to counter it, but I didn't encourage it either.

Why not? How truly wonderful to be proud of yourself and happy in your ability to try new tasks?

We come into this world full of self-belief. We try, we fail, we try again, and ultimately, we succeed in learning so many incredible new skills. Why, then, do we so swiftly learn, once we understand that other people have an opinion about us, that we must doubt our ability, quieten down, become less, be smaller, not take up too much space in this world lest we annoy people with our presence? How depressingly early all that need to fit in starts in life.

We go from being pretty damn pleased with ourselves as toddlers, showing anyone who shows a passing interest our pictures, our dancing, our singing, our latest Lego creation, to running down our own creative projects and telling anyone who will listen that we lack talent in a host of different areas.

What is it about society that feels it is in our best interests to take us down a peg or two?

I remember loving ballet and dance when I lived in Holland and was excited to join a ballet class at my local pre-school when I came to England. We went to this magical shop, where I tried on the most beautiful ballet shoes with ribbons that criss-crossed up my legs. I bought a leotard that I pirouetted around my living room in. You cannot imagine how excited I was when I first lined up for that ballet class with all the other little girls.

Yet within a few minutes of that special class, my teacher told my mother that I danced like an elephant, was clumsy, and would never become a dancer.

Now, I have watched *Strictly* religiously on the BBC, and I have seen adults who have never danced before transform over a matter of weeks with the right training.

184

Could the teacher really be so sure that I would never be able to dance? What kind of a teacher was she?

She was absolutely right, of course, in that I never believed I could dance, felt horribly self-conscious every time I was required to participate in a movement class, and carry, to this day, a feeling that I'm clumsy and dance is not for me.

I believed her when she told me I was not enough, and unsurprisingly, I never allowed myself the opportunity to get any better.

What is it with ballet?

It happened to my daughter too, at the age of seven, when she was told not to shut her eyes when she danced. She was lost in the moment and berated for it.

Luckily, we left the class. She did not take the advice to heart and still loves to dance, which she does incredibly well.

So, how does all this relate to my difficulty with Positive Psychology?

Criticism was my comfort zone. Self-deprecating humour was my go-to way of interacting with people, pointing out my flaws so it would be less painful when someone else noticed and commented on them too. I didn't even notice my self-chat was all negative, that not everyone pointed out a million faults in themselves for a laugh, and that even a compliment would be swiftly batted back with not only a denial but a further example of how that good thing could not be further from the truth.

I was set on negativity by default.

Lots of us are.

The idea that other people might swan around life being all sunny, happy, and confident in themselves was deeply unsettling.

What was wrong with these people? I certainly didn't want to stand out from the crowd...

Only, I *did* want to stand out from the crowd, secretly.

I'm not classically conformist at all, and everything about me, from the way I dress, the opinions I express, my values, and the way I see the world, often differs from the mainstream approach. Back to that ADHD diagnosis, maybe. So, why could I not own my right to positivity?

It just seemed kind of geeky. Who in their right mind goes around being relentlessly happy? Surely, no-one really feels like that? I guess what I was reacting to was the 'marketing' of positivity. The constant selling of the way to happiness. Buy this course, join this workshop, try this technique—I can sell you happiness for a price.

I get it. Everyone needs to make a living, and if you feel you have found the answer to true happiness, maybe if you invented a new gadget or discovered a cure in medicine, you might expect to make money from the discovery. It just feels like happiness is not something that should have to be bought.

It feels like every minute of every day, somebody is trying to sell me something based on my underlying human feeling of 'lack' that society drummed into me as I grew up.

I feel like a block of beautiful stone that starts to disappear because it has been chipped away at too many times on a quest to achieve someone else's idea of perfection.

Society bludgeons you into submission, then sells you a selection of wholly unsuitable things that promise to make you whole again, be it positive psychology courses, fancy diets, or exercise machines that offer miracle cures.

Despite my soap box chat above, though, I do feel I need to do something to counter the negative chat etched into my psyche from parental criticism, schoolteachers' 'feedback,' friends, enemies, passers-by in the street, and anyone else who frankly fancies having their two pennies worth about my abilities, or lack thereof.

It doesn't feel right to me to just let it chatter on.

I'm certain that low self-esteem has gelled incredibly well with my anxious way of being.

It kind of appears to the me now that my younger self did not feel she could be trusted to have a positive self-image.

What would I be like if I believed in myself?

Surely, I would be an absolute nightmare, and I would run around the world causing havoc.

I was certainly conditioned not to brag or 'blow my own trumpet.'

Yet, if I'm honest with myself, I'm definitely not at my most creative when I feel down about myself. I'm certainly not great with others. I withdraw from people and can even be unkind when I feel defensive and low. This is making me question the genius (or not) of letting my negative thoughts roam free.

I am now considering that my years of dedication to putting myself down might (read definitely) have been feeding my anxiety. It is an absolute fact that when I'm low, I feel anxious. Therefore, is innocently feeding myself constantly with negative thoughts directly contributing to my anxiety? Could force feeding myself a bit of positivity—in the same way any new habit needs to bed in for a minimum of twenty-one days to become second nature— to tip the balance of comments from negative to positive, have a direct impact on my anxiety?

The possibility was too good to ignore.

I secretly joined the dark side and began to gorge on positivity books and, dare I say it, chant upbeat affirmations.

I became one of 'those people.'

I felt absurd saying positive things to myself at the start, and I'm still mortified if anyone walks in on me, but I can't begin to explain how good it felt to change the dialogue in my head.

I now notice if I say supremely mean things to myself and stop and retract them—quietly to myself, of course.

The acid test for me is, would I say that statement to my children, and if I wouldn't, then I won't say it to myself either. Simple.

Who knew there was a whole world of comedy that doesn't rely on running myself down or others? I have to work a little harder on my stories, but it's worth putting more effort into my conversation rather than falling back on the go-to insults about myself that I have trotted out so often over the years.

I have now consumed countless self-help books on positivity, found brilliant TED talks, online free courses, and people to follow on social media that remind me to look for the good in things, and although I know it's a cliché, what I focus my attention on does seem to become my experience.

When I was at the peak of my anxiety, I would walk down the road and feel threatened by cars, the graffiti on the walls, young people going about their lives, the bustle of the crowds, and the pollution I was inevitably breathing into my lungs, reducing my life expectancy by who knows how many years.

What I didn't realise was that it was my negative outlook that was having the biggest impact on my life expectancy.

I can now walk down the same streets and see cars that make me smile and remind me of my son (he used to be obsessed by the MX5, which I now see everywhere), graffiti that I see as beautiful street art that enhances my local area, young people being creative and brilliant, and reminding me the future is in good hands, streets buzzing with energy, and the many incredible trees that fill my city streets and make my community a healthy place to live.

I'm not saying the negative things don't exist. I just now see the many positive things that outweigh them.

I guess it took me force-feeding myself positivity through the various positive books I read to remind my brain that it was allowed to focus on positive things too.

I had, for years, been dining out on my fears and catastrophic imaginings, all washed down with a big dose of self-abuse, and I had forgotten how good it was to see all the beauty that exists in this world.

I believe positivity resides within us all, and it is, in fact, our default state, but I have found for myself that it needs to have space to grow.

I liken it to letting a well-planted garden get overgrown with bindweed. As pretty as the bindweed looks, if left unchecked, it will choke out everything.

When I feel up and happy, my anxiety doesn't arise.

Now, when I feel low and anxious, I don't turn away from it but accept it and acknowledge I need to do a bit of 'mind gardening,' clear the weeds, and plant some positive seeds.

Too many metaphors, I know, but I reluctantly have to accept that I truly benefit from positive thinking. Perhaps I will be brave enough one day to own it rather than keep it as my guilty secret…

Notes

Chapter 23 – Anti-depressants

The concept of a quick fix for my anxious feelings has always deeply appealed, but it has been closely accompanied by my deep-seated fear of drugs and the potential for unexpected side effects that could wreak havoc on my delicately balanced sanity.

Anti-depressants have been such a dilemma for me over the years. That a pill might exist to potentially remove my anxiety overnight was a thing of dreams. The itch to try it was so strong.

However, at the same time, I was terrified of anything that might make me feel different, as the 'different' feelings might be the signal that a panic attack was on the way.

It was all so confusing. It really messed with my head.

Quite a few times, I would rock up at the doctors and ask for anti-depressants. He would patiently tell me that there would be a period, while the drug was kicking in, where I might feel more anxious, not less.

Knowing how my anxiety worked, he would then reassure me that this stage would pass quickly, with a decent chance that the end result would be a big improvement on my anxiety symptoms. They might even go away.

Then would begin the agonising decision over whether to give them a try.

Many a time, I was issued the prescription but didn't pick up the medicine.

Other times, I would pick up the pack, full of temporary confidence, only to leave it on the kitchen side, where it taunted me with its potential for a cure. It was an overthinking nightmare.

I did, in a moment of true desperation, once try to take it for a few days, and I felt like I was hallucinating. The effect was so strong on me. I genuinely felt like I was drunk. I couldn't think straight, was confused, and struggled to get my words out.

I can now appreciate that much of this was probably just my fear kicking in, giving me a massive shot of adrenaline and making my breath shallow and my thoughts race. I imagine I would have had much the same effect with a placebo.

I don't think I even lasted three days on them, so no chance to test whether they could help to calm my anxious mind. I was also fearful of the idea of becoming dependent on the drugs and going through a withdrawal process.

So much thinking. My poor brain spiralled, and my body flooded with fear. It was exhausting.

Being a little kind to myself, maybe it wasn't right for me. My gut feeling was certainly screaming no, and I was getting more aware that this might be something worth listening to.

So, after many years of this should I, shouldn't I thing raging on in my head, I eventually decided, much like the brown paper bag, that this medical solution wasn't for me. The search moved on once more.

Notes

Chapter 24 – Sleep

I was thinking this morning as I walked to my garage, where I write, that there will be a host of professional people who, should they ever happen upon my book, will smirk at the blindingly obvious reason I have been in this anxious predicament for years.

To recap the life events that brought me to this place:

- Challenges in childhood

- Constantly moving house and always being the 'new kid'

- Working and partying too hard

- Drugs and alcohol

- Too much caffeine

- Poor diet

- Comfort eating and bulimia

- Academic pressure at university

- Low self-esteem, low confidence, and perfectionist leanings

- Lack of exercise

- Poor sleep

It doesn't take a genius to work out that all of the above might be a heady combination for my poor body to cope with, though, the list before took me the full thirty years to piece together.

I was like a jigsaw puzzle missing its box. A jumble of pieces with no picture to guide me. I was clueless about how to make myself 'whole' again. That said, though, my intuition was shouting great instructions at me from the sidelines and, on occasion, a message would land on target.

Sleep was one of those things.

My problems with sleep go back a very long way.

I remember being scared of the dark as a kid, homesick at sleepovers until I was much older than most, unable to get to sleep (I would read for hours) and plagued by nightmares. I was grateful to reach my teenage years, when not sleeping and ruminating in the early hours was no longer frowned upon but viewed as a kind of superpower.

I remember going to a psychology lecture at university and the lecturer making a persuasive case that there was no scientific evidence that we needed sleep at all—talk about only selecting evidence that supports your view. Music to the ears of a bunch of party-loving nineteen-year-olds.

All this in the late eighties when the then UK Prime Minister, Margaret Thatcher, claimed not to need more than four hours sleep, though one could argue her decision-making suggests she needed a whole lot more. Working endless hours was promoted as the only road to a successful career.

Despite all the eighties propaganda, I knew I needed to get more sleep.

I read books on the subject, took herbal supplements, cut out caffeine, and worried endlessly about it.

I became quite the expert on preparing for sleep, was well-versed in the nap versus no nap debate, doused myself in lavender following a hot bath, lay in a cool bedroom with the window open, and awaited sleep.

I waited and I waited.

Approximately thirty years, as sleep evaded me at every turn.

The more I thought about everything I needed to do to improve my sleep, the longer my bedtime ritual became, and the less I slept.

I guess you're seeing the answer here a bit quicker than me.

I became fearful about sleep. Fearful that I was damaging my health, that I was not coping emotionally, that my work was suffering, that I was not a good mother as I was always exhausted, and the more I worried, the less I slept.

Much like my anxiety, I ran a negative video on repeat in my head, telling myself I wouldn't sleep, and so I didn't.

I piled thought upon thought onto the problem, and it didn't solve it.

Much like anything I consider difficult, endless negative thinking on the subject does nothing to improve my performance. I self-medicated with alcohol and took prescription drugs, but nothing improved my sleep.

Now, I sleep.

Not perfectly and not always, but I get tired, go to bed, and very much of the time, I sleep, and I love it.

So, what changed? All I can think is that all the work and focus on getting to grips with anxiety, understanding the power of thought, and getting a bit curious about the unhelpful thinking going on in my head got me noticing that sleep was one of the many areas where overthinking was not my best friend.

I stopped paying so much attention to my sleep. I stopped fixating on it, which meant I stopped the 'loop of doom' going around in my head, telling me how catastrophic it would be if I didn't sleep, and I, surprise, surprise, decided to try and face my insomnia rather than panic about it.

I stopped fearing not sleeping and welcomed my insomnia. It had that same interesting outcome. When I stopped resisting my insomnia and made peace with the idea of not sleeping, I found myself getting drowsy and often just dropping off.

If I'm going to abandon any semblance of cool (okay, that ship has long since sailed), I would also tell myself I was a great sleeper. 'Wow, Helga, you really are the master of sleep. Who knew you were such a sleep goddess?' Ridiculous as it may sound, and I accept that much of what I was up to at the time was a bit unconventional, it started to work. I lost the desperation around sleep, and everyone knows desperation is never the way forward.

As I started sleeping, my mental health, unsurprisingly, improved too.

The jigsaw puzzle pieces of all my self-help attempts, small in themselves, came together, and the beginnings of a picture were emerging.

Positivity improved my anxiety, and I slept better, which made me happier and calmed my fearful thoughts.

I felt better in myself and had more energy, so exercising seemed more appealing, and the more exercise I got, the better my energy and my sleep got again. I then felt more capable of cooking, and as I was exercising, eating poor quality food lacked appeal, so I improved my diet, and I felt calmer and slept better.

I started looking healthier, which improved my self-confidence.

I felt bolder to try things.

And on it went.

Things were beginning to shift. The future was looking decidedly brighter.

If you are struggling with sleep right now, what I would recommend is not worrying about it. The well-meaning health professionals who stress how vital sleep is for your health and the long-term consequences of not sleeping are scaring the insomniacs rigid.

At least this ex-insomniac.

Yes, sleep is important, but even more important than sleep is being kind to yourself if you're finding it a challenge. I did all the sensible things like dropping caffeine after midday, having a regular bedtime, and not drinking alcohol at night (game changer), and then relaxed and left the rest to my clever body. I tried to calm my mind with writing and wearing myself out physically, and eventually, I tipped over to becoming a sleeper. I am still a light sleeper and an early riser, but those long, wakeful nights are, thankfully, now a thing of the past.

I think this has been an enormous help to my nervous system.

A random aside – A leaky ego dam

A chunky way through my anxiety journey, I got an idea that I had this whole anxiety thing nailed.

I felt way better in various places, and my bubble expanded. I was still living in a bubble, but a much bigger one, and I started getting a little, dare I say it, arrogant about being 'over' anxiety.

I obviously didn't see it like that myself, but my ego kicked in, and I got all sorts of ideas about how I had worked out this anxiety thing and got stuck into some serious overthinking.

My ego fluffed up, and I started 'advising' people on their anxiety. I thought myself a bit of an expert. I had thought my way out of anxiety by being rather clever. Uh-oh! My ego rising up was rarely a good thing.

This whole journey was beginning to look a lot like a game of Snakes and Ladders. One minute, I was throwing six after six and whizzing up the ladders, able to cope in so many new situations, and the next, I hit a major anxiety snake, and it felt like I was right back at the beginning.

The big issue with this particular game was that I didn't have a set of rules to follow.

My authentic self wanted me to take a proper look at what was at the root of my anxious thinking. What was my fear trying to tell me? This didn't feel comfortable at all.

My ego wanted me to get clever, fix things, and think my way out of this tricky situation.

In the peak of my anxiety years, I was terrified of even taking a sideward glance at my anxiety, let alone listening to anything it might be trying to say. A powerful 'fear of my fear' became the perfect fuel to whip up my anxious thinking. Unprepared to accept these uncomfortable feelings, I worked insanely hard to attempt to hold them back, and it was like building a leaky dam to contain a tsunami. Anxiety kept breaching my defences.

The more scared I became of my anxious feelings, the harder I tried to run from them. This created the unintentional outcome of making the feelings even more intense. My body was clearly trying to tell me something. It took many more years before I was brave enough to stay around when my anxious feelings showed up, to find out what that might be.

The role my ego played in all this was an interesting one. The birth of 'ego Helga' can't be traced to any one particular event, but Nottingham University is a decent place to start.

After years of not feeling good enough at home and at school, 1987 revealed a strange new reality to me.

Undiagnosed with ADHD at this point, Nottingham Uni was where I discovered that when genuinely interested in something, I could go into mental overdrive and achieve preposterously high grades. From being thrown out of classes at school, there I was, bizarrely getting top marks and being heaped with praise from the professors. I worked harder, faster, smarter. I disregarded my body's needs and focused on getting the next fix of validation. I became utterly addicted.

Ego Helga was born, and she decided I needed to be the best at everything (or not try at all). This created huge internal pressure, as with any success came an accompanying intense fear of failure; the perfect breeding ground for anxious feelings. Ego Helga thrived on excess, whether it was not bothering with sleep (pointless activity for the dull), partying hard, or studying for forty-eight hours straight as a deadline loomed. I wore my extremes like badges of honour, desperate to cover up deep-seated feelings of inadequacy lurking below.

I believed I was happy. The only thing that put this in question was my hideous self-image, the jealousy, insecurity, and a few other flags that hinted that my new confidence was built on shaky foundations.

Then Glastonbury happened.

The years after university wore similar hallmarks. Desperate to get the highs academia had offered, I threw myself into work, hoping for similar moments of glory. I would go to insane lengths to prepare for job interviews, landing jobs I felt utterly incapable of doing. I would get off to a flying start, setting the bar impossibly high for myself by achieving what might be expected in a year within the first couple of months by secretly working ridiculously and unsustainably hard in the evenings. I thrived on the praise but panicked that I couldn't sustain my efforts. I was also unable to travel due to my secret anxiety, so I had to make endless excuses about why I couldn't attend training days or conferences outside of my tiny comfort zone. Imposter syndrome, combined with the need to hide my 'dirty' secret, resulted in me quitting job after job, rather than risk being exposed as a failure.

This insane pressure led me to drink more and more to unwind at night. I was stuck in an anxious loop, and no amount of trying to use my new 'thinking' superpower made any impression on the anxiety. Counter to everything I had learned about myself to date, the more I thought, the worse the anxiety became. Anxiety had even robbed me of this thinking 'gift.' I felt utterly at war with this evil force that had taken over my life. Again, not helpful thinking.

My need for control grew in perfect tandem with my fears. More and more things needed to come under my influence for me to feel safe. Working for others became too stressful. Too much of my flawed personality had to be hidden. Everything about my anxiety was about me trying to control the external world. One might say it was impossible.

I wanted to control what people talked about, as it might trigger my anxiety.

I wanted to control any transport I used so I could get on and off at any point I chose. If I could only fly the plane or drive the train...

I wanted to control distance, so that when I started to panic, I could instantly teleport myself to safety.

The list was endless. Crowds at events, where I sat in the cinema, whether lift doors would open, whether locks would work before I locked them.

If I could control everything, nothing bad would happen to me, and I would be safe.

Far from being laid back, I was desperate to control every element of my environment. There was zero acceptance of anything. It all needed tweaking, changing, and controlling in some way to make me feel safe.

This was rather stressful, as I am not a superhuman being with ultimate control of everything in the universe.

If I believed my happiness rested on being in control of everything, it's easy to see how I was forced to retreat to a smaller and smaller space to get even a half chance of feeling in control.

At some point, I had to give up and accept that I was not the controller of very much at all.

If I was going to have a more comfortable relationship with the rest of the world, I would have to accept that the only thing I was ever able to control was my response to things that happened.

I wasted a lot of time and energy in my pointless pursuit of control. I don't doubt that I still do this to some extent, but it has now popped into my awareness, and my focus has 100% shifted towards working on my own stuff.

Being an entrepreneur was a great cover story for my inability to travel. I had the excuse of needing to be near home at all times in case the businesses needed me. This allowed me to holiday only a few miles from home. Although people questioned why I never went abroad, I had an excuse at the ready. My husband and I set up restaurants, a gift shop, an ice cream parlour, a cycle café, and various Airbnbs. I would generally throw everything I had into the new venture, overwork to the point of burnout, and then move on and start again. The businesses were successful, but the toll on my health was huge.

From the outside. I looked like I was living the dream. In reality, I was battling growing fears, struggling in relationships, and burdened with a mind that would never switch off. Sleep became a distant memory.

I was obsessed with appearing to be successful from the outside. I was terrified people would find out that the real me was weak, afraid, and utterly incapable of seeing anything through. My fear of failure skyrocketed, and my self-worth plummeted. This was no place of healing for anxiety. I drowned it out as best I could.

Fast-living 'Ego Helga' was causing big problems for my body. I would get signals that things were not okay. Maybe a tension headache, some fatigue, a tense shoulder or upset stomach. Did I listen? Well, to be fair, the music was turned up too loud, I was comfort eating to shut down emotional signals in my gut, and drinking to block out any warning bells in my head.

When 'Ego Helga' became out of hand, my body stepped up to get heard over the noise, and you guessed it, the only thing I really listened to was intense anxiety. Give me a headache, I would take a strong painkiller. A pulled muscle, and I would get a heat pad and some medication. Not sleeping? I would drink more strong coffee. The only thing that stopped me in my tracks in the end was serious illness and unrelenting panic attacks.

Severe panic episodes were like putting sugar in my petrol tank. Things immediately ground to a halt. My externally focused, addicted self would be forced to roll over and get into bed. My carefully crafted ego would fall away instantly, and I would desperately try to understand what my body actually needed. Feeling like I was sliding down the snake and back to the start of the anxiety game, I would stop drinking coffee and switch to camomile tea, ditch alcohol, and Google foods to calm my system. I would instinctively improve my self-care and turn to things that genuinely served me, like sleep, time in nature, and nutritious food. As a strategy, I have to applaud it. These massive meltdowns got my attention and forced change upon me, but they were painful and exhausting. There had to be a better way.

At the time, I thought extreme 'Ego Helga' was my true self, and I always wanted to get back to her. Why couldn't I go back to how I was before Glastonbury? I conveniently forgot that this incarnation of myself had, in reality, sat her finals from a hospital bed. I also hadn't considered that the loud, brash, fast-talking, attitude-packed me might not be who I was born to be, but more a reaction to a strict, controlling home life.

Desperate to shake off these shackles of childhood, I sought loud and rebellious role models, and my introverted self was forced to step up into a new, improved mould, with copious amounts of alcohol to drown any doubts. Whether it was claiming I enjoyed sleeping around, being overbearing with my 'adopted' views, or taking more drugs and alcohol than I felt safe with, all these patched-together behaviours created a hyped-up 'monster' version of me that clashed vehemently with my truer self.

Of course, I was unaware of any of this. I nurtured this 'wild and free' version of me, thinking her smart and sassy, and delighting in the attention she started receiving. All so new to me!

Excess became my calling card, from being the only one at the bar still doing shots to the last person clocking out from work, braying about working an eighty-hour week. I realise now that friends were more bemused by me than in awe of my antics, but this was not the story I told myself. Hitchhiking around Exeter drunk made for a great tale to recount in the pub but was a lot less fun to experience. A friend once said to me, 'Why are you so drunk again?' when I turned up for a night out, having yet again necked a bottle of wine in the street outside. I honestly believed no one would have any time for me if I calmed things down.

Crashing and burning regularly, I had phases when I would be forced to go into DIY recovery, and it was during one of these that an old school friend came to stay. 'Domestic Goddess Helga' temporarily replaced knackered-out 'Wild Helga,' and all weekend, I cooked, ran around after him, and basically behaved like a demented concierge. Rather than thanking me when he left (or tipping), his only quip was to say, 'What has happened to you, Helga?' It was extremely confusing to an ADHD people pleaser. For years, I was mad with him for being so ungrateful, yet I now see he was reacting to all the fakery. I had just shed one role model (Alice Cooper) for another (Mary Poppins) and I was not one bit closer to being my true self.

It sounds like I'm having a go at my younger self, but I'm not. I just didn't see how far I had drifted from who I was born to be. How wrapped up I had become in trying to please the external world. Trying to work out what people wanted from me was confusing, and relationships seemed to swing from intense Thelma and Louise style bonding to massive falling outs.

I have always wondered why I 'broke up' with my best friend from school. We would go from being 24/7 in each other's pockets to falling out for months without speaking a word. The truth is, I didn't just look up to her, I wanted to be her. Lock, stock, and barrel.

Endlessly reinventing myself to gain external validation was exhausting. Deep down, I knew I needed to stop. My body would continue to send out subtle signs that things weren't working. If I ignored them, they would get stronger until, crash, anxiety would step in and off I would go, marching submissively back to bed.

Interestingly, the one area of my life where I allowed myself authenticity was when I became a mother.

I love being a mum. I loved it from the moment I was pregnant right through the 'terrible twos,' which never happened, to the 'teenage years,' which have frankly been hugely fun, as I have seen my children freely experiment with who they want to be. In parenting, I have weirdly not copied anyone else, not tried to be perfect, read almost no books, and not engaged in overthinking.

And I have never been happier.

The only times I have had issues were when 'Ego Helga' temporarily popped in with unwanted advice, or when I got rattled in that transition period where it became obvious my kids knew way more about a whole load of world issues than I did. Up popped my big ego, but thankfully, my love for them meant I got over myself pretty quickly. This was maybe where I started learning that connecting with who I really am, rather than trying to piece together a 'society-acceptable' version of myself, might be where the gold lies. Hallelujah!

Being myself, if I truly allowed myself to be, would involve doing all the stuff that's good for me. I would read books, work with people I liked and respected, work hard. Not just to be perceived to be the best, but because I felt inspired and interested. I would go to bed early, eat nutritious food (because that's the food I like) and get out and about in nature with my loved ones. Not so tricky, surely?

I'm working towards being brave enough to be authentic, and it does take bravery. I wonder if it's the same for everyone. Some of the wilder parts of me are definitely me too. I'm not just a clean-living, wholesome person, and I will always enjoy punk music and things that get my heart racing, but now I get more of that zingy 'high' feeling when I connect to my passion and write, rather than seeking chemically-induced highs which block out my true feelings.

So, bottom line, at the time, anxiety was the most effective tool my body had to rein me in, and the reason I feel anxiety is calming down now is because 'Ego Helga' has finally taken a back seat. I look after myself better, do breathing to stop my mind racing, and generally have some self-respect for my amazing body that is doing its utmost to keep me alive.

When I get the first rumble in my gut that I once read as a precursor for a panic attack, I now look for what is out of kilter in my life and see if I can rebalance. I no longer need anxiety to do that for me.

As a result, I do make a lot of changes.

Maybe other people worked out how to be themselves at a much younger age, but I am a bit like a toddler learning to walk, regularly falling on my behind but getting up time and time again, learning as I go. This involves changing jobs, relationships, re-evaluating how I spend my days, and generally making life tweaks. If that causes a raised eyebrow from others less willing to question their choices, so be it.

I think it has been a crucial part of my learning to accept that making choices that are right for me will likely ruffle feathers (and stir my fears), but as long as I'm not intentionally hurting others and I'm making choices from a place of authenticity and integrity, I'm becoming more and more willing to challenge the status quo.

I have still failed to complete the challenge where you are 100% honest for twenty-four hours. No polite comments, no 'sorrys' or 'thank yous' that are not truly felt, no agreeing with another person to make them feel better, no false compliments, insincere acts of kindness, or claiming to enjoy food you hate. I tell you, it's tougher than it sounds.

The plus side of moving towards becoming truer to who I really am is that I no longer feel I'm playing Snakes and Ladders. No more big wins, but also no more huge losses or feeling I have 'failed' to overcome my anxiety. I accept that I am a calm person in training, and every step I take is part of my training to be less dependent on anxiety to push and pull me through life.

However I might feel in the moment, I'm never back at the start of the game.

My battles with anxiety have required me to look at my ego and the direction it takes me in.

When I'm on a mission to people-please, I ignore my physical and emotional needs, pressure myself to achieve goals that are meaningless to me, and quickly get overwhelmed and spiral into anxious thinking.

The only thing that keeps me sane is being authentic, keeping what I think, what I say, and what I do aligned, and focusing on things that are important to me, my true passions, rather than seeking to jump through hoops to please others.

When I'm doing something I truly want to do, my energy shifts and I get this wonderful buzzing feeling that anything is possible. When I'm feeling anxious, my energy drops, the world looks terrifying, and I feel I'm best off retreating to my home and getting under the duvet.

I used to find it odd over the years that my anxiety attached itself to things I loved doing: going abroad, flying on a plane, going by boat, long hikes in nature, finding remote beaches, going to big concerts, going to festivals, even going to supermarkets.

I now wonder if maybe it's not that odd at all. I'm certain my anxiety feeds on my low self-esteem and negative self-talk. Other factors, such as the drugs, a virus I had at university, too many antibiotics, and lack of sleep, all contributed to messing with my brain chemistry and severely lowering my mood, with those external situations creating the perfect breeding ground for crushing negative thinking. Berating myself (sometimes consciously, very often without even realising) becomes pretty commonplace, so it makes sense that I would tell myself I wasn't worthy of doing good things and self-sabotage the very things I used to love doing.

When I clocked this, I considered this might be something worth keeping an eye on.

I do know that doing things I love re-energises me even more than a good night's sleep. So, if raising my mood shifts my energy, I have played with the idea of seeing if I can 'tempt' myself to do more challenging things when the payoff is high.

Much like the child standing at the top of the slide or hanging on to the edge of the pool, contemplating letting go, I've found that when I truly want to do something, I get a burst of resilience that makes stepping into my 'stretch zone' slightly less terrifying. The payoff comes if I succeed because then I do the thing over and over again, unable to believe I can now add this new activity to my repertoire. I did this with a short boat trip across my local estuary. At peak anxiety, I could not get my mind to accept that it would ever be possible for me to get on that boat. I ran the movie in my head repeatedly that starred me as the miserable captive, unable to step onto the boat. I would look at the sparkling blue water, think of the numerous times in the past that I had loved being on the water, yet I felt paralysed from taking action.

So, what changed? I think I just really wanted to feel the wind in my hair, the gentle rock of the boat on the waves, to take a small step that might lead on to something bigger. I just got curious and started playing with the idea in my head.

Every summer, I would go to the beach and watch family and friends get onto the little ferry to cross the estuary, whilst I got into my hot car and sat in traffic, queuing to get around by road.

Eventually, my desire for change and to experience a little river trip grew bigger than my fear, and I made the journey. Can I admit I felt sick getting onto the boat? My legs felt like jelly, and I couldn't speak to anyone for fear of losing any sense of control and possibly screaming and jumping out to swim. Again, though, something happened when I got onto the boat. The fear melted gently away (about halfway across the ten-minute crossing), and I started to get excited. I didn't just like this crossing; I bloody loved it! It was like eating ice cream after you've been on a diet for years. I did that trip again and again with anyone who I could talk into crossing the water.

I was so insanely proud of myself. You might have caught me saying nonchalantly, 'Fancy getting the boat across to Shaldon,' whilst inside thinking, 'oh my actual goodness. I, Helga Beer, am crossing the water in a boat. This is a flippin' miracle. I am so excited I could burst.'

It flicked a switch in me. Whilst my anxiety was still in the driving seat, I was keen to shove it out of the way and have a go at steering the car myself. When I tuned into what I truly loved and had a reason that made sense to my authentic self, my self-sabotaging Helga moved over, and I slowly but surely allowed myself to do a few more things I loved. This, combined with the myriad of positive things I was introducing into my life, from challenging my negative thoughts, to eating nutritious food, exercising to regulate my hormones, meditating to quieten down my internal chatter, all came together to produce some more positive outcomes in my anxiety challenges. Things were beginning to shift for me.

There has never been a point in the last thirty years when I can honestly say I didn't want to find a way through my fear. If I said I was happy to stay in Devon and never go away again, I wasn't being truthful with myself. I didn't like the feeling that I had restricted choices. Fair enough, if I really didn't want to go anywhere (Devon is gorgeous and there are many sound arguments for not travelling unnecessarily), and I can see a time where that might be true for me, but it hasn't been true in the past thirty years, and I have lied to myself when I told myself I was content with my lot. I want to be able to choose. I want to decide on where to go for a walk, a holiday, a business trip based on what is best for me and not based on what I can manage. The reason to stay on my quest to make peace with my fear was because I wanted to feel free and not feel my hands were tied by invisible ropes I had created myself. There had to be another way.

I want to do more of what I love from this day forth!

I know I sabotaged myself by attaching anxiety to things I loved, but my anxiety was ultimately no match for my creativity and natural optimism.

If I couldn't have holidays abroad, I would come to love my holidays on my doorstep, which ranged from a local hotel (two miles away) to Brixham (about twenty miles) and if I was very bold, Lyme Regis (more like forty). I went to gigs in my very local area, went to the theatre to see London musicals in Torquay, and built in as much of what I loved into what I felt able to do within the self-imposed limitations of anxiety. It started to make a difference.

If the reason for doing something was strong, I seemed to have more energy to give getting out of my comfort zone a go. I became increasingly aware that feeling happy and excited was a tough opponent for anxiety. Happy was increasingly winning over fear.

Hmm. Maybe this could be cultivated.

This was probably one of my favourite anxiety-busting phases. Finding creative ways to do things I loved within the scope of what felt achievable to me at the time and then taking a tiny step to nudge myself a little further. This meant I was constantly seeing small wins, rather than bashing myself for being a failure. Who knew this could make such a difference?

I was about to type, 'I have never felt good enough,' but that's not strictly true.

I remember feeling supremely happy and confident when I was very young, but as with most people, going through school and then onto work, society wastes no time chipping away at the perceived rough bits and sculpting us into a more conformist shape. I lacked the self-belief to stay true to myself, and as early as eight, I understood that to fit in, I was going to have to make some fairly hefty adjustments.

As an adult, I have been diagnosed with ADHD, but as a child, I just felt different and confused about how best to fit in.

As I approached my fiftieth birthday, to realise that the persona I had spent years carefully creating was not serving me—possibly even crushing my true spirit—was hard to digest.

I was attached to my ego. I was attached to people praising me. I was attached to being perceived as successful. I was attached to external validation. More than attached; I was positively addicted.

Notes

Chapter 25 – The Online Anxiety Programme

I came across this programme whilst mindlessly scrolling on Facebook.

I was at a massive low point. I was almost fifty, and my anxious thoughts felt like they had taken over my life completely. Despite this, on paper, I was living the dream. I had two brilliant children, a house with a sea view, and I was running my own beachside cycle café.

I loved being an entrepreneur. My creativity appeared to have found an outlet. I even had the occasional spare hour to write a children's book.

I had spent the last ten years setting up three restaurants, a gift shop, and an ice cream parlour, all in beautiful seaside locations, so according to every book titled 'My Dream (insert business) by the Sea,' I should have been very happy indeed.

Cycling to work (on the big bike with the basket at the front), walking my dog for miles along the stunning sand dunes, opening my beautiful little business in the mornings to a queue of regular customers. It was everything twenty-something me had dreamed of, yet I had rarely been more overwhelmed by anxiety in my life.

It seems there are many sides to every story…

The truth was, I was working far too hard and missing out on seeing my children.

My husband and I discovered but ignored the fact that we simply couldn't work together. Best case, we would end up divorced, worst case, the lucky one of us would be serving a life sentence, and I simply did not love what I was doing.

I loved the idea of it, but I now see it didn't sit well with my values.

I was serving food I didn't believe in—the husband loves nothing more than a bacon baguette and cheese toastie; I'm more plant-based, healthy food. We were creating environmental waste (albeit using the best eco products available) and peddling high sugar ice cream milkshakes I wouldn't drink myself and were not improving the health and well-being of anybody. It didn't feel right to me.

I'm not criticising other food outlets doing the same thing. We all love a treat, but I'm very clear that this was diametrically opposed to my core values, and I was paying a big price; anxiety.

There were good things that kept me there longer than I should have been. The brilliant customers, opening up in the mornings and hearing the seagulls, being my own boss and the freedom that came with this, seeing friends drop in, getting great reviews, and generally feeling that I had got things right, in terms of the business, at any rate.

Yet there I was, mainlining caffeine, double espresso filling the gaps where sleep had failed. There were endless nasty rows and upset. I was wracked with guilt from never being at home.

Couple that with a poor diet, no free time, lacking sufficient time to write, dropping all my creative classes, and feeling the internal strain of not being true to my values. It's not surprising that I got myself into a spiral of stress. This only a few years after very nearly losing my life to a tear in my carotid artery and with advice from the doctors to take things easy.

The cogs were starting to come off the machine called me.

I think the only thing that saved me during those years was my cycle to work. The calming effect of cycling through the tree-lined lanes seemed to recalibrate me.

The trouble is that when these things happen, they do not announce themselves in a bold and helpful way. The pressures creep up slowly and quietly, so you just don't notice that things are getting out of balance.

Okay, so maybe someone with greater self-awareness might have been looking out for the signals, but I liken it to going grey or losing your hair. Can you ever pinpoint the very hair whose loss made you bald, or the last grey hair that tipped you from brown to grey?

Anxious thoughts have this stealth effect on me too.

Whilst it often appears as if they explode into my life unannounced, felling me with their overwhelming power, the truth is, they appear gradually. The anxious feelings creep up subtly over time. I, on autopilot, put in coping strategies that make sense in the moment, like cancelling social arrangements, turning down opportunities, and avoiding travel until I get to a point that I really DO need to do something and realise I haven't left my hometown for months and the thought of even going to the closest city fills me with abject terror. Bugger!

This is the point I had reached when I saw a Facebook advert pop up for a Freedom from Anxiety Programme.

I think it was October. I was forty-nine years old and in rather a shabby state.

Here was this smiling, carefree woman, talking on a video about how, if I looked at things differently, my anxiety could disappear.

For some people, the anxiety fell away instantly when they looked at life in a new way. For others, it took weeks and months, but I, like her, could go from being a captive in my home to being free to travel anywhere in the world feeling calm, happy, and balanced.

She had a six-week programme, and I signed up immediately.

This was a bit of a revelation for me. Here was someone talking about all the same issues as me and how she had moved on from them.

Catnip for the anxious!

She had the same issues with distance from home, supermarkets, trains, planes, tubes, crowds. You name it, I felt them too.

There was a Facebook group jam-packed full of similarly anxious people and some who had been trying the techniques for a varying amount of time. Some people were talking about being better and verging on what looked to me like anxiety-free. It was beyond exciting.

The classic 'run before you can walk' me imagined that I too would be completely free from anxiety in six short weeks. No doubts at all. I would ace this course and be totally ready to go about my life without another anxious thought ever bothering me again. Hmm.

So, ever the optimist, one morning, when my husband idly mentioned cheap flights now being available from Exeter airport to Naples, Italy, I wildly suggested to him that he book them for all of us immediately.

No bother that I hadn't stepped on a plane in twenty-five years and was still having trouble travelling to the next city, let alone leaving the UK. It was all going to be fine; I'd signed up for a course!

I do love the fact that whatever happens in my life, a small part of me still has the capacity to rise up with unrivalled optimism.

It also helps if the challenge is a comfortable few months into the future and I don't have to do anything scary or challenging right now in the present. Given those conditions, I do latch onto the positive and believe anything is possible. It's a handy skill to have.

This is how I always go into a new treatment for anxiety with extremely high hopes. Things only fall apart when I have to put in the hard work and edge out of my comfort zone. Then, my negative chatter whips up like a storm brewing.

But hey, at the start, I'm always fully committed and confident. That was how I approached this six-week plan.

The first thing to mention is the Facebook group. I had to join a group of anxious people sharing stories. To be fair to the coach, she nipped any anxious ramblings and cries for help in the bud, only allowing people to wallow in anxious gloom on a Friday; 'Freak out Friday,' as it was called.

This seemed so harsh to me at the start. Should we not be supporting our anxious friends in their struggles?

As with everything for me, given time, things make more sense. Anxious thoughts pass, and generally, if I'm feeling out of my mind with anxiety on Wednesday afternoon, by Friday morning, I will be seeing things differently.

Also, focusing on anxiety when I'm anxious feeds my thoughts and increases the physical symptoms, releasing more adrenaline, which in turn gets me thinking a million more anxious thoughts, feeding my symptoms in an unhelpful loop.

I totally now get why talking about my anxious symptoms just makes me look for more anxious symptoms in my body, and without fail, the one certain thing in life (along with death and taxes) is that if I go looking for anxiety with an anxious mind, I will definitely find it.

Instead, if I get curious and look for anything positive to truly get excited about, my anxiety doesn't get a look in.

I can see why it made way more sense to have people sharing stories about their progress over time and how they were getting their lives back on track (a perspective issue, but we will let it go for now - smirks).

231

The stories were fantastic. People were mooching around IKEA for the first time, doing the weekly shop again, travelling on trains, planes, having holidays, and seeing long-lost relatives. As I said, catnip for the anxious.

Interestingly, not everyone was pleased with the other group members' progress.

As time went on, I have to embarrassingly admit that I found myself getting jealous at times.

My holiday to Italy, which had seemed like such an exciting thing to book when it was six months away—we were going for my 50th birthday—had become like a huge weight around my neck.

I couldn't see how I was going to get there. It was mid-November, the course was ending, and I wasn't feeling any better.

Certainly, I didn't feel I was improving quickly enough.

Much of what she was teaching me was about seeing things differently. Widening my perspective. Letting go of overthinking. But I just went into overdrive, overthinking how to think less.

I wanted to be the best at thinking less on the whole course, so I got busy thinking more about thinking less. Oh, the sweet irony.

My ego wanted me to succeed at this. I threw all the big guns at it. I read everything I could on the topic, listened to all the podcasts, and filled my head with information that kept my poor, overworked brain thinking long into the night.

I wasn't sleeping. I crammed as I had for exams. I didn't get any better. It was all very confusing.

Everything I had always believed were my superpowers: the ability to think quickly, multi-tasking, having a brain that could solve problems easily, working hard, being able to control huge amounts of information (and people) were considered by the coach to be part of the problem.

This wasn't good.

My fragile ego did not like the idea that my perceived strengths might actually be my greatest weaknesses when it came to anxiety. My ego didn't like this AT ALL.

So, I looked for faults in her technique. When someone shone a light on me and it was not favourable, my go-to mechanism was to get defensive.

So, that's what I did.

I got super defensive and negative and Googled, 'is this a cult' and other such helpful searches. The coach was saying some tough-to-hear things. That my thinking was causing my anxiety. That all my anxious feelings were not a result of conditions in the outside world, such as the supermarkets, planes, and motorways, but purely a result of my internal thoughts.

This wasn't comfortable at all.

I got to week six and, not willing to do the internal work, caught the coach using the 'God' word once. I convinced myself she was running some kind of weird brainwashing cult and demanded a refund for my course fee in an outraged email worthy of a Daily Mail reader lambasting the latest outburst from a Labour minister.

She returned the money immediately, but I'm pretty sure now that I owe her that money back.

The truth is, coach, you got me thinking and questioning my thoughts.

I found myself saying, 'Is that really true?' for the first time.

There seemed to be a newly created space between my thoughts and me buying into them that had never existed before. I started to see that much of what I considered to be true crumbled with the smallest amount of interrogation.

Obviously, I should have been cock-a-hoop about this if I could only have seen that this put the ball firmly back in my court.

If my thinking was making me anxious, and I knew my thoughts could change incredibly easily, then this was my ticket to overcoming anxiety.

Anxiety wasn't a thing I had been zapped with at twenty-one after taking too many drugs. My anxious thoughts were of my own making and could be calmed almost as easily as they could be stirred up.

I obviously didn't see this at the time. Hindsight is a beautiful thing.

I do have to give the coach full credit for this change in my thinking.

Unbelievably, it wasn't until I was the ripe old age of forty-nine that I discovered the idea that just because I think something, it doesn't make it true. I feel an apology to the entire planet coming on. I think thoughts that have not an ounce of truth fairly often, and exclusively when I'm in a low mood and feeling out of sorts.

At times, when I have thought I was being so cleverly insightful about my friends hating me, the people at work being awful, the world being a dark and difficult place, I now see all that was amiss was my thinking.

Feeling anxious is my body's way of telling me, yes, something is amiss. Most often, how I look after myself with diet, sleep, relaxation, and exercise, and this self-neglect leads to poor quality of thought, subsequent low mood, physical anxiety symptoms, more negative thoughts, and more anxious feelings. Knowing that enables me (sometimes) to spot the early warning signs, make a few changes, and have way better outcomes.

With all the anxiety techniques I have tried, it's clear to see that the worst time to try and persuade me to do anything positive to overcome my anxiety is when I'm peak anxious and need help the very most.

That's when I turn up at the therapist's office.

When I'm overwhelmed with anxious thoughts, I'm spectacularly negative and unable to access my rational mind. I can find danger in eating buttered toast (choking hazard, cholesterol risk) and see the catastrophic worst-case scenario in every situation I come across from the person holding a door open for me (obviously a stalker) to the therapist trying to calm me with hypnotherapy (clearly trying to take over my mind with scary 'mind magic'). You get the picture.

I exaggerate for effect, but when I'm feeling anxious, everything seems dangerous, all people seem untrustworthy, and every drug I'm offered (prescription) is potentially able to cause me complete mental derailment.

When I feel like this, the chance of seeing the positive and good in techniques aimed at helping me is slight, and instead, I bring an unhelpful wallop of fearful cynicism to every encounter. It's why I don't take all the advice given and can't see anything through properly.

Looking at all this now, I can see how I could have potentially calmed my anxious mind many years ago, but I guess I had a bit of learning still to do.

Even though I'm naturally optimistic and can't help but keep bouncing back, it's not surprising that when asked to try something new that is going to involve trusting another person and relinquishing control, it's not going to seem very appealing to me when I'm in a low and anxious mood.

When I most need help, I'm least open to it and most likely to tell myself nonsense stories that stop me from taking the help offered and trusting people who offer me a way out of my anxious thought spiral.

I can see now why it has taken me over thirty years to work through some of this. It's a bit like Alice falling down a rabbit hole. Nothing with anxiety is quite as it seems.

A radical thought from me now is that it does seem my anxiety might possibly be my superpower, the one thing that redeems me from the worst excesses of myself. A radical thought, indeed!

I have, historically, been completely unable to regulate myself and keep on piling the pressure until something, usually my health, gives in. I can't deny that anxiety works as an emergency alarm system for my body. When all else fails and I'm not listening to my body's signals that

I'm overdoing things, anxiety kicks in and puts on the emergency brakes. Everything comes to a halt, and I go to bed.

This got me thinking…

Could I view my anxious thoughts as helpful? The final warning system?

I clearly don't enjoy feeling the physical symptoms, so by logical conclusion, could I put in a better early warning system, so I don't need to push my body to collapsing point before I change the way I tackle life? Skip anxiety altogether?

It slowly dawned on me that my anxiety was possibly my greatest ally, the last emotion standing when I've pushed myself too far.

If this is true, could I possibly build a better relationship with my anxiety response and learn to be grateful for it? See that all the times I have berated it for stopping me in my tracks, it has actually been saving me from myself?

Interesting idea!

It is true that when the anxiety kicks in, I do ALL of the following: stop drinking caffeine, stop drinking alcohol, go to bed and rest, change my diet and research healthy foods to combat anxious feelings, meditate, walk in nature, cancel all stressful activities (which often means leaving terrible jobs that are not suited to me), and do some serious self-care. If all that is true, could I do all the self-care stuff BEFORE I'm at the end of my tether and give my anxiety response a break? A holiday? Oh, the irony! I also needed to deal with my ego.

I love to feel good about myself. I have developed low self-esteem, so getting external validation for who I am is deeply appealing. Addictive, even. I love people complimenting how hard I work, how quickly I achieve things, and as a result, I have continually pushed myself harder to gain praise from others. My ego can quickly get out of hand if I'm feeling confident, and even in well-meaning situations, I can appear bullish and keen to hear the sound of my own voice.

The coach suggested that my ego was the problem.

I needed to let go of my carefully crafted persona to make way for my true self. My ego was not keen on this, so the simple thing to do was to rubbish her ideas and not make the necessary changes. Are you beginning to see a pattern?

Getting back to the stressful times in 2018.

The Italy holiday was looming, coach's methods had gone out of the window for the time being, time was running short, and I was beyond desperate for a new solution.

What could I possibly do to get myself onto a plane within three short months?

I did what any desperate woman might do. I went on the hunt for 'The Bee Man!'

Chapter 26 – The Bee Man

If you are an anxious person trying to find a way out of your anxious feelings, hearing tales of people being 'cured' of their phobias is akin to offering cool water to the thirsty.

You can't get enough of it.

I was forever on the lookout for that elusive fix and, waiting at the bar for a drink after a creative writing workshop, a tempting anxiety carrot was dangled my way.

I overheard one of the course participants talking about how her son had gone from being terrified of bees to donning a full bee suit and making hay, or should I say honey, in an apiary in mid-Devon. All achieved with only two sessions of hypnotherapy.

There it was! The answer to all my problems.

If someone could go from terror to happiness in two short sessions, surely, if I had ten, I too would be free from it all.

I muscled my way over to the woman talking and segued myself into their conversation. So, who was this mystical person who could achieve such incredible results? Where did he live? How could I get hold of him? Annoyingly, she couldn't remember all the details but promised to get back to me. I gave her my email address and, ever the optimist, assumed I was but a couple of phone calls away from being cured at last.

She didn't ever send me that email, and as we drifted away from the workshop and lost contact, all I knew was this bee story and the fact that he lived in the village of Dingley Dell in Devon. I Googled him a few times and nothing came up.

It was a rather remote village, and I felt sick at the thought of facing my anxiety to travel there.

I put him and his magical ways to the back of my mind and forgot about it until my Italy holiday was looming and I had no choice but to find some major new source of help.

The thought of the Italy holiday was all-consuming to me. The only similarity I can draw to it is grief. I couldn't bear to think about it— although that was all I ever did—couldn't eat, sleep, sunny days brought no joy, and I felt like I was permanently in this uncomfortable, anxious haze. Why couldn't I get out of this hideous holiday? It felt like some slow drip torture technique my family was inflicting upon me, with no moment of my day being free from the anxious thoughts.

The closer it got, the more impossible it felt to get on that plane.

My family was super excited, and all their keenness simply acted as a big dial to crank up the pressure.

I remember walking along my favourite country lane and lacking the capacity to enjoy seeing my first snowdrop, a sure sign spring was on the way. Why? It signalled my holiday to Italy was getting closer. This was not like me. My mum was worried about me and told me to cancel the trip. I tried, but naturally, experienced massive pushback from the family.

I unfairly started hating my husband for booking it, accusing him of deliberately putting me under pressure, forgetting conveniently that it was me who had told him to book it, and basically getting myself into a defensive, angry state of mind fuelled by intense fear and dread that I would show myself up to be a complete failure.

I was terrified.

I felt like a cornered animal. I see now that I desperately wanted to go and succeed but was delirious with fear. I was scared for my health due to the tear in my carotid artery, scared I might have a mental breakdown, ashamed that my children would see me as weak and not a reliable mum. You name it, I had worried about it. Every kind of negative thought was pumping around my head 24/7, or so it felt.

I remember being at work and one of my colleagues saying how she had overcome her fear of flying, having just returned from a brilliant holiday in Ibiza. Normally, that would have made my ears prick up, desperate to hear how she had achieved it, but I was way beyond all that. I was now coming face to face with my absolute worst fear and was in no mood to be uplifted by anyone else's success story.

I was jealous, anxious, fearful, and any other negative emotion you might be able to conjure up, with little space for anything else. At that moment of utter desperation, I decided to Google the Bee Man again. A different result! This time, I did find a hypnotherapist registered in Dingley Dell. Could it be him?

I picked up the phone and he answered. We chatted for almost an hour. He asked me some tough questions over the phone like, 'Are you honest?'

I answered, 'I try to be, but it's always subjective as nothing is black and white,' and other tricky things. I seemed to pass whatever test he had in mind, and he agreed to work with me. I was shaking when I got off the phone in my small café in Dawlish Warren. I had a lifeline!

The first meeting was in Exeter at my friend's house. I was so anxious that driving for at minimum an hour, along often very minor Devon country lanes, seemed impossible. I would get so overwhelmed with anxiety at the thought that I felt like there was a weight on my chest and I couldn't breathe. He only let me off that first time.

The next session was in Dingley Dell. The Bee Man was tough. He was ex-military, and although kind, had no intention of letting me off the hook, always pushing me to take the next step. He wanted me to drive alone. I resisted for weeks but eventually drove, arriving shaking and gripped by anxiety, dizzy, and unable to concentrate—not sure how clever driving was—but always left calm and in control.

Italy got closer. He got me to write stories about being there. Descriptive pieces that detailed every sight, sound, smell, and taste of Italy. Stories about exactly how I would travel there, every last detail of the journey, all interspersed with positive stories about how I would feel when I was there. We had sessions right up to the day before I was due to go.

Early the next morning, my family, packed and ready, waited for me in the car and watched me try to get into the passenger seat, but I simply couldn't do it. I had failed. All that preparation and I couldn't break through my fear.

Tearfully, I said goodbye to my confused children and promised them I would come on a later flight. I had no intention of going anywhere.

I spent three days recuperating. Eating good food, sleeping for hours, reading relaxing books, and walking in the countryside with my mum.

I went from feeling emotionally floored to coming back into myself within a few days. The relief of being back in my comfort zone.

I spoke to my children, bluffed to them that I would try and get a flight out there if I could, and resigned myself to having a relaxing mini-holiday in my home.

I had to go out in disguise because I was so embarrassed that neighbours, customers, friends, and work colleagues would all know I hadn't gone to Italy. I had no intention of confessing my failure to get onto that plane to anyone.

A couple of days into my 'home holiday,' my mobile phone rang and, making the mistake of answering it without checking who was calling, I found myself talking to The Bee Man.

Bee Man: Where are you?

Me: Umm. Topsham.

Bee Man: Why on earth didn't you go?

Me: I was terrified.

Bee Man: Book a flight. I'll come with you to the airport.

Me: (embarrassed and thinking I could agree now, get him off the phone and then cancel later), I said: Yes, great! That would be amazing, thanks.

I was thinking there was no chance of me getting on a plane to anywhere, ever.

That night, though, I spoke to my daughter, and she asked me when I was coming to Italy. When I suggested that maybe I should stay at home, she broke down in huge, emotional sobs. I had expected that from my son, who was a year younger yet seemed unfazed about me staying in the UK, but not my resilient little girl.

My daughter appeared genuinely heartbroken.

'You promised, Mummy,' she sobbed numerous times.

I was shocked that she was so inconsolable.

I promised her, there and then, I would come. This time, I meant it. I went straight online and booked an evening flight to Naples. Please do not think I was anything other than absolutely terrified. I knew what I had to do. The 'how' was yet to be revealed.

The Bee Man took me to the airport.

I think he must have pulled out every trick in the book to get me on that plane.

I arrived at the airport, and even looking at the planes made me feel like I was going to throw up. My mind was screaming, 'you can't do this,' but I saw myself, almost like watching myself in a movie, taking step after step in the direction of the departure lounge.

Bee Man was with me right to the last gate, to the very last point that only passengers were allowed.

If I had begged, I think he might even have come on the flight with me.

Yes, I was terrified, but I am so grateful to this day that I took that flight. A night flight on my own to Naples, twenty-five years after my last disastrous flight to Germany. The plane took off, I sat in my seat, gripped by fear, the doors closed, and we ascended. No going back!

What it has taught me is that if your mindset is determined, you will do whatever you set out to do. When I had first agreed to the holiday, my commitment was not 100%. I always thought I could get out of it. It was a cheap holiday. We could cancel and go somewhere easier.

What is interesting to me now is reflecting on my thinking around that time.

When faced with the thought of going to Italy, everything that had seemed difficult to me in my everyday life but was easier than going to Italy suddenly seemed possible. As long as I didn't have to go on that plane to Italy, I would have agreed to do almost anything else. London, trains, motorways, all the things I allowed myself to get anxious about before this trip, seemed easy and achievable when compared to the mammoth obstacle of overcoming my fear of flying. It seemed that the 'bar' of what was possible or not possible was not a real-world, physical bar but something movable.

When I realised my daughter's happiness was at stake, Italy became (just) possible. When the focus was on her and what she needed, something primal kicked in, and I found an inner resilience that was entirely new to me. It was super reassuring to know that when I needed it most, I was actually strong, independent, and capable. This was my key learning from Italy.

If you had asked me before my late-night chat with my little girl if it were possible for me to get on a plane, on my own, at night, and fly to a strange city, I would have said no. It seems nothing is impossible if it's something I truly set my mind to do. I have to really want it, though, to push through my fear. Someone else telling me what I should do doesn't cut it. This is about me and my WHY. Why did I need to get on that plane? Because my love for my children is second to nothing, and when I fixed my mind on my little girl and the fact that she needed her mum, the WHY was set. How? Well, that's something you have to let go of. It was revealed at exactly the moment I needed to know.

Italy has also taught me to question the stories I tell myself and others.

When I first got back, all I could say to my husband was, 'Thank goodness I'm home. What an ordeal. That was horrific for me.' Yet, this was not a true reflection.

Yes, I was anxious for periods of time each day in Italy. Not surprising, as it was the first time I had been abroad for over twenty-five years.

There were also so many times when I had great days, experienced new things, and felt genuine joy. I try and catch myself now when I tell myself things that aren't true.

Yes, there were tough patches on that holiday, but many more hours when I was fine. I am so unbelievably grateful to that holiday. It was the beginning of some big changes. Nothing happened overnight, but I started taking conscious steps in the right direction.

All in all, my biggest thanks go to The Bee Man.

He taught me so many things in those frantic days before my holiday. Obvious to most, but he taught me how focusing on my breath can quickly calm me, and unconsciously holding my breath causes me stress and that weird lightheaded feeling I thought was just anxiety. It works without fail. It's something I always have with me. No fancy gadgets needed. My breath is always right there to quickly bring me back to calm. Who knew?

Also, he encouraged me to question my thinking. So much of our learned experiences we digest as fact, right down to the 'right' way to load the dishwasher. With some pretty clever examples, he showed me that what we take for absolute truth doesn't always neatly stack up, much like the dishwasher, and warrants a bit of further probing. Thank you, Bee Man!

This may seem like a silly example, but for years, I thought that the only way you could show compassion to someone was to try and feel what they were feeling. I did this unconsciously, so I would hear something sad, fill myself up with sad emotions, and end up crying with the person. I thought this was the only way to honour that person's feelings.

It didn't occur to me that not only was this not the 'right' way of behaving, but it was not the number one choice of most other people. Story of my life! How this played out for me was that if I then told you about something that was distressing to me and you didn't become distressed alongside me, I would imagine that you didn't care. An innocent mistake on my part, but also massively unhelpful.

In addition, can you imagine how confused people were when I started crying when they took the time to tell me a difficult personal story?

Where they might have been looking for a listening ear or someone to witness their tale and allow them to get it off their chest, my crying probably made them think I was self-centred, probably not listening, and even a touch unhinged. It was all so confusing!

I began to realise that, quite often, I was blind to my behaviour, thinking it was true just because it was familiar to me. Now, I am open to the idea that what I think is just my perspective, and engaging with others is the best possible way to gain a new insight. Phew to learning! Life is a steep learning curve, maybe more for me than most, but I'm guessing other people fall into old patterns of being that don't serve them too.

When we consider that what we think is neither right nor wrong but just our perspective, one way out of a billion possible ways we could look at a situation, the world opens up and looks a whole lot more inviting.

Well, at least it felt like that to me.

I went from seeing everything as black and white to seeing the world as many more than fifty shades of grey.

Whether it's wearing my lucky socks for an exam, or brushing my teeth before rather than after breakfast, it's worth checking out how useful my habits are to me now. Many of the things I do without conscious thought are things that maybe I didn't even choose for myself but picked up from my parents, school, friends, and my work colleagues.

For one, telling myself constantly day in and day out that I'm not good enough and it's only a matter of time before people find out definitely doesn't serve me well now and isn't even true.

That message has played on a loop for years.

Now, I tell myself more positive things, but not to the point where I lose all social awareness, obviously. I don't tell myself I'm the greatest being of all time—although there is no reason why you shouldn't—but I do give myself some credit, rather than minimising all things that go well and making a full-blown West-end style performance out of any minor setback.

Do what works for you, but I was definitely not being honest with myself. I told myself a lot of harsh things that weren't true, and they held me back unnecessarily. I have no time for that now. I have really benefitted from trying to notice my autopilot responses to see what is still serving me. Slowing things down through meditation has helped, and the best way I meditate is by taking a long walk in nature.

Taking a Leap – Naples April 2019

I was looking through a stack of my notebooks (I have a notebook addiction —other ADHDers will relate) and came across a bulging notebook crammed with train tickets and receipts from my trip to Naples. Accompanying it was another massive notebook with pictures, hand-written notes, affirmations, vision statements, and photographs. It was a huge creative undertaking with a beautifully designed cover and an elastic band around it to keep its contents in place.

The bigger book was a project I was encouraged to do before my first trip abroad in twenty-five years.

This creative book exercise was devised by the Bee Man, who said if I bombarded my brain with stories and images about the holiday, it would trick me into thinking I had already done it and I wouldn't be so afraid (or something like that). I wrote long essays in the first person, as if I was there.

I would cut up tourist brochures or read up on internet facts about the village we were staying in, and then, in as much technicolour glory as I could muster, write as if I was there. It felt very odd in the beginning and used to make me feel a bit sick before I got properly into it. However, when I realised I was 'safely' at home, I could get into the flow and find myself enjoying practising having a calm holiday. In retrospect, I see I pointlessly fought the process at times by running down the likelihood of it working. Lack of trust in myself and offers of help has been an issue for me. If I had simply poured positive energy into seeing a calm and happy version of myself in Italy, my subconscious might have had a better chance of being ready for this trip. I have used this technique to far greater success since Naples. Will it come as a big shock to you that it's not the technique but my application of it that is a bit askew?

'I'm sitting in a shady spot on the terrace of our villa in Sant'Agata, a warm citrus-filled breeze drifting in from the lemon groves. I'm reading my book, engrossed in the antics of Heathcliff, revisiting Wuthering Heights for the first time in forty years. I'm relaxing on a sturdy wooden sun lounger with Audrey Hepburn sunglasses shading my eyes from the strong sun. In the distance, I see row upon row of grape-laden vines from the vineyard on the organic farm further up the hill. The aroma of

strong espresso that Elizabeth, the host, has brought me infuses my senses as I simultaneously bite into a freshly baked cannoli, the flaky pastry disintegrating on my tongue. I can hear the distant shouts of children running free in the play area backing onto the garden. Elizabeth is lighting her wood-fired pizza oven, and the wood smoke mingles with the lemony air.' You get the picture.

I'm not great at description, but I had to write it as if I was there, as if it were a diary of my holiday, complete with pictures and anything else that would bring that notebook to life.

I wrote my complete experience, from leaving the house for the airport, through every day of the holiday, to my flight home on my birthday. The more detail, the better. Every stage was captured from stepping onto the plane, the doors closing, the safety announcements being performed. You name it. I wrote about it all. And it was awful. I remember thinking, 'Why am I doing this? There is no way on earth I am putting myself through this ordeal. How can people want to go on holiday?'

I find it hard now to fully grab onto my feelings of the time, as they have changed so much since. I can almost relate to the people who say, 'So, you're going to a stunning place in Italy, to eat pastries, and drink coffee. Poor you,' but I do still remember that fear.

I remember not being able to picture any of the scenes I was writing about without imagining myself screaming, losing my mind, needing to be flown home—sedated possibly—or worse still, not even being capable of flying back, stuck in Italy for the rest of my life. The deeply held fear that I would lose my mind permanently. That I might experience a breakdown so intense that I would never recover. I cannot begin to explain quite how frightening that was.

So, what happened, I hear you ask?

Many things.

We know I didn't get on the plane first time, but I did go a few days later. We know it was hard; not surprising considering this was my first time abroad for twenty-five years, and a flight to boot!

There was nothing easy about that trip. I pushed back those anxious thoughts like I was Sisyphus pushing the eternal boulder up the hill (Greek mythology). It was hard. The metaphorical boulder would slip back, threatening to crush me. I pushed it back again. I arrived home exhausted. It had felt like living through a nightmare.

Or had it?

That was certainly how I felt while I was there and also when I first got back home. However, given a chance to unwind on the sofa and sleep in my own bed, I could remember other times too. Not such horrific occasions when I was eating pizza in Positano, travelling on the tourist train in Sorrento, sampling the delights of the little gelato shop in the village, and yes, sitting in the garden of our accommodation, breathing in the scent of fresh lemons.

The place also felt more familiar than I imagined as I discovered in real life all the places I had optimistically pasted into my vision notebook. There is actual photographic evidence of me smiling. Of course, there are others where I look more 'rabbit in headlights,' but I went on this trip, and in so doing, shattered a massive myth that I would never go abroad again.

It was hard, but nothing makes me prouder than seeing the photo I now have as my screensaver on this very laptop, of me with my amazing kids standing by a wall, overlooking the sea in Sorrento and smiling. I have a ceramic yellow lemon proudly displayed in my writing area that confirms I did go, even if, at times, it felt like a weird dream.

And the moral of the story? If I had not wasted my energy fighting my anxious feelings and accepted them, I would have had a totally different experience.

I just wasn't ready to do that in the moment, and that is totally fine. It is a hard thing to do when you are ticking off a huge list of firsts all in one go. I had not yet built-up sufficient trust in myself, to know I could cope with anything that my anxiety had to throw at me, but being in Italy for the first time didn't feel like a safe place to try.

I now see that I could have been practising at home in much less stressful locations. I could have allowed myself to feel the anxiety in IKEA rather than trying to embrace the acceptance technique abroad. I guess I needed to build up more confidence at home first. That's not how I roll, though. It's like revising for an exam rather than cramming the night before. Great idea in theory. Naples was a leap for me, but ultimately one I am glad I took. I could absolutely have coped having a panic attack in Italy. I wouldn't have loved it, but I would have survived. I didn't trust that to be the case at the time, so I used every ounce of my energy to contain my feelings until I got home.

Of course, that's only how it felt to me at the time. In truth, I relaxed on so many occasions when I was not paying attention. I forgot to feel anxious in between the noticeable tense times. I just didn't clock the calm times in the same way as I noted my anxiety. Funny that!

Notes

Chapter 27 – Music

I have used music to shift my mood for as long as I can remember.

The only answer to overbearing people in my life was always to turn up the stereo and try first to drown out the shouting and then the banging on my door to 'turn the bloody music down.'

No night out in my teens was ever good to go without Martha and the Muffins belting out *Echo Beach* or *Walk into the Sun* by the March Violets. Being gothic was all the rage at the time, and there was something in that black uniform that spoke to a certain darkness in my life.

Music was like a relationship to me. My first love was Bob Marley, then The Smiths, before losing my heart completely to The Stone Roses at nineteen. I have never quite recovered from that. *Made of Stone* is still my ringtone, and *This Is the One* is my song of choice when I'm feeling bruised and need to sing loud and harsh to banish hurt feelings.

It wasn't until the Bee Man that I made a more conscious link to music and my emotions. I realised I could use it to my benefit. I could play certain tracks and feel different, in a way that suited me.

I had mainly used music in the past to innocently punish myself. Playing *Man on the Moon* from REM was a dead cert if I wanted to feel particularly sad after a row with my husband. On a good day, he would play this on his acoustic guitar. Sounds hideous, but love is all about the cringe—wry laughter.

I could use music to lift my mood. To feel more resilient. Maybe tap into that tiny part of me that still very much believed I could get better from this overwhelming feeling of anxiety.

I experimented.

We Are The Champions? Okay, way too cheesy.

I Am The Resurrection? A great one for my over-achieving ego, but maybe not a long-term winner, although I love it, obviously.

Destiny's Child's *Survivor*? Belting it out gave me a taste of those good feelings.

Weirdly, *Hall of Fame* by The Script was one I loved to 'crucify.'

On it went. Singing badly to Indigo Girls' *Closer to Fine* was a complete joy, as was *Maria* by Blondie. All turned up far too loud. All annoying the hell out of my tinnitus and any neighbouring houses or cars in traffic jams.

I had to release my ego and any concept of guilty pleasures and just go for it. Trust and let go.

I started to play around more and found this really was something that could make a difference. And interestingly, music that had been so crucial to me growing up (massive vinyl collection, towers of CDs and singles) was one of the things I had let slide from my life in the anxious decades since my teens.

This was beginning to look like a pattern. Identify something I love that could be useful to help me edge out of anxiety, and then abandon it fully just as my anxiety takes more of a hold and when I need it most. Interesting strategy.

I'm not saying music could 'cure' my feelings of anxiety, but I was beginning to see it had a place within the puzzle, along with replacing 'should' with 'could' and allowing myself to reconnect more with my passions. It was clearly time to dig into who I really was as a person. Not the me propped up with drugs and alcohol, but the me who loves nothing more than dancing on my own with the tunes whacked right up. That me needed to get a few more chances to spin the decks of life.

Not noticing any of this at the time but seeing something subtle emerge for myself right now, it's time for younger me to march on in search of her elusive anxiety 'cure.'

Chapter 28 – Nature Therapy

I have always loved nature. My childhood was spent running wild in fields and woodland. Ultimate freedom and endless adventure. When I was young, I was adventurous to a fault. I climbed trees that were too high, built rafts that weren't safe, tobogganed on rickety sledges, played in derelict buildings, and generally sought out anything that felt wild, different, and free.

I had no fear.

I broke bones regularly and skirted in and out of trouble on a weekly basis. I feel my body took a long, hard look at the younger version of me and thought, 'if we're going to get this one to a reasonably decent finish line, we're going to have to rein her in.' My anxiety has the unenviable job of acting as the fence at the top of the cliff as I, *Thelma and Louise*-style attempt to crash right through it. I have come too close too often.

So, whilst I may have used up my brave quota (reality check—there isn't one), my love for the freedom I find in nature remains unchanged.

Nothing makes me happier than lying on the grass, looking up at the sky, watching the clouds float by overhead, listening to the birds, and feeling the earth beneath my body. I love country lanes, watching the sunrise and sunset, seeing the hedgerows change with the seasons, touching trees, feeling their incredible energy, paddling in rivers, and sensing the wind and rain on my face. I adore being outside with every fibre of my body.

So, when I consider the times when I felt lowest, what had I been doing? Working long hours, not being outside, stressing about pointless things, and not getting exercise. You know the score.

Being in nature puts me back into balance.

I'm now studying for a Forest Bathing qualification (reader update – it's sitting in a file in my inbox, gathering dust) and am enjoying finding out more about the science behind something which instinctively feels beneficial for me. Having a look at the research, it's clear that time in nature has some real, quantifiable benefits.

When I became pregnant with twins unexpectedly at the age of forty-seven, nature came through for me. It was not long after the serious health episode with my torn artery that I found myself pregnant, and whilst delighted with the news on so many levels, I was also terrified I would not survive giving birth. I was recommended not to put my head back over the sink at the hairdressers if I was having my hair washed, not to trampoline, not to go on fairground rides... even vigorous sneezing wasn't considered entirely safe. Giving birth to two babies was a scary thought, but also something I had dreamed of for my entire life. I always wanted to have twins.

It was a challenging time. I was terrified of leaving my two amazing children, both under ten, without a mother.

The only thing that calmed me down was walking for miles, often in a small loop, as I was still scared to go too far.

As the weeks of the pregnancy went by, and my nature walks continued, I felt myself calming down and getting more excited about my wonderful new arrivals. I named them Tom and Alice and indulged myself a little too soon in painting a wild and wonderful childhood for them in my mind.

When I sadly miscarried at twelve weeks, nature was, again, one of the only things that helped me to heal from the grief. Long walks through the lanes close to my house helped me to gradually come to terms with my loss. Nature, coupled with a very beneficial session with The Bee Man. It was painful, and I still feel sad that I didn't get to extend my family, but nature helped me to find a way to make peace with the situation.

Now, when I feel life getting a bit too manic, I grab the dog lead and head out into the lanes with my border collie, Titch. Within minutes, I'm drawn into the colours of the hedgerows, dodging the muddy puddles, throwing the ball for Titch, and if it's autumn, running around like a woman possessed, trying to catch the leaves as they fall. I breathe in the fresh smells, and without even trying, my mind quietens down. It's magical.

Where others dream of big houses and fast cars, I dream of my own little woodland with a small cottage for the family and our animals. Ideally by a stream, a few miles from the next house, and with a space to grow vegetables and wildflowers. I get that it's a bit of a rose-tinted ideal, but it's what gets me through life's tougher patches. When all is in chaos, I visit my smallholding in my mind. Considering all I used to do for most of my life was revisit hideous comments and ugly situations, may I say, this is a vast improvement.

It's only recently dawned on me that it's not obligatory to listen to all the negative chatter that used to tear me to pieces on a daily basis. I don't have to revisit every failure, humiliating remark, or embarrassing situation. I can now (sometimes) catch those pesky thoughts and say, 'No thanks,' allowing my mind to move on to pastures more pleasant or, God forbid, stay in the present moment of my life. Whilst this lack of self-flagellation does remove a rich vein of comedy from my life, it also preserves my body from daily beatings, which I no longer choose for myself.

Notes

Chapter 29 – Mindset

The reason this gets a chapter of its own is because I think it's one of the key pieces of this whole 'anxious life' puzzle.

Of course, every section in this book ultimately refers back to mindset, but it's so incredibly important that I want to go over it again and again.

When it comes to mindset, repetition is my friend.

According to a 2009 study published in the European Journal of Social Psychology, it takes 18 to 254 days to form a new habit. When you ask most people how long it takes to change a habit, they will say 21 days, but we are all different, and making changes is a variable process for everybody. I seem to take longer than most, and I find repetition hard, probably down to my ADHD. I do find that if I mentally commit to making a change and totally connect to the point of making that change (my WHY), then with enough repetition, it eventually becomes second nature.

I have done this with every good new habit I've decided to embrace. I can't help but think about how my body will feel when I'm picking food to eat each day. Gone are the days of guzzling mountains of cheesy chips, doughnuts, and other less healthy food choices.

I don't claim to be perfect, but I do value my body now and acknowledge what a Herculean effort it goes through to keep me alive. I feel weird doing things now that I know cause it damage and risk my health.

It's not that I have any judgement on what other people do, it just no longer makes sense to me to 'treat' myself with things that shorten my life. Although in the true contradictory style I specialise in, I am still addicted to those ultra-thin Naples-style pizzas and can't give up yummy sourdough bread, whatever anyone says about carbs.

Overall, though, I'm having way too much fun in life and have skirted close to the edge too often to do anything that doesn't give my body the best possible chance of staying alive—with the odd slip-up that I try to rectify with a day of eating lots of veggies.

I feel similarly about how I speak to myself.

I have worked hard on changing the inner dialogue in my head, both the noisy one that stops me fast in my tracks with its loud, hurtful insults, but also the more insidious one that whispers cruel criticisms, attempting to bypass my conscious mind. I am getting way more clued up to listening out for that one.

Why, oh why, would I want to fill my head with a load of negative bunkum that is likely untrue and serves only to clip my wings and send me back to my cave? Seriously, no more!

Now, I pause, reflect a moment, and try and catch myself before I mindlessly unleash an unnecessary harsh remark on my poor, unsuspecting self. Just as I'm about to blurt out that oh-so-clever, self-deprecating remark for comedy effect, I stop and instinctively change the comment. I may not get as many laughs these days, but I also spend fewer days in bed feeling like the world hates me.

That old saying, 'if you can't say something nice, don't say anything at all,' applies not only to those people I come into contact with in life, but to myself also. I feel nearly as affronted when I insult myself as I would if someone was insulting my family. It's not good enough, and I won't tolerate it (unless I have slipped into a low mood and lack the capacity to fight my demons, but this rarely lasts for long these days).

I feel the same way when I hear others run themselves down and always feel tempted to challenge them. Once you are on the lookout for it, the number of times people say truly awful things about themselves is depressing. To compound this, if you think for everything they say out loud, they are probably adding a further thousand or so even more poisonous comments to themselves, you can see why our mental health takes such a regular bashing.

If the only thing you take from this book is to look out for the times you run yourself down and then stop doing it, you will have done yourself the most enormous favour.

Once you have stopped all the name-calling, the next obvious step is to add in a few positive remarks. I appreciate that this feels pretty awkward and might take some getting used to. You need to get to a place where you can talk to yourself like you might to one of your good friends—and I don't know many friends that would stick around if I called them a useless bitch as I regularly called myself.

Also, friends like compliments. The kindness trend that is going around, to tell people the good stuff rather than only thinking it, can be applied to yourself too.

How often does a friend leave the room or can't make a party, and everyone else will say, 'I just love Joanne. She is so funny. She always makes me feel better just by being around her. She's such a flipping amazing mate.' Imagine how much Joanne might benefit from hearing that stuff. Before you scream at me that we shouldn't need external validation, it is nice to hear a few good things once in a while.

When we are anxious, and often even when we aren't, we imagine people are finding fault with us, seeing the tiny tear in our jacket, are horrified by the state of our hair, appalled by our grammar in a presentation, or bored by every story we tell. Multiply that by a million if you have ADHD.

No doubt, some people will be looking at us to find fault, but the very vast majority are not thinking any of those negative thoughts and are probably just wrapped up in their own insecurities.

Also, seeing as we have no idea what people are thinking and have zero control over it anyway, why not think fabulous thoughts like:

'Blimey, that Helga girl looks amazing. What natural style! What a cracking singing voice. The way she grooves on that dance floor.'

What does it matter? As we have no idea, why not imagine the best possible scenario rather than the absolute worst? Okay, this could go too far, but you get the general gist.

I have this soap dish called 'the soap of flattery..' Every time I wash my hands and pick up the soap, it reveals, 'Hello, gorgeous. I bet you look incredible naked.' Yes, it's a joke, but it makes me laugh many times a day, and what's the harm in that?

So, if we can imagine telling people the good stuff and how that might make them feel for a day, imagine if they did this for themselves instead, or as well.

The massive bonus of not relying on others to build us up is that we don't have to jump through hoops to get our dopamine hit. We can be ourselves and tell ourselves the good stuff at any time of the day.

Not only is it free (and therapy is expensive), all you need is a bit of creativity to devise an endless supply of nifty compliments to suit all occasions.

No more people pleasing, just solid self-esteem to be our authentic selves, which (hopefully) people will prefer to the 2D version of us that is insecurely looking for the next way to get some positive attention.

Don't get me wrong, I am a work in progress, but it has been a real pressure-off for my family and friends that I'm able to build myself up and no longer scurry around in a desperate search for every little scrap of kindness someone might choose to throw my way. Bye bye to that tedious and exhausting way of being.

I'm not saying I don't appreciate people being kind to me, I absolutely do, but I'm so much less needy and complicated to be around. I let people do their thing, and I do mine. The point is, if you are going to run a movie in your head, why not make it a good one? Take a starring role, be the hero of the piece. Why cast yourself as a villain in every situation? Positive reinforcement benefits us all. If you are good to yourself, it will be so much easier to be good to others, and that unleashes a ripple that benefits more people than you realise.

So, for everyone who thinks positive self-talk is absurd, selfish, narcissistic, and whatever else that stops you from trying it, I would ascertain that the results of decent self-esteem achieve quite the opposite. If others suddenly think you have become an ego maniac, chances are, they may have some work to do on their own sense of self.

I admit that was all a bit intense, but I can't over-emphasise the benefits of doing the work and really looking at your habits and cherry-picking only those that serve you well. Then adding a whole load of lovely new ones like being kind to yourself, taking time to relax, exercising regularly, eating great food, moving your lovely body, and trying things that take you closer to the life you would love to live.

Whilst I sound like a stuck record, this is a chapter I'm happy to play on repeat. Repetition is everything! It took years to get into bad habits, so why not give the good ones a chance to bed in just as well?

Notes

Chapter 30 – TED Talks

Many years ago, my friend excitedly phoned me to tell me that TED Talks were coming to Exeter. I think I muttered something vague in reply, and the conversation moved swiftly on. What on earth were TED Talks? I forgot about them, and life continued unaffected by this new concept.

Then I went to The Bee Man, and he too recommended these TED Talks. Specific ones that might help me get a handle on my anxiety and help to get me on the plane to Italy. The carrot had been officially dangled, and I set about greedily consuming all the recommendations and a whole host more.

Who knew these brilliant little talks existed? How had I survived without them up until now?

The TED Talks ('concise and enlightening talks') were online and could be anything from three minutes to a maximum of eighteen minutes. A huge range of topics were out there, but two that stood out for me were

Sir Ken Robinson's talk, 'Do schools kill creativity?' and Kelly McGonigal's 'How to make stress your friend.' Wow! Mind officially blown. Bite-sized chunks of informed opinion that gave me a totally different spin on things.

Who knew that if I thought about my stress differently, as something that could enhance my performance much like sports people do, the impact on my body could change for the better? The concept of 'a biology of courage' totally turned things around for me. I think I had underestimated how my close brush with death in 2015 had affected my fear of stress itself.

Much like fearing being an insomniac doesn't help you to sleep, fear of stress only caused me to ramp up my stress response. 'Stress is dangerous' was the message I was picking up everywhere, and this obviously made me more stressed, which was even more dangerous. Could I have been any happier than to hear a scientist, after endless proper research, say that by simply changing my mental attitude to my stress, I could reduce the harmful effects it was having on my body? This was a game changer. This was something I could do. Rather than stressing about the danger of all the stress I was piling on my body by being hopelessly anxious, I could now start re-labelling my stress in a more positive way as my 'biology of courage.'

Out went the fearful thinking, and in came this new, resilient way of looking at things. Every time I feared I was in a stressful situation, I would say, 'Wow, this is your biology of courage in action.' Over time, I became less scared of my adrenaline rising, and guess what? There was much less adrenaline.

What it made me realise was the impact all my negative thinking was having on my 'real-life' experience and how a shift in my thinking might change my health and my anxious life experience. What a radical idea!

More recently, I have also benefited from Tim Box's TED talk, 'How to Stop Feeling Anxious about Anxiety,' and Shahina Jaffer's talk on 'Art and Perception.' I have watched a lot of talks. As Albert Einstein said, 'You can't solve a problem with the same mind that created it.'

Considering that my beautiful mind had created a whole host of anxious scenarios for me, a few short TED Talks offering me a different perspective could surely only be a good thing!

Notes

Chapter 31 – Niksen

Finding a way through anxiety is tough. Something I thought, at worst, would last a few months when I was twenty-one was still in my life thirty long years later. This was not part of the plan. So, why was I still working through all these anxious feelings?

This made me question whether I was working through them at all. Was this another one of my core problems? I was still fixated on looking to other people to 'mend' me, some external wizard to wave a magic wand to make all those anxious feelings go away. Did I need to have a bit more of a deep dive into the possible purpose of all these feelings, and whether I had something more to learn in all of this?

The one thing that seems clear is that feelings have a reason for being. A positive purpose. We clearly need them to help us communicate with others, to make us act quickly when we're under threat, and I think for me, some of these things might not come easily. Particularly communicating what I really think and feel.

Without getting too deep, I think that, whilst growing up, certain feelings were deemed 'acceptable' and others very much less so.

Feelings had to be 'fixed' not felt, and I ended up confused about all my feelings and how to not only accurately label what they were but also deal with them when they arose.

I took to self-harm purely out of extreme frustration and lack of opportunity to let my real feelings out. I had this seemingly out of control range of feelings coursing around in me, and cutting myself altered the focus and made me feel I had some control. It was a massive cry for help probably; physical proof that I needed a chance to express who I was.

The list of things you couldn't say, do, or feel at home was long and stifling. It wasn't until I was in my late thirties that I found out self-harming was something other people did too. It was just my dirty secret and something I thought was carried out by me alone. Nobody talked about it in the 1980s. It's so strange how we turn all our pain on ourselves when we feel we don't have any other options. I am so clear that my days of harming myself both verbally, in my thoughts, and in physical acts of violence are now behind me forever. Thank goodness I have found new ways to release my emotions safely.

Back to the story, though. As a result of my early experiences, the idea of facing my feelings had always been unappealing, and given the choice, my default option was always to run, hide, or block things out.

Why search my soul for an answer when I could pop a pill, drink some wine, or eat the entire contents of my fridge to smother my feelings?

The lesson I took from my upbringing was that when I left home at a young age, I sought out peace at all costs, avoided conflict, and pushed away any thoughts and feelings that didn't bring me joy. I was firmly from the 'sticking plaster' school of thought. The past needed to be shoved firmly into my subconscious. Out of sight, out of mind.

I know I've mentioned this before, but when someone said to me, 'What do you stand to gain by holding on to these anxious feelings?' I was confused by the question and more than a little affronted.

Like anyone would choose to feel this way.

However, once stated, that thought niggled at me and I couldn't help but ponder if I ever did use anxiety, unconsciously even, for some gain in my life, possibly to create boundaries with challenging people and distance myself from difficult situations. In the absence of being confident to say no, did I use anxiety to say no for me? A voice more valid than my own?

Was my anxiety a tool to hold people back?

Without naming names, there were many people in my life who couldn't take no for an answer. People who would override me and push endlessly at my boundaries until I was at breaking point.

Where I felt I couldn't say what I really thought and push them back with words, I wonder if anxiety, bizarrely, was one of my coping techniques.

Not initially, but when I saw that people stopped when I genuinely couldn't do something when crippled with anxiety, did I then learn to use this new 'power' as a tool to create peace and space for myself? When 'no' had been ignored so often, did I sometimes use anxiety as a way of reinforcing my position?

The truth is, I'm not sure, but what I do see is that it took me a long time to find my way out of it, and I wonder if at times, on a subconscious level, I valued my anxiety to be able to kick arse and get me what I needed in life—usually some time on my own and the ability to stand my ground.

It gave me a crutch, an excuse that was outside of my control that I could point to and say, 'No, I simply can't. I'm too anxious!'

I'm not saying this relates to anyone else with anxiety. I'm just pondering on why it took me so long to find the way through my anxious feelings. Why I so often held the recipe for ending my unhealthy relationship with anxiety, yet I would always fail to take that vital final step.

I baked the metaphorical bread but always left out the yeast or forgot to turn the oven on. In every potential solution, I rushed a few steps and never, methodically, saw any technique through. Did I, on a deeper level, even want to let go of my anxious response?

These big thoughts about my anxiety and all the striving to overcome it was deeply exhausting, so you can imagine my delight when I came upon the Dutch concept of Niksen in my quest for a cure.

'Niksen' is the Dutch art of purposefully doing nothing, 'Doing nothing, but with a purpose to do nothing or no purpose at all.'

How wonderful!

Having spent the first five years of my life in Holland, before I had any awareness of 'fear of travel,' and with Dutch being my first language, it made sense to go back to my roots to find a solution to my anxiety predicament.

There was so much I loved about living in Holland as a child. My amazing bike with a back-pedal brake (note to parents: do point out that UK bikes have front brakes and pedalling backwards does nothing to slow you down on an English hill), whippy ice cream vending machines outside my village shop, the obsession with sausages, chocolate and anything sugary for breakfast (this is not a contradiction; I was five) and endless hours playing outdoors with my neighbourhood gang.

The Dutch way of life is laid-back, the country ranks well on happiness indicators, and I have a backstory there, so surely there was no better place to seek a solution to my anxiety than in Holland.

How I stumbled across Niksen is not entirely clear. I think I read about it or heard it talked about on a podcast, but why it is so dear to me is that the instructions for use are beautifully simple. You literally look out of a window and do nothing, ideally for two minutes or more, every day.

This I can do now, but weirdly, and you will get it when you try, it takes quite a bit of practice.

You scoff, but sitting still and doing nothing for two minutes was a massive challenge for me. When I started meditating, I was listening to someone talk me through it. Someone else was doing the legwork, and I could just focus on the voice and try and zone out. With Niksen, it was all down to me. I had to purposefully do nothing, and it's way harder than it seems.

The first time I tried, I started playing with my phone. Attempt aborted. Playing with my phone is not Niksen. Then I started looking out of the window and would get distracted by a cobweb and get up to move it away, and so it went on. Whenever I purposefully sat down to do nothing, I felt an overwhelming desire to do something. I think I'm contrary by nature. When I need to get down to writing, I can happily procrastinate for hours, so I thought doing nothing was something I would ace, but I had epic fail after epic fail. Note to self: you can't fail at meditation...

The interesting part of Niksen is what I learned by trying and 'failing.'

First lesson learnt; not everything in life is a competition and I don't have to be perfect. Failing at meditation (and I include Niksen in this) is not a thing. I can allow myself to get better at it over time, and the day I think I have nailed it puts me right back to day one in my practice. Meditation is my own personal *Groundhog Day*, but much like Bill Murray, I'm learning to become more creative and appreciate new details in every day.

Secondly, it does get easier, and relaxing in a chair and properly looking out of the window and seeing what's there, in that moment, is deeply calming and beneficial.

I look out of the same window each morning, at a time so unheard of to the rest of my family that I can guarantee I will be alone. I get myself all settled in a comfortable chair and just look. I have come to intimately know the trees in my garden, learned to observe my lawn and pot plants without feeling the overwhelming urge to start weeding, seen a wider variety of garden birds than I'm able to name, listened to the cooing of the wood pigeon, watched incredible sunrises, and before you know it, ten minutes or more have passed. This Niksen thing is addictive.

The best bit is, I can now do it anywhere. Delete from your memory every teacher who told you not to stare out of the window and daydream. It feels very intuitive to me to do this, and I now think back to my younger self, who would do this for hours, watching the rain making patterns down the windowpane. I have to apply a degree of subtlety to it sometimes, like when I'm in meetings and I'm looking out of the window rather than listening to a presentation, but it does wonders for my blood pressure. It's easy, it's free, and anyone can do it. If you need a break from trying to find a way forward in your life, I can recommend nothing more than having a go at a spot of Niksen. I just love the Dutch!

Chapter 32 – Self-Help Books

This journey to find a way out of my travel restrictions has not been cheap. I have spent many thousands of pounds that might have been better spent on cocktails in the Caribbean than on 'deep discussions' in Devon with therapists from various disciplines.

Sixty pounds an hour seems to be the going rate as I write, and when I'm quite often earning minimum wage, keeping up with this kind of expense is tricky to say the least.

This is where self-help books come in. Especially those picked up in the local charity shops. It's a great hunting ground for books purchased with good intentions, never actually read, and sent to the charity shop during spring cleans or house moves.

As I look at the shelves overhanging my desk, I can count at least sixty such books keeping an eye on me as I type. I should confess here that I have a full-on book addiction. Every space I spend time in (including the loo) has an accompanying teetering pile of books just waiting to grab my attention. Fiction, which I absolutely love, is being pushed to the sidelines at present as I gorge on book after book packed with ways to shape and improve me.

I have read so many excellent books, but regrettably, like good films, when pushed to remember the salient points, I flounder even to recount the basic plot points. Despite this, the information must go in somewhere, surely. What I like about self-help books is the different approaches and perspectives on offer. The books may or may not 'gel' with me, but what they always do, like or loathe them, is make me reflect on a topic in a new way. This is generally fairly useful for me.

Chances are, I wouldn't have considered the myriad of different ways that exist to think about anxiety if I had only been churning around the questionable thoughts in my own head. If it has taken me thirty years WITH the help of countless therapists, books, the advice of friends, podcasts, and various evening classes, how long would it have taken if I had been going it alone? I might be on my hundredth lifetime by now, still sussing out how to get on a plane and chill out enough to enjoy a break in the sun. Ooh? Imagine if I actually am?

Just for fun, I thought I would list a few of my confusions.

Some of the many things I had no idea about before entering into the wonderful world of self-help books:

- I have to have a thought before I get a feeling. I may not notice the thought, as it can happen rather fast, but MY thinking creates MY feelings. This means I can potentially change how I feel about something in the external world by changing my perspective on it. Whaaaat? So, when I'm feeling rubbish, as I was at three a.m. this very morning, chances are, my thoughts are askew and might be better disregarded, or at best, written on a piece of paper to baffle future me.

- When someone is sad, they don't expect me to cry with them to show empathy (I honestly thought this was essential. I am an accomplished crier).

- When someone is telling you a story, it does not show you are listening to bring up a story from your own life that is similar. I did, again, believe this was true rather than, as I have more recently discovered, simply annoying behaviour. I have wasted so much energy trying to 'dig deep' to dredge up such tales, thinking I was bonding, when I now know others thought I was just completely self-obsessed. Whoops!

- I cannot control how another person treats me. EVER. It's not just that I'm not good at it, it's because that's not my job. Phew! Endlessly trying to find new strategies to control other people is about as useful as trying to hold your breath and beat the free diving record without training (which I have obviously tried and failed).

- You don't have to say YES to everything to be liked.

- You don't have to be liked by everyone to be happy.

- You can say NO, and the earth won't stop rotating.

- Money is neutral and not 'evil,' and it is how you use it, for the benefit of yourself and others, that makes the difference. You make the difference with the choices you make.

- It's not my job to 'make' my family happy. If I work on doing things that make me happy, I'm way more fun to be around than when I'm trying to be the good fairy from *Cinderella* and make all their dreams come true, which are invariably my idea of the other person's dream, and thereby not their dreams at all. I refer, amongst other things, to the massive pile of presents gifted to my loving husband over the years, which have been listed on eBay within the same week of purchase.

- When I feel low, the thoughts that are swirling around my head, giving me unpleasant physical sensations in my body are not my intuition speaking to me but a load of old bunkum that I have absorbed from the external world that I can feel free to ignore until I feel better.

- My best, most useful thinking shows up when I'm calm and never in the middle of a screaming match with my partner (possibly about said pile of unwanted gifts).

- Peak argument is never the best time to make solid plans regarding the future of my relationships.

- Celebrities don't have superpowers, and all humans have similar worries and insecurities. Everyone is scared to do new things; it's how they handle the fear that makes the difference. It was incredibly reassuring to read that Sir Ranulph Fiennes and the adventurer Chris Bonnington felt fear just as I do, but they labelled it differently and channelled it to push them forward rather than grabbing their duvets and pulling them over their heads. I have a choice too, in how I respond to my fear. I can use it to push forward and prove to myself how resilient I am, even if my definition of resilient means going 'all the way' up to Taunton on the M5 motorway. Horses for courses, always.

- It was worth digging deep to find out what lay beneath my problem. I was not scared of being on a plane, motorway, train, or whatever. I was scared of losing control, not being safe, fearing I couldn't cope, lacking the trust in myself to find the 'right' way forward. When I took the time to dig a little deeper, I could see that all these external things I was attaching my fear to were fairly neutral external objects that were easier to fear than the bigger fears buried inside me. They were just signposts.

- A few key things underpin my health: diet, exercise, sleep, and relaxation, and I have to work on all of them if I want to feel much better. Everything I choose impacts on my body either positively or negatively. I have historically fixated on one thing, say sleep, and worked on sorting that out to the exclusion of all else. A combined approach works wonders.

- Sleeping with headphones in and constantly listening to 1970s sitcoms on a loop is not good for achieving a restful night's sleep. That's not from a self-help book. It's something I worked out for myself after fourteen years of keeping this habit. Time to 'fess up... I still do this sometimes, and I know it's not helpful. Saying that, it might help future me to write a sitcom, but only if I can keep my eyes open for long enough.

- I am a habitual being and habits, good and bad, can be changed, but it takes a big bit of work and much repetition for me to make a change.

- I am a habitual being and habits, good and bad, can be changed, but it takes a big bit of work and much repetition for me to make a change. (get the gag?)

I could go on for quite some time, but it was interesting to see how many things I believed to be absolutely true and helpful were not based on any scientific facts but things I had mislearned growing up.

I've thought about the number of words I mislearned growing up by mishearing them until, at a later stage, I read them and saw their true meaning. A few classics include:

'To all intensive purposes.'

'You've got another thing coming.'

'On tender hooks.'

Yet, it was so much easier to see when I had misheard language in childhood and taken it unassumingly into my adult life (and been publicly humiliated by some pedantic ego-maniac), than when I misunderstood emotions or behaviours. Much the same with other people's thoughts and ideas that had been passed on to me when I was too young to question them. Things I took as truth from parents, friends, or teachers that later proved untrue gave me the insight that many of my beliefs would benefit from further scrutiny.

The world moves on, science makes new discoveries, and even parental information needs regular updates. That's why I find it helpful to listen to new ideas, whether I agree or disagree, as it enables me to question my truths. I have certainly identified a huge number of unhelpful beliefs that I assumed were true but crumbled under the microscope. I love that about life. If I change how I think, everything changes, and I am the one who can influence that!

Chapter 33 – Walking Therapy

I am a chronic overthinker. My brain is whirling at a hundred miles an hour, and frankly, it's exhausting. Of all my over-developed muscles, the capacity for rapid-fire thinking is one I have done the metaphorical weights on, so strong is it in its ability to continually rampage through my mind. I like to take it on long walks in nature and attempt to wear it out, like the enthusiastic and out of control puppy it is. I even throw a few distracting balls for it to chase.

Distractions come in so many forms for me whilst out on a walk. I especially love looking at the sky. The endless ways it changes. The clear blue, cloudless days, the misty early mornings, the dense grey, rain-filled blanket clouds. Even the moody, metallic light just before a storm. I feel my exhale lengthen right now just at the thought.

Nature is my quick cheat's version of meditation. It moves me out of my mind and into my body, my senses running amok amongst the hedgerows and the earthy scent of the soil after the rain. Even the cold, muddy puddle water that invariably seeps into my boots keeps my thoughts firmly placed in the here and now. Then there are the blackberries in August. Impossible to resist yet always plunging me headlong into a game of Russian roulette. Will they be sweet or sour? No clever thinking can help me pick the perfect purple berry. I simply have to take a chance. Isn't that a concept I've heard somewhere before?

It's when I'm walking the lanes that things start to make sense. When clarity pops in out of nowhere, and that unfathomable problem suddenly finds a simple solution. It's when I'm walking that I have ideas, that my dreams seem achievable, and moving forward with plans is just a matter of taking a few simple steps with no need for spreadsheets or worksheets, although I am partial to capturing an idea on the notes in my phone.

I'm never disappointed in a walk. How many things in life fall into that category? I can be lying on the sofa, feeling entirely devoid of energy, unable to keep my eyes open in front of the TV, and someone will suggest a walk. I will, in that moment, consider this possibly the very worst idea available to woman. Yet I know from experience that it's worth pushing through my pain barrier and shuffling into my coat. Within minutes, I will find myself lifted by the colours of a winter sky, the bird song chirping from the hedgerows, or the whisper of grasses being whipped by a gentle breeze.

When absorbed watching leaves bouncing along the path on a windy day or seeing the silhouette of a family of oaks standing strong on the hillside, tricky thoughts and uncomfortable feelings I've been doing full-on battle with somehow lay down their weapons without me doing a thing.

It never ceases to amaze me how quickly my mood can shift in nature. Not if I allow my worries to come with me, neatly encased in my mobile phone, clicking on emails and answering texts. No, then I will walk hunched and head down, stressing about a poor signal whilst missing the sun setting and the hares playing in the field alongside the path. On those days, so wrapped up am I in my self-created stress that I divert all my energy into winding myself up further, rather than taking in the healing benefit of nature, right there, just outside of my field of vision.

At least I'm aware of this now. I have a half chance of catching myself missing the point of my walk and am able to self-correct and get back on my true path. Maybe this is what all this learning is about. It's not that I won't continue to make mistakes and take the wrong path, but that my internal auto-correct will now be set with greater sensitivity.

It's the same with my feelings. I have more awareness and can now allow more subtle feelings of unrest to alert me to check in with myself instead of calling on the juggernaut of all emotional responses that is full-blown panic. I guess it's like putting a fence at the top of the cliff rather than an ambulance at the bottom. I now see that all my feelings are just a response to the quality of my thinking. When I'm feeling a bit off, I know my thoughts have gone AWOL, and the best thing I can do is put on my shoes, grab the nearest jacket, and head out of the door (rain or shine) and walk myself to a better mental state. This happens without fail every time.

I walk to work now whenever I can, as the hedgerows and trees seem to suck up all my unwanted stress. When I arrive home to my family, I have already cast my work stress and worries into the passing breeze, with all crumbs of concern falling from me as I walk the mile or so back to my house.

What I love about walking is that I don't need to 'do' anything for the benefits to appear.

If I *do* want to do something, like scream in a secluded space, even that is open to me.

I recently caught a programme on TV that my children were watching about screaming. As part of an experiment, people were asked to carry out a number of tasks. One of these was screaming at the top of their voice. The smiles after they had finished were incredible. Seems we are all desperate for the freedom that letting go and screaming unleashes in us. I remember screaming in childbirth. I mean, really letting rip (apologies to anyone nervously waiting for a pregnancy check-up) but truly loving the feeling. I know that sounds weird. It was that complete release. Maybe that's why people love rollercoasters. The freedom to scream until there's no scream left.

So, screaming in a quiet woodland is another unexpected pleasure from walking. It can be best summed up for me as the freedom to be myself. Honestly, unapologetically, authentically. I don't think the oak trees or the sheep in the field are passing judgement on me any more than I am judging them. I don't get caught up in the need to please, and as a result, I feel the true joy of just being. That is what makes walking so healing for me.

Wow, writing that down felt good. It explains why I love walking so much. I love any activity where there is no 'right way' to do it. I guess I just want to feel free to be myself. Nature allows me to do that.

Notes

Chapter 34 – Cold Water Swimming

As a child, I loved to swim in the sea. The excitement of seeing the ocean for the first time as I arrived in Cornwall, whooping for joy and screeching 'I can see the sea. I can see the sea' at the top of my voice. Big competition in our car for who could capture the first elusive sighting. That smell of the salty air, the seagulls cawing, the thrill of being somewhere different yet familiar, whether it was Porthleven or Coverack. I found that merging of the known with the new genuinely quite thrilling (interesting). Uncovering my bucket and spade from the previous year, yet finding a shell shop that had freshly opened. Seeing a familiar face, but also meeting a new friend on the beach, as we dug for hidden treasure in the sand.

And how I remember the cold! That first toe in the water. The push and pull of the sea. Can I, can't I bear to go in further? It's exactly the same reason I like Haribo sour sweets. That, 'Ooh, I can't bear it, yet I want more' feeling. I seem to be drawn to the extremes. The cold makes me single-minded. All other thoughts disappear, and all I can focus on is the icy water. Hmm.

As a child, I enjoyed the scream, the very drama of the cold. The shrieks as my sister splashed me and the cold went further up my body than I felt able to bear. And then the complete acceptance as I let go and dived right under. Taking the full shock of the cold, teeth chattering, brain discombobulated, waiting to acclimatise, much like waiting for an ice cream headache to pass. Maybe this doesn't sound much like fun, but to me, it was life-affirming, invigorating, real. I have never felt more awake than when diving into a cold sea. I have also never had a quieter mind. The only chatter comes from my teeth....

Then the relaxation that follows, when I've finally made friends with the cold and the salt from the water gently takes my weight, the sense that I'm part of something so much bigger, as I float freely upon the waves.

Until a few years ago, I had only ever swum in the sea mid-summer, on the kind of hot day that warrants an icy dip. Increasingly, I was hearing more and more about people who swum all year round. Particularly women my age, who benefitted from the mental health benefits of the cold. I was intrigued. I thought back to those Cornish summers. The cold sea, my quiet mind, a single focus, letting go, complete acceptance? I could think of another context in which these skills might come in super handy.

So, it was my lovely friend Von, who suggested a wee while ago, that I should join her and a group of scarily cool women, for a daybreak swim in the sea at Teignmouth. In early March. I hadn't been in the sea, outside of August, for years. She said it would be great for my wellbeing. The sea temperature on that day was a chilling nine degrees. A temperature better suited to a cold glass of something, surely?

As an aside, for years when walking along the seafront to work at my ice cream shop, I would regularly stop and chat to a very elderly woman getting into (or out of) the sea for her morning dip. She swum daily. Our timings neatly collided most mornings. She looked in amazing shape, and often invited me (not in phenomenal shape) to join her. I was intrigued, but certain I was categorically incapable of getting into a cold sea in winter. She was somehow made of tougher stuff than me, but she certainly piqued my interest.

Back to Vonnie, she suggested we have a dip in the sea and then afterwards we could do lovely female bonding things like have a campfire on the beach, eat cake and generally have a good time. The cake did the trick, as she suspected it would, and I decided to give it a go. I remember feeling serious trepidation on the day. For one, I was fairly overweight and embarrassed to be getting undressed in front of women I didn't know. Then there was the cold. The wind was howling. Huge waves were crashing onto the beach. I dipped a toe in and wondered about the collective sanity of the group surrounding me.

Wisely, I kept this to myself and plodded on with getting disrobed. I had committed now and felt uncomfortable pulling out. I plunged, rather heroically, into the water in my swimming cossie (the others sensibly had wet suits), froze the living daylights out of myself and ran out, teeth chattering uncontrollably - just as the sun was coming up over the water.

And then it happened. That incredible feeling you get when you have done something brave. Something shifted in my brain. I felt like I had been plugged into an electric socket, so intense was the energy coursing through me. I had found a new tribe – the small band of people brave (or stupid enough) to get into an arctic sea. I looked around. Surely people would be looking at me differently now? I was looking at me differently now! I had regularly passed other groups of sea swimmers on morning walks, wistfully looking over, yet never once believing I could become one of them. And here I was. I took photos. I posted them in group chats. Not my normal modus operandi I can assure you. I didn't even give a hoot about running around the sand in my swimmers. The photos will attest to this.

Then came the regular two-minute cold showers. I dined-out on the knowledge that I could stay put under an icy downpour, even when my brain was telling me to run. It was a lot like staying put during a panic attack. Over time, my brain stopped telling me to run and I started to kind of weirdly embrace the wild cold, dare I say it, even like the intense (previously unbearable) physical feeling. Same external stimulus, entirely different reaction. Hmm.

So, what was the learning from all of this? The bottom line was the cold hadn't changed one bit, but I had. I now viewed the cold sea differently, and as a result I had an entirely altered experience of swimming in it. My thoughts had changed, and my experience transformed to match. This created a new curiosity about areas of my life, where I might apply this new thinking.

Back to the swimming though. I now can officially say, I adore swimming in a chilly sea. I no longer need to scream and shout about it. That's not to say I don't miss the days when I used to shriek like a fool when I got into the water. Maybe next time, in fact, I will allow myself the whole childish drama of shrieking at the cold once more. Abandon my new 'too cool for school' ability to cope. A useful reminder that it's not a requirement to be so adult all of the time. The point though, is that it will be my CHOICE. I will be choosing my experience - and this is quite the key to unravelling anxiety.

Notes

Chapter 35 –
Podcasts

Words guaranteed to fill my husband's heart with dread are, 'I've found an amazing new podcast.' This is usually followed by some pretty rapid-fire U-turns on my behaviour, and inevitably, a fairly expensive shopping trip.

The danger with me and podcasts is that the information always sounds irresistible, and the changes feel like they must be made immediately. Oh, the excitement of turning my world upside down on the promise of a better tomorrow. It's intoxicating!

Hours after listening to a new podcast, expect me to be signing up for an expensive new online course, getting tested for food intolerances, starting a fasting regime, or doing some revolutionary weight-bearing exercises to help me through the menopause. All great ideas in principle, but the hallmark of them all is that I rush headlong into them, often having listened to only half of the podcast. Change is just so flippin' exciting!

This morning, waking early at six a.m. with the intention of writing, I instead listened to three podcasts back to back about the gut/brain connection and the needs of my microbiome.

A couple of hours later, I was queued up in Waitrose (a twice-yearly treat for me), having purchased expensive prebiotics and probiotics on the internet, with a trolley packed to the rafters with turmeric, ginger, kimchi, sourdough bread, raw dark chocolate, kale, and chamomile tea. How I spent close to £100 on this little selection is impressive. To be fair, two bottles of Sauvignon Blanc also slipped in. Not mine, I promise! The husband shook his head at me and titled my new hobby, 'podcast shopping.'

I was determined to eat all the items I'd purchased but secretly already wondered what the turmeric and cauliflower sauerkraut would actually go with. I was confident, though, that my gut would love all the new ingredients, and I would be growing an abundant rainforest of healthy gut bacteria, all vying for the chance to balance my brain chemicals and bring me some calm.

Unfortunately, the promised calming benefits were quickly replaced with surges of anxiety as I digested the cost of my new eating regime. I assessed I could afford to keep it up for approximately one day. The turmeric cauliflower made my stomach turn. I did a spot of deep breathing and focused on the benefits. As ever, the excitement of the podcast was waning, and I wondered if all of this was entirely necessary.

I resolved not to re-listen to that podcast, still eat the good stuff, but not overthink healthy eating. The whole idea felt too complex (all the fasting and fermenting) and it stressed me out. So much so that I begin to think, as I do in times of trouble, 'what would my German Oma do?' - and defaulted to believing the answer must lie in some form of patisserie.

And herein lies the problem.

Not in the podcast itself, but in my desire to make radical, unsustainable changes at the drop of a hat.

The hard part for me is that no matter what the topic, the person talking will always be passionate in their view, and it's their passion that I find so compelling. I'm open-minded and rather too easily influenced (but I'm working on it).

I'm very drawn to the idea of getting big wins from making seemingly small changes. The trouble is, I never change just one thing. I'm either horizontal on the sofa, lamenting my inability to get going, or waxing lyrical about fasting, speed-walking, wild swimming, and replacing my coffee with Matcha. One minute, I'm eating quinoa and kale at every meal, the next caught up in a box set of *The Outlaws* because inevitably, the stage that follows any new podcast fad is overwhelm. Despondency kicks in, wine is reached for, and the house gets purged of sugary products (by purge, read 'I eat') to prevent future sabotage of my self-improvement plans. It's a vicious cycle.

I do want to make changes, but the choices on offer are too bewildering.

Even the reputable doctors with genuinely useful podcasts offer a new technique each week, and it's a bit too much for ADHD me. Do I really need to walk backwards, use my left hand to eat my cereal, exercise in a sauna, and walk barefoot to work? It makes my head spin.

I was a nightmare well before the invention of the internet, buying too many new self-improvement books, but at least these took time to read and gave me a chance for the dopamine to subside before I went out shopping. Now, I can listen to three back-to-back podcasts in one morning like today and have spent the best part of my month's salary before I've even finished my Matcha. It's too easy to be caught up in the frenzy of change.

It's quite a shift from picking up anxiety leaflets in the GP's surgery in the early nineties, and even then, I signed up for far too many random therapies that promised me a fix.

The pep talk to myself today is: listen in moderation.

Podcasts are valuable sources of new knowledge but also a phenomenal way for me to procrastinate, stress myself out, and sabotage my self-esteem. I know it's not the podcasts doing this, but when I find myself listening to creative writing podcasts all day and doing zero writing, you may start to get the picture. Same goes for exercise. Learning numerous new techniques is no replacement for getting moving.

Once more, I'm beginning to realise the podcasts aren't at fault. Yet again, it's my expectation that they will deliver an instant, easy fix.

Seems there's no replacement for doing the work, and no amount of listening to other healthy people talking can substitute me making real changes myself. Darn it!

Thanks, podcasts. You have been great, but now I need to digest all that learning and put a few simple things in place that I know can make a real difference.

I'm going to dust off my swimming membership, keep my promises to the dog to walk whatever the weather, eat the jars of fermented food cluttering my cupboards, and make time to write every day, even if it's only for ten minutes. Every little counts.

Maybe I need to start a podcast on this.

Notes

Chapter 36 – Workshop Addictions and Self-Help Courses

That I have an 'addictive' personality will come as no surprise to you at this point, but thankfully, my addictions now have a healthier focus, and drugs and alcohol have been replaced with well-being courses and self-development in my search for a 'balm' for life.

For example, I have just spent the last half an hour 'preferring to see less' of numerous self-development categories on Facebook because I'm such a sucker for a self-help course. I sign up for these wonderful free workshops on pretty much every subject mentioned in this book in the hope I can tweak my happiness and get myself even more on the straight and narrow.

This has made me realise that my perfectionism has not been erased by all the mindfulness and other learning, but that it has a new focus; my desire to be 'perfectly' healthy and calm. This realisation has made me belly laugh this morning, which can only be a good thing, at least according to my laughter yoga workshop. Could I be any less on track than mindlessly chasing mindfulness? So caught up am I in the search for the next perfect cure that my addiction to finding happiness has me manically chasing my tail as much as my search for perfectionism in any other area of my life.

I may consider myself too switched on to buy into the idiocy of attempting to look perfect or have the perfect job, yet here I am, attempting to 'perfectly' master being chilled and living in flow. Ha!

What prompts me to think about all this is that I have just signed up for another eight-week workshop on Joyful Living. Part of me thinks I might be more joyful if I simply lived rather than studied living joyfully, but despite the fact that I do spend a chunky amount of time in workshops, being around people chasing their dreams and taking exciting steps does snap me out of autopilot.

So, here I sit on the fence. Do I keep doing more courses which inspire me to make exciting changes (like writing this book instead of working for the Department of Work and Pensions) but risk exhausting myself with all the positive actions I'm taking? Serious question: can you burn out on self-improvement?

Tongue removed firmly from cheek for a moment, it does create a predicament for somebody with my personality type, as I can't help but run headlong into whatever I'm doing and risk being wiped out on well-being.

I feel I need a nap just writing this. To be fair, though that may have way more to do with the massive toasted teacake and scone I consumed with coffee, just to ready me to write. I am, of course (pun intended), going to continue with the courses but try and stay off the online ones and keep to the ones where I get to meet real people.

So, I have signed up today for a 'Joyful Living' workshop, and it will be great because the group leader herself has golden energy, and an evening spent in her company is akin to plugging yourself into a human charger overnight. Honestly, she really is that good, and I always come out believing anything is possible which, whether true or false, is a whole lot better than giving up and settling for a somewhat reduced life.

These night-time gatherings also make me laugh loads, and I generally leave energised yet ready for a good night's sleep and feeling much less uncomfortably anxious. Happy days!

With the online courses in contrast, I usually end up hideously overdrawn, don't actually do any proper studying, feel supremely guilty about the aforementioned fact, and carry this constant niggling anxiety about whether expensive Shamanic Drumming really is the answer to life's big question after all. I think it's time to get back to updating my ad preferences on social media pretty smartish. I have signed up for an online procrastination bootcamp for this evening. Maybe I should just do some writing instead.

I was having a conversation with a work colleague only this week (poet, musician, and generally epic human) about whether being massively open to learning new things made me worryingly gullible and at risk of being drawn into dodgy things OR fabulously open to learning and capable of seeing the world in new and exciting ways? The jury is out.

Ironically, as I type this, an email has just popped into my inbox offering me a FREE course on Stoicism (Ancient Wisdom for Modern Life), which promises to address all my usual concerns, and its effect is genuinely much like offering a T-bone steak to a cartoon dog. I am absolutely itching to watch the trailer, but these online course offerings are never-ending, and I am seriously in danger of lying on my deathbed cursing twenty-five years of my life spent watching YouTube videos rather than going to the beach or finishing this book. I have been known to scoff at my children's TikTok wisdom, but am I any better? I think we know the answer. I'm going into my inbox now and deleting that email before another eight hours of my life vanishes right before my blurry 'too much screen time' weary eyes.

The real-life courses can stay for the moment. There is something special about the energy a band of cheery souls can bring to a community centre on a wet evening in October, and whilst my younger self would no doubt be screeching with laughter if she caught me happily sticking pictures on my vision board, I would gently ask her, 'Who got us into this mess in the first place?' whilst simultaneously thanking her for waking me up from autopilot like only crippling anxiety (or a life-threatening illness) really can.

So, to answer my work colleague's question, am I just super gullible or looking to understand myself better, and thereby live a more fulfilling life? I'll answer that one at Don't Panic's press conference. Please do remind me.

Notes

Chapter 37 – Creative Writing

The desire to write has been with me for as long as I can remember. I was an avid reader as a child and still find reading one of the greatest pleasures and quickest ways to drop into deep relaxation. I remember a psychic, who I was hounding to uncover why an ex-boyfriend had dumped me, suggesting between my relentless questions about why he hadn't called that a thing to fix my anxiety might be hunting down a new creative outlet rather than bugging her. I must have been a massive pain. I was paying her £40 a pop. I guess tear-streaked clients aren't a great look for any business.

After her advice, I wrote sporadically and certainly enjoyed the escape it created, plus the diverse people I met on courses, but I don't think I made the vital link between writing and my improved mental health.

One reason it helps so much is that I struggle to express myself fully when speaking. Maybe it's a concentration thing, or maybe it's just the clarity I experience when a thought moves from out of my head and splurges into a sentence. I can look at it for a start. I can consider it from many angles. In my head, it's all nebulous, and a rogue, unhelpful thought can slip by unnoticed. On the page, it looks me boldly in the eye and demands to be considered. I find this super handy.

Also, when I'm writing, I'm on my own. I don't write well in a group setting (although I love the energy of fellow writers) and it is beyond impossible for me when someone is looking over my shoulder. I don't want external input at the writing stage. When I write, I alone can contemplate my thinking quietly, unhindered or influenced by others. I can always delete it or lock it away if I'm unsure.

When I'm speaking, I'm talking to another person, and my overthinking around what they might be concluding about my deviance as a human being gets in the way of what I'm trying to say. Unless I'm with loved ones and I'm able to relax fully, or on the rare occasions when someone has pushed me into fully-fledged rage, then I can be surprisingly eloquent.

If I ditch the concern about what that person might think of me—and that goes right out of the window if they breach my values and make me mad —I can swiftly gather some impressively powerful arguments. Likewise, in job interviews, a strange setting where I unexpectedly feel I have full permission to be myself and to say what I really think. I appreciate that this is a fairly unorthodox place for expressing my unfiltered opinions, but I so sincerely don't want to get yet another bad job that I'm keen to represent my true self—for better or worse. I'm working on being more unapologetically myself in a slightly wider range of settings too. I might branch out into speaking my truth in IKEA. Who knows what might ensue?

Anyway, back to the writing, as I easily digress.

I find clarity on the page. If I can get past the need for perfection and get over the fear of getting started, I find writing freeing. It's amazing how quickly hours can pass when I'm hunched over a keyboard. I guess it's the freedom to be entirely unfiltered. There will always be an opportunity to edit the words at a later stage. I have a lot of ideas. They can clog up the processing space available in my brain. On the page, they are free to go off into a story now or be saved as a character note for a future book. All the wild and wonderful things I think up can find a home in my writing. It gives a purpose to the unconventional place I call my mind.

Likewise, in every difficult situation in the external world, I can always think about how it might apply to a new, developing character. Every person who screams in road rage at me as I get into the wrong lane of the motorway, or every rude cashier at a supermarket who barks at me, 'This checkout is closed,' can get an interesting backstory and find a way into my creative writing. It's a game changer for dealing with tough situations.

In real life, I also often feel a need to filter my speech. I genuinely believe this has a value. I can think 100 thoughts in any moment. Expressing every one of them is not only boring for the wider world, but extremely confusing as they do not come out in any sensible order.

The page allows me to move these ideas around, delete the confused ones, archive some for another day, and group others together to give them cohesion. It's my very own space. It's blank for a start. Putting your own stamp on a blank space is a rare treat. In most areas, whether it's work or home life, there is some compromise. When I'm writing, it's just me deciding on what is allowed in and out. I am the curator of the page with no other initial influences.

It's only when I allow the work to escape into the outside world, for society to peer over my shoulder, that things might change. That's the point when my babies leave home and I am no longer responsible for their destiny. The words will find meaning with the readers, even if it wasn't the meaning I intended to convey.

Bottom line, writing is freeing. It teaches me to be more in touch with what I really think and feel. That, for me, is beyond invaluable.

A Random Aside – The Magnetic Pull of Anxious Feelings

During the panic years, it was an unwritten rule that no one should ever say anything that was likely to trigger my anxiety.

It was an unwritten rule, and no one knew about it except me.

I should have written it down. I might have spotted the flaws in my thinking.

As I was saying, I assumed that all my close family would understand that even mentioning anything vaguely related to the wildly varied and ever-growing list of things I was scared of would kickstart my anxious thinking.

In retrospect, I see that this was unfair.

The one who most often felt the brunt of this was my poor mum.

I would decide on any given day that this was the day to stretch my X-zone, and I would need someone to come with me. Doing anything new felt super tough, but that escalated to near impossible if I was on my own.

What if I had a panic attack that rendered me immobile and I could never get home again?

What if my mobile phone packed up? What if there was no reception?

What if my car suddenly developed a fault? The list went on and on.

This was handy for keeping numerous small businesses trading, a classic being my local car garage.

Mechanic: What's the problem with the car?

Me: Not sure. Can you check absolutely everything? Just in case?

Mechanic: So, is anything actually not working?

Me: Please check everything. Just in case. A full service, yet again. That would be ideal.

A huge garage bill later, and I would drive off a very tiny bit happier that at least the risk of one of my catastrophic thoughts was slightly less likely to happen.

I did this with tyres too. Mobile phones. You name it…

Anyway, back to the story.

To mitigate against any of the above happening, with me potentially descending into a fearful mess that would render me incapable of driving, I always had to get someone to come with me.

As you can imagine, the queue of people keen to join me on my 'mad escapade' from Sainsbury's to the other side of town wasn't enormous. Weirdly, it wasn't everyone's idea of a great day out, hanging out with a seriously uptight person on an outing to travel a few miles up the road.

So, the people most often roped in were my husband (and after twenty-five years, his interest 'unreasonably' had waned), and my mum.

The greatest thing about my lovely mum was that she almost always said yes.

The downside was that she often forgot the rules for travelling with me. You know, the ones I had never explained properly to her because even I wasn't fully aware how they worked.

We would be trying something new, and I would be feeling fairly okay. It would be going a solid seven out of ten. What she didn't know was that I would be simultaneously frantically trying to distract myself from the panicky feelings. Working very hard not to do body scans (whilst obviously checking up on myself every few seconds).

This would be hard work and make it challenging to have even a basic conversation. I would easily snap as I tried desperately not to get dragged into my anxious thinking. The magnetic pull was strong.

My mum would then drop some innocent comment into our chat.

Mum: This road is longer than I thought. It feels like we've been driving for ages.

This was because she was no doubt a bit bored, but for me, it was like lighting the touch paper to my anxious thinking.

I suddenly couldn't think about anything other than how far we had come, and I immediately started to feel intensely anxious.

Me: Please NEVER say that when we're driving, Mum.

I started crying as the hopeless realisation dawned on me that I was never going to get better.

Mum: Sorry, darling. What did I say?

Me: Never, say this is a long way, or look how narrow the road is, or I wonder when we'll get home. All of that triggers my anxiety. You made me anxious today. Now we have to go home.

Mum: Oh, sorry, darling. I just meant…

I looked at her, exasperated, and added her to the long list of people who didn't understand.

Other people talking about things which triggered anxiety at a time when I was desperately trying to keep a handle on things and push those thoughts away did feel seriously unhelpful.

Over time, however, the safe topics people were allowed became fewer and fewer, as the triggers for my anxiety expanded like bread dough in a warm airing cupboard (is it only me who puts the bread dough there?).

I used to think my husband was positively bullying me with his harsh words around my anxious feelings. I realise now he was caught between a rock and a hard place. My thinking was wonky around what created my anxiety, and it was hard for me to keep up with what triggered me, let alone those close to me.

This got me thinking about sticky thoughts.

My anxious thoughts felt magnetic. They pulled me in so forcefully. One thought would quickly trigger another, and soon they would be firing off more spectacularly than fireworks over the Thames on New Year's Eve.

The truth is, I have a brilliant imagination. Yes, deep in the anxiety years, I used it mainly to tell myself catastrophic horror stories, but I did know that when push came to shove, I could also use it to mentally escape fearful situations long enough to get me home safely.

When the train broke down in the Channel Tunnel and we were plunged into darkness for hours, I was forced to tell myself a story that I could cope. I was forced to distract myself and get a grip on my anxious feelings. I tapped into an inner reserve and did not run up and down the train screaming, as was my greatest fear.

What I was close to seeing at this point, but never quite grasping, was that there were a few fundamental flaws in the stories that underpinned my anxious thinking.

A whopper was the one that said I WAS an anxious person, rather than a person with some anxious thinking. That my normal, sometimes negative human feelings, were a sign I had an abnormal problem with anxiety.

I get why I believed this.

The story that I was somehow broken was one I was told over and over again.

I guess it kept a good few of the therapists in employment as they delved deep into my serious anxiety problem and diagnosed me, unhelpfully, with Generalised Anxiety Disorder. Yikes! They also declared this was a tough one to fix—a bit like when the plumber comes round to fix a leak and says, 'This one is going to be expensive.'

Then I think about all the other stories I've told myself over the years. Like the drugs flashback story. Have I ever even had a drugs flashbacks? More likely, I've just hung on to my fearful thinking around the drugs experience, and every time a scary memory resurged, I labelled it as a drugs flashback. A scary piece of labelling.

Shame was another dodgy narrative for me.

When I brought up a shame-based thought, it would cause an actual involuntary physical reaction in my body. Most commonly, a jerk of my limbs or a noise escaping from my mouth. The emotional impact of the shame was so intense. It was embarrassing when it happened in public. The shame would bounce around my body like a rogue pinball, fired up by imagination. Often, it would launch a rapid-fire attack, with ball after ball being expelled in quick succession, intense shame ricocheting around my nervous system like a toxic shock.

Why couldn't I have harnessed my fantastic imagination to better effect?

Someone said recently that the mind is a bit like a radio station, playing the same old songs on repeat. You can choose to notice what is happening and change the station, or turn the radio down with meditation, or even off if you are one of the enlightened few.

So, this random aside is more about thoughts and the massive part they played in my anxious experience.

I always survived every anxious period and panic attack. I might not have liked them, and often the repercussions in terms of feeling wiped out afterwards added to the challenge, but I was always ultimately okay, and the 'repercussions' afterwards were really just me piling more anxious thoughts onto whatever difficult incident had occurred.

Phew! That's a lot to think about!

Notes

Chapter 38 – Manifesting, Storytelling, and my Brain

I love a bit of manifestation. Give me a vision board and some magazines, and I will cut and paste for hours. It's remarkable how many of my visions have come to pass. I have replayed positive situations in my head, imagined new goals coming to fruition, and fate seems to twist in my favour. The cues I give my brain to focus on make all the difference. The revelation is that this applies to my anxious feelings also.

How anxious I feel is a direct response to the story I tell myself. Always.

I hope this ability to tell a scintillating tale will be put to better use when I write fiction. My brain is forever fizzing with thoughts and ideas, and in the absence of using them to bring characters to life, it seems I may be directing this unspent energy towards creating anxious thoughts.

What I'm seeing lately is that my brain helpfully amplifies what I'm focusing on. Much like when I manifest. I focus my thoughts on what I want, and my brain goes about busily pointing out things that could usefully relate to me achieving that goal.

This is brilliant when I'm envisioning myself at a book signing at Waterstones in Bath, with my trilogy of books (this is the first of three) all lined up on the table with pretty colour co-ordinated covers. It feels like a leap, but it has resulted in me writing every day, noticing new courses, joining writing groups, which has all got to help to get those books onto the Waterstones shelves. I'm sure there is way more spiritual learning to consider on top of this, but in my simplistic way of looking at the world, this is how manifesting works to me. Plus, it's fun to cram my brain with positive and exciting plans for the future. ADHD heaven!

This helpful brain trait is always at work, but less appreciated when I negatively obsess about fear and danger. When I make danger my primary focus, my brain will highlight problems everywhere. When I want to change my car for a Fiat 500, I see Fiat cars at every road junction.

My brain notices what I pay attention to. When I believe that motorways are scary or that Dartmoor isn't safe and causes panic attacks, it will point me towards further evidence to support this belief, noticing news stories about M5 accidents or breakdowns on the moor.

I see signs everywhere. To be fair, I guess I'm looking for them. 'Am I doing the right thing?' I ask myself, stuck in traffic, and a number plate rushes past with YES as its last three letters on the plate.

I appreciate that this is a convenience. When it suits me, I choose to see signs everywhere. Relevant messages posted on billboards, graffiti on the underpass, or simply a book opening at the perfect passage I need to read in that moment.

I don't know what it all means. Probably that, deep down, I'm not yet fully trusting my intuition and still looking for validation from the outside world that I'm on track.

On a plus point, though, it is fun looking for little positive signs each day, from the heart-shaped stone on the beach to the radio show discussing just the topic I've been contemplating writing about. I know the science. It's the reticular activating system in action, but it's also something I actively enjoy. A little pick-me-up daily.

Just a quirk of mine, but one that gives me a bit of hope that I'm going in the right direction.

We all have to do what works for us, right?

The interesting thing is that now I have become aware of this, I find I can also change the story.

A classic example of this was driving back from a gig in Bath with an old friend. She'd had a fair few glasses of wine and was finding life hilarious. It was late at night, I'm not a big fan of driving in the dark, and it was foggy.

There is fog and *fog;* this was the can't-see-anything-in-front-of-me kind of foggy. I couldn't see the road signs, and to make matters worse for me —and even more belly-achingly funny for my bestie—there were road closures and diversions everywhere. The sat nav was screeching 're-route' in the most stress-inducing way whilst still insisting that I drive up single route 'roads' that had more grass than your average suburban lawn.

I was lost, totally freaking out, and being encouraged by my lovely but excessively tipsy friend to pull into a layby and sleep. 'What's the big deal? We'll just have a little rest until the morning.'

One hangover from my history with anxiety is that I still have my homing pigeon device set on permanent standby.

Things get tough, and I want to go home.

This was not boding well for me in the lanes on 'pea soup' night. The other thing worth telling you is that I'm not the most confident dual carriageway and motorway driver. Another hangover from the anxiety, I guess. This has actually receded since, but at that time, I always fervently sought out the non-motorway route as motorways made me anxious—or that was the story I told myself.

Not that night.

Lost in the lanes with zero visibility and a sat nav that may have been on the tipples with my friend for all the use it was being, I was desperate to find a motorway. When I finally got onto the M5, I was fist punching the air, so relieved was I to know where to go and have a wide and straight road to follow.

This, though, had me scratching my head after the event.

How could I, someone who is terrified of motorway travel, suddenly switch narratives in my head and see them as my salvation?

The answer was exactly that.

The story I had told myself about A roads being good and motorways being dodgy just didn't stack up in the moment. When it suited me to get away from my pea soup nightmare, I could suddenly embrace motorways with love in my heart.

This made me wonder what other stories I could rewrite if it suited me.

With a little investigation, I realised, rather a lot of them.

I now see that I do this all the time.

The only difference between the times I get uncomfortably anxious and the times I get 'normally' anxious (or excited, apprehensive, or whatever that very normal emotion is that other humans experience when trying something new) is the story that accompanies the feeling.

If the story is nonsense, and I can truly see that, anxiety passes through in seconds. This used to happen in Exeter. I decided at one point that Exeter was okay and no longer somewhere I should panic. I rationalised I could get home easily, so it moved onto the safe list. Symptoms would rise in the city, but I would tell myself, 'Not here, we're okay. It's Exeter,' and the feelings would dissipate.

In a different location, the very same symptoms would appear, but this time, I would launch into a full catastrophe story, and those same initial anxious feelings would be dialled up and result in a panic attack—or more likely, me running home to avoid a panic attack.

To panic or not to panic came down to whether or not I believed the anxiety story churning around in my head.

Now, if I do get caught up in a story and anxiety ramps up, I think, 'Hang on. If I'm feeling this hideous, my thoughts must be off.' Just noticing this makes my anxious feelings recede.

Storytelling held the key to my anxiety.

I was terrified of my anxious feelings, so I gave them false powers. I believed the narrative that they had control over my life, and because I believed it, they seemed frighteningly powerful.

It reminds me of *The Wizard of Oz*. The wizard is super powerful until the moment Dorothy realises he is just a man behind a curtain with no magical powers at all. His strength is directly proportional to her belief in him. When she sees him for what he is, she can't go back to her old beliefs.

When I was finally bold enough to come face to face with my fear, it just turned out to be a normal emotion; no more dangerous than any of its more palatable counterparts, such as joy and happiness. Running away from my fear was what was fuelling it and making it look so frighteningly large.

When I stayed firmly put and allowed my fear to 'do its worst,' there was no terrifying ghostly spectre, just a quiet calming of my anxious response.

Without fear, I couldn't respond to genuinely dangerous situations, and it's an important part of my emotional toolkit. I can't get rid of it, and it would be dangerous to do so. Having spent more than half my life being terrified of fear, I now see that a long, cold stare, Paddington Bear-style, brings it back into line fairly quickly. It's just there giving me the heads-up that there may be some issues to address. All I need to do is take a quick look, check all is well, and then fear is more than happy to stand down. Way better for us both.

Going back to the earlier manifestation thing, I realise I'm telling myself powerful stories all the time. My brain responds the same to a real disaster as it does to my fictional ones.

In the past, just thinking about getting onto a plane would result in a full flood of panic feelings. Waves of anxiety would course through my body at the merest mention of getting stuck in a lift. Even if I was thinking about the lift at home, sitting on my sofa, in my comfiest slippers with a hot chocolate in my hand. I told myself the story, saw it in my mind, and the panic feelings downloaded. Today, I have had different experiences, which makes it hard/impossible to bring up those same anxious feelings once more. They no longer make sense.

Where your thoughts flow, your energy goes, as they say…

I start contemplating the good stuff, and my brain puts equal energy into highlighting opportunities there too. I am more in charge than I realised. It seems I have the option to call out the bad thoughts and say, 'Thanks, but no thanks,' and fuel my dreams and ambitions instead.

Call it manifesting or positive thinking, we anxiety peeps turn out to be absolutely genius at it.

If you are prone to strong anxious feelings like me, you have been successfully envisioning incredibly powerful stories for years. It's all a story, so why not tell yourself a fabulous one and see what happens?

When I changed my story, I changed my experience. Manifestation in action!

Notes

Chapter 39 – The Box Technique

I came across a TEDx talk by Tim Box called, 'How to Stop Feeling Anxious About Anxiety' a few years ago. Right from the opening statement, I was riveted.

'Feeling anxious, whilst seemingly unhelpful, is understandable. Right now, anxiety makes sense to me, but there was a time in my life when anxiety didn't make sense. The main thing that has changed, whilst I still experience anxiety, is that I no longer suffer with it. I didn't experience this shift by getting rid of it.'

'You don't get rid of anxiety by trying to get rid of it.'

Whaaaat?

'You don't get rid of anxiety at all.'

This rang true for me.

He then goes on to say how he has spoken to so many anxiety sufferers, and every single one of them expressed the exact same desire. The desire to get rid of anxiety completely.

This man understood what I felt, and he was funny. He was able to laugh about it and make it okay, normal even, to experience anxious feelings. Major game changer! He went on in his talk to say, 'Anxiety is the feeling that demands our attention. There are two groups of people who don't experience anxiety. The first group. Dead people. Dead people don't feel anxious. The second group is those we might refer to as psychopaths. Those people who lack any ability to have concern for the consequences of their or anyone else's actions.'

He then questions whether any of us would want to fall into either of these two categories.

A resounding no. So, then he asks, 'If being free of anxiety is such a bad idea, why do we view anxiety so negatively?'

It was like when Maria, the reflexologist, probed me about my X-rule, gently questioning if I had one foot on one side of the line and the other foot on the other, what would happen? Would half of me be okay? 'No, obviously not,' I retorted. So, she asked where the actual line was. It was an interesting question.

Back to the TEDx talk. Tim then goes on to discuss a wide range of things that can't happen without some level of anxiety. The list is long and covers many everyday things.

I remember finishing watching that talk and thinking, 'Wow, this guy actually gets what I'm feeling.' And more importantly, I got what he was saying. This man could help me.

My Nice holiday was a few weeks away.

I had been feeling increasingly nervous about going. I think I had told myself I wasn't going to go by this point. Yet I was still watching the Nice live webcam for hours on end and scouring the internet for new things to make me feel calmer.

I needed to see this Tim Box man. He was the answer! I found his website and fired off an email.

He was lovely and got back to me straight away but didn't have time to give me the necessary sessions before my trip to France. He did have other therapists, though, that he had trained in his Box Technique. He directed me to his website. I scrolled through the site and found a well-travelled creative type that jumped out at me. She was living the life I wanted to live. She looked super friendly and kind and was based in Plymouth, Devon. It felt like the stars had aligned.

In all fairness, the sessions were online, so I could have had a therapist anywhere, but this woman was calling to me. Let me assure you, I was not disappointed.

It has come to my attention over the years that it's not just the therapies that have made a difference, but more so the humans delivering those treatments. This woman was heaven-sent.

She was a no-nonsense, animal-loving, seasoned traveller, who was never once dismissive of my barrage of fears around travelling. She made me feel normal. That some of the things I was thinking, in terms of preparing myself for the trip, were not anxiety but part of normal planning for a holiday. Okay, maybe just the top three of my list of 436 essential things to do before any trip, but still, overall, nice work Tim! She had certainly embraced his concept of normalising anxiety.

I arranged to have three sessions prior to Nice. The rest is history. I properly relaxed and actually enjoyed a holiday abroad, for the very first time since my Glastonbury meltdown of 1990.

She has since helped me with many other issues, sometimes more as a security blanket, as I have slowly found my feet after years of anxiety, but she has helped me nonetheless. I am beyond grateful.

The Box technique is based on hypnotherapy, but nothing like other versions of hypnotherapy I have tried previously. I get agreement from my subconscious to release certain things that no longer serve me and possibly adopt other new ideas that might bolster me in situations where I might otherwise feel anxious. The results have always been surprisingly good.

I was certainly going in the right direction with my anxiety before discovering this technique, but the Box method moved things along more swiftly. It was like jumping off the anxiety cliff with a parachute, rather than bravely free-falling. It still took courage, but it was so much less intimidating.

It was the technique that swept away any last remaining pockets of unnecessary anxiety. The 'auto pilot' anxious reflex that was just an old habit –like reaching for popcorn every time a movie trailer comes on. Anxiety would still be there for the real emergencies, but not the trip to the supermarket to buy carrots.

I was getting close to the end of my quest, but a new lesson was winging its way to me. It would soon be time to bump into the Quiet Coach, Nano Ponce.

Taking a Leap – Nice August 2023

So, I just got back from a week in Nice. No big deal, you might think. She has this nailed. Let me take you back to a few hours before we were due to leave.

Basically, I had allowed my fear to take over, and it was on the rampage throughout my body. I would describe it as an over-exuberant puppy that had not yet had its daily walk.

Unwittingly, I think I had been trying to control my fear in the run-up to going away, and all that pushing down of my feelings had resulted in my fear having loads of extra, bouncy energy. When I let it out, it threatened to overwhelm me. I was terrified. It was sweeping over me in waves, and this got me thinking about all the stuff I had read about fear. How there was no sense in fighting it. Fear was a normal part of my emotions.

Could I abandon the need to keep fear on such a tight leash? Maybe once the excess energy had dissipated, I could perhaps have a more routine relationship with it again. If everyone has fear and others don't respond to it with the same alarm as me, could I trial having a different experience? This was a new approach.

So, I went for the 'bring it all on' technique. The 'all feelings welcome' approach, and every time I said this to myself, the fear didn't get worse but actually eased a little.

I know we've been through all this before, but there is learning to be done here. It feels weird for me because I'm a fifty-four-year-old woman doing the learning, but in relation to my travels, I'm coming at it with new eyes. As a child, when I did something new, I felt fear and tentatively had a go. Sometimes, I jumped right in, whilst other times it took a few more attempts. No judgement applied. Some things just took longer to get to grips with than others.

Now, I embark on something that takes me out of my comfort zone, and I don't look at the progress I have made. I compare myself to so-called 'normal' people and feel surprised when things are hard. New things are hard for everyone. I have to recalibrate. Get used to the new normal for me, which is travel.

Back to the trip. So, I gave in to my fear, it bounced through me, and I fell for all my old tricks. The storytelling part of my brain started telling me plausible stories about how I didn't want to travel anyway. I called friends, giving lengthy, well-thought-through excuses as to why I shouldn't go. The ones who knew me well batted them right back at me. Newer friends indulged my storytelling and agreed it was just the wrong trip at the wrong time. Not true. I was lying to myself, allowing my fear of fear to call the shots. I went back to bed and tried 'being with my fear.' Terribly New Age!

The fear itself was not so bad. It felt uncomfortable yes, but many things in life were uncomfortable but they didn't prevent me from taking action. I realised that hooking up my powerful storyteller in my mind with my fear, was where I was going wrong. I found myself fearing not the real physical feelings experienced in my bedroom in Devon (not nice, but ultimately bearable), but some future imagined fear which I surmised would be more intense, more overwhelming and would likely render me entirely unable to cope. My ramped-up narrator speculated that should this fear be allowed to freewheel in Nice, I would be plunged into very real danger at the bare minimum, whilst probably leaving me doomed to dwell in a state of insanity, for the rest of eternity. Hmm.

Quite a compelling story to dissuade me from even having a go.

Fortunately, at the same time, my children were telling me how much they wanted me to go, how much better their holiday would be if I was there, how much it would mean if I tried.

My brain shifted a little. I wanted to go. I to-and-froed between terror and curiosity, but overall, decided it was too hard to try. A good friend, who is a life coach, told me to take a step. Get out of my comfort zone. I got mad at her. Another friend didn't buy into my excuses. I hung up, cross (secretly) with her too.

My daughter told me to pack a bag, even though I wasn't going. Just to give me the option. She did it for me. I had zero intention of travelling. She packed almost nothing except some clean laundry she found in the kitchen, my passport, and my medicine.

It was one a.m. and everyone was getting ready. I rowed with my husband about not going. I was crying and sitting on the toilet, listening to the family in the final stages of leaving.

Suddenly, something came over me. A strong feeling. I got this sense that I had to do this. I saw my daughter and said, 'I think I'm coming.' She looked surprised but pleased. I tentatively picked up the travel bag and headed for the car. At that point, I didn't allow myself to think about anything travel-related. My son was beyond overjoyed and said it was the best news ever. I got in the car and the family piled in too.

We drove to the airport. My fear was certainly there, but at a low hum. It had receded massively from the intense unbearable high I experienced when I was struggling with my decision about whether to go. Committing to going had eased it for the first time all night.

I arrived at Bristol airport and got out of the car. It appeared that I was still going. Through airport security we went, into the departure lounge, onto the flight, looking out of the window, all the while thinking, 'you've done this now. No turning back.' I felt surprisingly okay.

I landed in Nice, and it felt surreal. Of course it did. I hadn't slept all night. I was doing something that was still very new for me, but I was aware that other feelings were rising too. Pride, for a start. I couldn't believe I had been so brave. Curiosity too. It was so warm. Everything looked and smelt different. I saw landmarks that I had seen from endless internet research and found myself walking across Place Massena, the 19th-century plaza I had been observing virtually for days on the Nice live webcam.

We stopped for a cool drink. It was so hot. I felt calm and a bit excited. Part of me was a little tentative. Why wouldn't I be? It had been years of overthinking about travel that had held me back, and I was still wondering if any of my far-fetched doom fantasies might materialise. Nothing did. I was exhausted and also exhilarated. I was abroad with my family in a busy and hot city, and I felt good (cue Nina Simone).

It was incredible.

If you have ploughed on this far, you will know this holiday could have been a trigger for so many past fears: crowds, distance from home, flying, trains, feeling trapped with no car—you name it. Yet, there I was, and I felt fine. Better than fine. I was enjoying myself, and I couldn't believe that a mere twelve hours earlier, I was a quivering mess, lying in my bed, awash with fear.

The reality of the situation was so much less scary than my wild, imaginative thinking. In fact, it wasn't scary at all. And so the holiday went on. I did amazing things. Swam in crystal clear seas, shopped in bustling French markets, ate incredible food, went on tourist trams around the Cote D'Azur. I found myself crammed onto an express train coming back from Monaco, and though I didn't love it, I was always okay. It was August in Nice. It was busier than at any other time of year and I was doing this!

I did spend the week wondering if the bubble would burst and I would suddenly be besieged with anxiety, but it never happened, and I had a great holiday. I still couldn't quite believe it.

That I had come this far, literally and metaphorically, was dream come true material. I would read stories like this about other people and think, at my lowest points, that it could never be me.

I am so proud and can firmly say that creating a new relationship with my fear is what sealed it for me.

The day I decided to let fear be rather than trying to squash it out of existence changed everything. When I let fear do its job, to alert me to potential problems, and accepted the feelings that came with this emotion, I realised I could handle the feelings.

What I couldn't cope with was my attempts to resist it, force it away, and to fuel it with horror stories. When I did that, like a cornered animal, it would always give me both barrels.

That was what needed to stop.

I needed to learn to trust myself. To trust my emotions and my ability to cope with my feelings. That was it.

I always thought I was trying to cope with the outside world, but really, all my battles were with myself. When the penny fully dropped that this was unnecessary, I decided to try just letting myself be.

All of me.

The scared parts, the angry parts, the frustrated parts, as well as the more conventionally positive elements.

Fear is not a flaw in the human design. I'm meant to have all the emotions I was born with. I do not need to cut out my fear. Then, I would indeed be broken. I'm supposed to feel it all—light and dark—and when I truly embrace this and allow my body to work as it is designed, things get a lot easier. Resistance is futile.

Taking a Leap – New Job March 2024

It's a year to the day that I accepted a job as a fundraiser for a local environmental charity. I turned the position down initially—my ego couldn't handle the lack of status— but my manager artfully talked me into giving it a go. As a result, I walked away from another job with, on paper, a way fancier job title, and my ego was forced to wind its neck back in. So, why did I make this choice?

It ticked a lot of boxes regarding my values, but even more importantly, offered me a leap out of my comfort zone with regards to my anxiety triggers.

I was deep into learning that taking leaps was something I needed to do if I was ever going to call a truce with my anxious feelings.

I even applied to be on the BBC cult reality show *The Traitors*, thinking, *'Please do not pick me,'* but I applied all the same. That would have required me to stay at a remote castle in Scotland and do any number of scary things like potentially be 'buried alive' (I'm sure it's safer than it sounds), jump from a plane, you name it. I would have been challenged. Even the social aspect was terrifying. Showing up as myself with millions of viewers judging my every move. Horrific! Yet there was a part of me that wanted the challenge. That knew I needed to take more steps outside of my comfort zone.

The new job wasn't quite as terrifying as the castle, but it did offer me some grade A challenges. At the time of starting, I was still nervous about driving on the motorway and dual carriageways, had an irrational fear of Dartmoor, hated narrow country lanes (although I was getting way better at these, having moved to the middle of nowhere) and was still terrified of getting lost in unfamiliar places. I hated getting 'stuck' in traffic and felt sick at the idea of doing any of the above on my own.

So, my new job involved driving around Devon, often to very isolated areas, always on Dartmoor, attending crowded events in narrow rural areas, going to events where I could drive in before the event started, but then would be 'stuck' there all day until vehicles were allowed to move off the site. I would have to do all of this on my own whilst facing another fear; talking to random strangers about nature in great detail with the fear that someone would identify me as an idiot, or even worse, a fraud who knew nothing about the environment.

It was a challenge.

Fast forward twelve months and all the above is pretty much a breeze— other than maybe a touch of imposter syndrome. I can't begin to tell you how good it feels to be driving on the A30 on the way to Cornwall—a county I was too scared to visit for decades—going to a remote location to train people to do my fundraising job. Yes, you heard right, training, so you can add public speaking to the list of leaps I have made out of my comfort zone.

I just keep saying yes to things and, broadly speaking, despite moments of anxiety, I'm okay. Sometimes, I even have the luxury of not being able to remember precisely what scared me about the situation in the first place. It's the most incredible feeling. I can't stop grinning. It makes me look a little unhinged, granted, but I am more than happy to whisper gratitude to the universe (and any passing trees) as I go about living my life in this amazing new reality.

My life isn't perfect by any stretch, but I can cope with life's imperfections, and I have a growing belief that I'm okay whatever happens. I have to pinch myself as I type this. It's the most incredible transformation!

Update 24 March 2025

I'm going to Bristol tomorrow by train to meet up with two school friends. This probably doesn't seem like a big deal, and it isn't really, except this morning, my old brain patterning kicked in and the internal chatter went something like this: OT = Old thought, NT = new thought, F = feeling)

OT: So, you're off on the train tomorrow? We have not historically liked trains.

F: An anxious feeling shoots through my system.

NT: I'm okay with trains now.

OT: Are you really? You won't be able to get off. You'll be stuck! Check out how many stops there are between home and Bristol immediately.

NT: No, I'll be fine. Worst case, I'll feel anxious feelings, and they will go away again.

OT: We hate those feelings.

NT: We used to find them unbearable to even look at. We now know they will pass and may not even show at all. We are going!

OT: Thanks for checking it out for me. Appreciate the heads up.

F: Calm with the odd nervous twinge

As I said, I'm going to Bristol tomorrow. Period.

I had the most incredible time! Best day out for a very long time, spending time with two amazing school friends. Imagine if I had just stayed at home and not busted that myth?

This weekend was similar again. I had to visit an organic farm in North Devon. I checked the map over and over again, and no amount of scrutiny made the roads any bigger. These were Devon lanes, and the farm, as they proudly promoted on their website, was in the middle of nowhere. I decided not to go. Told myself I was too tired and it would be too much of a strain. On the day, though, I saw things differently and found myself in my car and en-route before I'd had much time to reconsider. Cut to the chase, I once more had a brilliant day at a beautiful, remote countryside location and drove back grinning like a fool, delighted with my success. What this taught me more than anything else was that every time I bust through the myths of my old thinking, I feel stronger and more resilient to take on the next challenge. A book launch in Dublin is next. I'm even a speaker at the event. I'm nervous, but it's not holding me back from booking my flight!

Taking a Leap – London June 2024

Despite things getting way better for me in terms of my anxiety, I had blind spots. The most obvious ones were Dartmoor and London.

It's easy to work out why. I had panic attacks in both places, which drew me to the incorrect conclusion that there was something inherently unsafe about going to either location. The mere thought of them made me anxious. They were easy to avoid, and as a result, my incorrect beliefs remained intact for too many years.

In fact, my anxiety about them grew as I piled more and more anxious thinking onto the idea of visiting them.

If I'm honest, Dartmoor is way better now. I have been there many times, but I'm still reluctant to drive right across the moor from Dunsford to Tavistock. I still associate it with panic. I'm now happy to drive from Bovey Tracey to Whiddon Down, which is driving horizontally across the moor as you look at it, rather than vertically—go figure. I'm hoping to bust through that fear before I write the conclusion to this book (as I edit this, I already feel okay).

London was another massive blind spot.

London was one of the first few places, after Glastonbury, where I had experienced a full-blown, overwhelming panic attack. I remember it now. I was standing in Covent Garden, people everywhere. It was a beautiful sunny day, and I suddenly became aware of the heat, the noise, the crowds, the tall buildings, and that I was in the middle of a dense urban area. I wondered if I might prefer not to be there, and that feeling rapidly escalated into an intense need to escape immediately. As this was not possible, I panicked big time.

There was more going on beneath the surface though. Information that might have been useful to consider. For one, I was massively hungover, and I was having 'love trouble.' I was emotionally all over the place, AND it was hot, there were crowds, it was noisy, I was dehydrated, and I probably needed a lie down.

That I felt bad is totally understandable. That I got quite so scared by the feelings maybe a little less so, other than I had recently had a massive bad trip at Glastonbury and anything that resembled that was triggering.

I did not see the parallels at the time. I just thought I was losing my mind again and wanted to run.

I got back home and thought, 'Well, I won't be doing that for a while.' Little did I know that 'a while' would turn out to be thirty-four years.

So, as the years rolled by and my anxiety worsened, the idea of going to London became even less appealing.

London would 'make me' have a panic attack, I told myself, as if London was emitting some weird energetic force to make me panic. With my frankly marvellous imagination, I created many scenarios in my head where I lost my mind in the city, and over the years, these changed from stories I told myself to concrete, unchallenged facts.

With time, as my anxiety receded, I became willing to try new things, even go abroad, but London and Dartmoor remained places to avoid. This was fairly easy. Everything I wanted to do in London, I could probably do somewhere else, so I was happy not to challenge it, until…

My daughter started getting into music. Not obscure indie bands, although she loves them now also, but big-name stars that played big venues. Big London venues.

One thing I'm absolutely useless at is disappointing my (not so) little girl, so when she excitedly proclaimed Taylor Swift was playing at Wembley, and SZA, Mitski, and Beabadoobee were playing at London festivals in the summer of 2024, just after her GCSEs, I boldly suggested we should get tickets. Even as I said this, I was thinking, 'For the love of God, please let them be sold out,' but I applied for those scarce resources, and as luck should have it, I got the tickets. Bugger!

Purchasing the tickets seven months before the first concert was scary, but nothing compared to how terrified I was the week before the gigs. We're talking full tears (in private to my mum), excuses tripping off my tongue faster than tickets selling out for the Oasis comeback tour, and back-up plans aplenty with friends lined up to step into my sweaty shoes at the last minute.

Bizarrely, on the day, though, despite sleep having gone AWOL for days, I found myself on a coach heading for BST Hyde Park, and again a few months later to Hackney for All Points East, followed by a 90,000-capacity crowd Taylor Swift concert at Wembley Stadium. Talk about taking baby steps!

The fear was right up there. As intense as I have ever felt it, but something inside me drove me to take one step at a time and to not think about the epic journey ahead of me. One step tentatively following another, until I got off the coach at London Victoria.

The first surprise was that London wasn't as crowded as I had expected and I could breathe. Also, the fear wasn't rising and suffocating me. I had, over the years, learned not to question this too much. I found myself stepping out into a sunny London street and feeling okay. I waited for the panic to arrive, but all that turned up was a big red London bus. I pinched myself. I was not dreaming. A grin spread across my face. I was doing this thing. It was nothing like I had imagined. Something registered deep inside. I was no longer scared.

At this point, I was doing a dance of joy inside. I didn't want to be too cocky. I knew things could change, but these little rushes of happiness kept bubbling up. I was doing the scary thing, and I was okay. And then it dawned on me. I would always be okay because I was no longer terrified of the worst thing that could happen. I wasn't scared of having a panic attack. I didn't want one, but I understood it wouldn't kill me. This changed everything.

I relaxed into being a proper London tourist. Photos of me can be found outside the Houses of Parliament, cruising up the Thames, queuing for tickets on the banks of the river; all things I imagined myself incapable of doing. My WhatsApp went crazy as I fired off photo after photo to my loyal band of friends. I fear there may be photographic evidence of me punching the air!

I went to the festivals. Watched the sun going down in a massive crowd over Hyde Park, witnessed a swaying wave of beautiful young people holding glowing wristbands into the night sky at Taylor Swift, and the entire time, I felt nothing but the purest of joy.

It tears me up now, typing. I can't listen to Taylor Swift without silently thanking her for my transformation. I felt those last elements of my panicky self release into the charged atmosphere of her insane concert.

The journey home was indescribable. I can't capture in words quite how good it felt as we drove down the motorway towards Devon. Me grinning inanely, finally allowing myself to fully immerse in that euphoric feeling of having climbed my own personal Everest. I felt giddy, light, and so powerful.

I'm not saying I will never feel anxious again, but I know it's not possible for me to fear panic in the same way I did. I will never be able to tell myself those horror stories anymore. I simply won't believe them.

Fear was an unreliable narrator in my head. I believed everything my fearful inner voice told me because I had not learned one critical lesson:

'Just because you think it, doesn't make it true.'

For years, I had assumed the voice in my head was giving me an accurate assessment of what was going on in the external world. *That person hates you, you are useless in that job,* or *London makes you anxious.*

Once I realised I was not listening to the voice of truth but the voice of fear, things turned swiftly (see what I did there) around.

I'm learning all the time, and I'm grateful for the lessons the anxiety years have taught me, but I also know I'm entering a completely new phase of my life.

The voice in my head is telling me a different story these days. One that makes me feel more accepted. No need to run away anymore, either from myself or the not-so-scary outside world.

I have passed through an invisible barrier to a new reality, and I have to confess, it feels amazing on the other side!

Chapter 40 – Quiet Coaching

Sometimes, lessons come along quietly, stealthily, without anyone announcing their arrival. They appear, observe, and gently steer me in new, more useful directions. May I introduce you to the world of Nano Ponce. Quiet Coach and anxiety-whisperer extraordinaire. A technique that crossed my path by complete chance.

I met him on a book project we collaborated on. I had to read my story out loud to a group of fellow authors, an abbreviated version of *Don't Panic*. Whilst others commented to similar effect on my writing style or how they felt emotionally impacted by my story, his feedback stood out for its difference. All he said was, 'I don't see an anxious person. You talk about this anxious person, but I don't see her. This person here is not anxious.'

I was taken aback. In a good way. I was in a group of people, way more senior than me, with bigger and better jobs—certainly financially more secure—and I was seriously apprehensive about reading my story. Old insecurities were rising. What would people think of me?

Then this human, a successful businessperson and coach, was noticing that I didn't look or sound like an anxious person anymore. Hallelujah! It felt good.

We got talking over the months, and I found the conversations subtly, quietly illuminating. Ideas I had considered before around how our thoughts create our feelings, how the lens of our perception creates our view of the world, all gained clarity the more we chatted.

It wasn't that he was saying something new to me, but more that the examples he used to illustrate his points enabled me to grasp the ideas more firmly. He often pointed to the noise in my head. 'Too noisy. You won't be able to hear your own voice.' He quietly made me notice quite how often I resorted to trying to think myself out of an overthinking problem. We laughed a lot.

Nano helped me with my overwhelm. I had written most of this book, but it was raw, unedited, and the word count was daunting. I was frightened even to glance at it. I don't think I had written a word in six months. I was blocked. He had a writing programme, 'The Writer's Wand' (I recommend this to anyone trying to get their book into shape), which gave me the structure I was crying out for, but it was also the Quiet Coaching I received whilst working on this book that impacted me with value. I noticed, over time, that I had more control over not just my anxiety response, but other emotions. I was a little more removed from the melee of my emotions. I could reset back to calm more quickly. I could observe the wild, stormy sea of my thinking and steer my way back to a quiet mind.

I was trying to think how I could explain this in practice. It's all a bit nebulous, I appreciate. So, here goes.

I had a big fight with someone. The usual fallout from this would be intense overthinking, shame, freezing with fear, writing off any plans I had for the coming days, probably either comfort eating, having a drink, or both, accompanied by losing myself in a sad film so I could cry about someone else's issues rather than focus on my own.

Back to the fight yesterday. I had a big argument, and I felt incredibly sad - but I had things I needed to do and I carried on with them despite feeling less than 'on top of the world'. I became absorbed in my work. My mind calmed down and I was able to enjoy my day, albeit a dialled down version, as I acknowledged I was feeling emotional and allowed those feelings to be there. Moderate overeating yes, (I had a slice of cake and some cheesy marmite crumpets) but no alcohol. I didn't partake in the drama of the occasion. My brain would normally be going into overdrive after such an altercation, creating nothing less than a full-blown tragic musical about it all.

Yesterday, I accepted it had happened and just moved forward with my day. This might seem like nothing much to you, but to me it was deeply significant. A seismic shift.

I'm still not entirely sure what magic he weaves, but seeking his help to gain control over my writing also helped me to gain more control over my emotions.

Organisational yin to my creative yang! As all the best teachers are.

A side note from Nano to Helga

I feel fortunate that destiny brought us together in that virtual room. Our work began modestly—just discussing your experiences and the book's purpose. Then you committed yourself fully to the process. I can't take credit for that transformation, truly.

When I received the first batch of chapters, I read them eagerly. I fell in love with your writing style and how vividly you pictured your experiences. They were so you!

And I sensed something deeper in the book—an underlying narrative connecting all the chapters. Yes, your book presents techniques and solutions for managing anxiety, but it's much more than that. Yes, it goes over more than forty approaches you've tried throughout your life, but that's not the whole story.

What truly shines through is your inner self—a part of you that refused to accept anxiety as your identity and kept searching for something better. This inner Helga—with a capital H—manifested sometimes as survival instinct, other times as a curious explorer.

I recall we had a chat about this over WhatsApp.

Helga: *That's exactly it! The methods were irrelevant. Not because there was anything wrong with them, but because I needed to find myself and they were just a vehicle for doing that. I couldn't go and trek across Africa or go on a Walkabout like the Aborigines, but this was my equivalent journey. Albeit covering a few miles of Devon.*

Nano: *The methods were your stepping stones, but YOU are the one deciding to keep jumping from one to the next, instead of giving up.*

This inner you didn't quit the exploration and the quest. And I know you never will.

I am deeply grateful that you allowed me to be part of this. Nano

Notes

Chapter 41 – Ebb and Flow of Life – Acceptance Technique

Resistance is futile. What you resist persists.

Scarily, this was a big part of the answer, and the thing I most shied away from.

The idea of accepting anxiety was deeply unappealing. I wanted to be rid of it. I didn't notice it being around before my drugs trip at Glastonbury, so why should I have to live with it now? It needed to go.

Yet, from the Linden Technique in my thirties to the Box technique more recently, and countless self-help books in between, the message coming through loud and clear from so many therapies was that I should go with my feelings and try not to resist anxiety.

This was a terrifying proposition.

If I felt unsettled with the first twinges of anxiety, how would I feel if I let the feelings come at me full pace?

What would happen if I didn't run away? Surely, I would be overwhelmed and unable to cope.

So many questions. I was too scared for years to find out.

This reminds me of being at a wave machine swimming pool in Germany many years ago, when I thought I couldn't swim The waves started gently coming at me, getting bigger all the time, and while everyone else was whooping for joy and jumping in time with the big waves, I was flapping away in panic, swallowing lungfuls of water, resisting the waves and getting near-drowned every time.

My brain took one look at that scenario and concluded from my flapping and screaming that this was one activity I might like to avoid in the future. My water confidence has been lacking ever since. Had I just jumped like everyone else in time with the waves rather than try to resist them, I might by now be an Olympic swimmer. Heck, anything is possible.

So, why did I resist the Acceptance Technique for so long also? Pretty simple answer really. The feeling of anxiety building and threatening to overwhelm me like a tsunami was not pleasant. I got soaked by the first few waves of anxiety (read: had a few panic attacks) and my brain again concluded that getting out of the way of a potential anxiety attack might be the best option.

To start with, it truly was.

I would have a panic attack, make a mental note of the situation, avoid it, and then feel much better. This was workable at the beginning. Avoiding going on the Tube quickly morphed into avoiding the bus and then avoiding going into London. Hard when this was where I lived. Same with travelling abroad. I had a panic attack on a plane, avoided plane travel, but then found boats suddenly worrying, and before I knew it, I was marooned in the UK, and so it went on. The mental list of no-nos kept growing, and my world kept shrinking, to the end outcome that the only plausible place to feel okay became my own home; the only place where I could control the vast majority of my experience. Job done, said my brain! Rather than having fancy holidays as a top priority, my brain was wired for survival, so deciding to stay at home forever was a brilliant option.

So, having spent decades trying to 'fix' my anxiety and delete it from my experience, more recent musings have led me to wonder what it might be like to be brave enough to go with my anxious feelings.

The basis for this thinking is that all humans seem to get issued with a package of feelings that routinely include sadness, fear, anxiety, and anger, as well as the more sought after ones of joy, calm, and happiness. If I hang onto the fact that we are nature, and that nature, by design, is pretty incredible, then maybe this 'factory setting' design is not what is flawed, rather my desire to feel only a small selection of my feelings.

This leads me to consider many things about the ebb and flow of life. I'm very different at different times of the day. Upbeat in the mornings, fuelled with excitement about the opportunities ahead, way more sleepy in the afternoon (I know this is diet too, as I am the queen of the carb-crash), often a little dejected as energy levels falter early evening, when my thoughts become considerably less 'bouncy' and everything seems hard, and sometimes even pointless. I see why the BBC put *Pointless* on late afternoon. Maybe I'm not the only one (I jest). I'm not one thing, one person, one point of view, but an ever-changing entity, and what shows up varies greatly from day to day. I believe this to be entirely normal for a human.

As a result, I always write in the morning and do more mundane tasks in the afternoon. This all makes sense to me until I ponder the concept that maybe I'm only writing in the mornings because I want to come over all light and upbeat and want to hide my darker and less socially desirable moods which might bleed out in the afternoon?

No surprise, then, that I've decided to shake it up and write in the late afternoon and dabble with honouring my less than chipper feelings instead of pumping out relentless positivity. It's interesting to me even to see the words that appear on the page. Afternoon me is more cynical, more tired, and not that up for embracing the positive and busting out my best self.

This is interesting to me for a number of reasons. It hadn't occurred to me quite how attached I am to my upbeat feelings and how determined I am to fix and tweak feelings that don't comply. In the same way I've failed miserably in every attempt to speak the complete truth for twenty-four hours, I also fail to sit with feelings that aren't textbook 'perfect' and endlessly try to root out the 'good' stuff. This, whilst concurrently telling myself I'm a changed being, living in the present, and embracing myself as I am. It's fair to say I'm a work in progress.

It is becoming crystal clear that I need to make peace with anxiety and let it settle down with all my other emotions to play a normal and healthy part in my life. I kind of think of my emotions as children, and boy, do I have favourites. Calm, joyful, and happy get all the loving attention, the appreciation and praise. Anger remains the quiet one in the corner, but anxiety, the one screaming for my attention because I ignore it gets precisely none of its needs met. Poor anxiety is undermined, treated with contempt, and banished from the family so I can concentrate on the nice emotions that I love.

Forget the fact that, when hard times come, joy isn't going to step in and save me from getting run over by a bus. In fact, if I'm too joyful and not paying attention, who knows what might potentially occur?

Maybe, if I could learn to treat all my emotions with equal respect, anxiety might settle down.

So, if I take a cold, hard look at how I routinely handle my emotions, I see that the minute any low vibe emotions turn up, feelings that don't have me purring with contentment, I reach for a fix. The fixes have changed over the years, from alcohol, cigarettes, and partying to now comfort eating, walking it off, watching a romantic comedy, escaping into a book, or blasting out a nostalgic tune—all fine things to do except perhaps the excessive comfort eating—but the underlying desire to fix myself remains the same. This needs looking at.

If I don't feel good, I get concerned and find tools to fix myself with. Now, I'm not saying there is anything wrong with that per se, but I do wonder if I couldn't try and live with the feelings a little longer and get used to feeling a bit off and not immediately need to change that. The meditation I do in the morning is all over this.

I know it always works for my anxiety when I'm in a situation where an easy fix is not an option.

If I can brave the concept of going with potential anxiety rather than pushing the feeling away, it tends to pass fairly swiftly and much less painfully than I imagined. Sometimes, it doesn't turn up at all, even when I'm terrified and certain it will overwhelm me (refer to a Taylor Swift concert, SZA in Hyde Park, Nice holiday to name a few).

Sadness is another emotion I shy away from, and I simply can't abide loneliness. I'm contemplating having a go at letting these feelings be when they show up. If I was the kind of person who could keep any kind of monitoring diary, it would be interesting to see how often the feelings come up and how long they last when they do. Also, if they come up less often when I don't interfere by running away or whatever else occurs to me that I should do.

I keep hearing these analogies about rivers and letting life flow through you. I now do this all the time, and it works amazingly well once I'm brave enough to get used to sitting with the unpopular feelings.

As a complete aside, I have damaged my Achilles, and all I need to do to improve it is four sets of short exercises that take a couple of minutes a day. Have I done them today? NO. The piece of paper is on my worktop, full of promise of a pain-free ankle, yet I limp around, bemoaning my painful joints without taking the small necessary steps to remedy it. The emotions exercise might befall a similar fate. But whenever I do remember, I'm going to try and hold off finding an immediate fix. Even hanging on for a few minutes would be a start.

Prior to this lightbulb moment, I had never considered that maybe comfort eating was also me hunting for a fix; a blocker for the tough feelings. I have always loved food. I think about it morning, noon, and night, and my instinct in every key moment in life is to bring out the appropriate food.

I still do this, but I'm becoming aware that there are other healthier ways to celebrate landmarks in life, and that I do use food to hold back my emotions.

I'm aware that I've done this to my children also, with everything that is good in life having an associated food memory. Again, this isn't necessarily a bad thing other than realising that I give food way more status in life than maybe is appropriate. I tend towards overeating for the dopamine hit and the association I have made between food and love. I'm working on focusing more on food's nourishing qualities rather than its abilities to heal my heart.

My go-to thought remains that love is food, and to show love, you give food, but I'm increasingly noticing that much of the food I assign this loving quality to is super unhealthy—a wolf in sheep's clothing. I'm going to work on tasty recipes for kale and quinoa.

So, why the ebb and flow chapter? Well, I am very much drawn to accepting that my basic human design is not flawed and that, therefore, there is value in all my feelings and I have things to learn from every emotion, not just the upbeat ones. I see I may have been missing a trick by ignoring the lessons of a vast chunk of these emotions and what they can teach me whilst blindly chasing the elusive joy and happiness.

I know the rich rewards of not chasing obvious wins, so why can't I apply this understanding to my emotional life? Perhaps because it has only just dawned on me. It's all a learning curve, after all.

A Random Aside – Trust and The 1970s Effect

I have bought my son a bike helmet for his racing bike, which he doesn't want to wear. He likes the freedom of getting on his bike and feels the helmet adds an unnecessary level of hassle.

I remember feeling like this when seatbelts were first introduced.

Today, I think both of the above are super useful. I'm sold, don't get me wrong, but there is something about shifts in recent decades towards making all situations 'safe,' that is causing me a few personal 'operating issues.' An unintended consequence of a good notion. I will try and explain why.

I am in the process of learning to trust myself again. To believe in my inherent capacity to get myself out of trouble, should a problem arise. If my catastrophic thoughts go into overdrive, that I am sufficiently confident in myself to let them pass without the need to step in with a million precautionary 'fixes.'

In an 'if you don't use it, you lose it' sense, my 'trust' skill needs to be dusted off and brought back into everyday use. I want to learn to distinguish between real danger and when I'm just following old, fearful habits of thought.

This has prompted a whole avalanche of thoughts on safety and trust.

During the anxiety years, I used to make myself super busy planning for every eventuality. A bike in the back of my car in case my car broke down (with puncture repair kit, the phone number of a bike repair person in case I needed a bigger repair, and a friend on standby should all the above fail), run flat tyres on my car so I would be able to drive even with a puncture, and that's without beginning to list the things in my handbag to fight off a possible panic attack (lavender oil, Bach rescue remedy, beta blockers, Kalms, travel sickness bands). You get the vibe.

Initially, each individual item made me feel safer, but over time, I worried about whether I had remembered them all, had they gone out of date, and so worry ultimately escalated, and the 'safety kit' became something extra to worry about too. An unintended consequence.

Post Glastonbury, I felt so overwhelmed that my brain took note and alerted me to other similarly overstimulating 'potential dangers,' such as crowds, central London, planes, the Tube, commuter trains in the south east, that might be worth avoiding for a while.

This made sense at the time. I certainly needed to take a raincheck on those hectic environments whilst I nurtured myself back into balance. Unfortunately, though, I took much more than a simple raincheck. I stored the incorrect lesson that these situations were somehow inherently unsafe.

I can see the logic in other similarly unhelpful leaps I made too. If seatbelts kept me safe in a crash, wouldn't it be even safer to avoid situations where I perceived the risk of a crash might be greater? Cue me avoiding roads at rush hour, during the daytime, and in no time, driving altogether. And so it went on.

Before the invention of mobile phones, I had no thinking about the need for a device to enable me to contact people I was meeting. I had complete trust in my ability to make arrangements, and generally, things did go hitch-free. If there was a confusion, it was swiftly resolved somehow.

I met my best friend outside Wembley Stadium before a big Madonna concert. No mobile phones for either of us, and she was heavily pregnant. Before Taylor Swift, I felt the need to have a fully charged

Don't Panic

mobile phone, a spare battery pack, had memorised my daughter's number by heart in case my phone packed up—no mean feat at fifty-five years of age—and agreed a place to meet in case all our phones packed up. It was quite some difference in thinking, and this was at a time when my anxiety was on the decline.

Student me met her boyfriend at midnight in a train station in Brussels without a thought entering her young mind that he wouldn't be there. Or that there was any inherent danger in travelling alone to meet him. She believed it would be fine, and it was.

My trust had somehow leached away over the years. To help me try to recapture that sense of freedom, I began watching the BBC's *Race Across the World* and a Netflix documentary series from 2017 called *The Kindness Diaries*. Deeply fearful me needed to remember that people travel around the world and have a great experience every day. Watching the contestants resourcefully get themselves out of trouble with limited money, no mobile phone, or any other crutches I believed were essential for travel, was refreshing.

These people had trust in their ability to navigate life and were loving using their savvy to get to their destinations quickly. So often, without prior planning, the race contestants would find themselves on the same train or boat, despite embarking on different journeys to get there. I had experienced the same phenomenon when I travelled around Europe by train as a student.

This ability to trust was a valuable asset. I needed to rediscover it in myself.

Six-year-old me, the one who wanted to become an explorer and spent all her spare time learning survival tactics for future adventure, had this in spades. I'm so glad she couldn't look ahead to see me sitting at home, too frightened to even see a film at the local cinema for fear they should lock the doors when I was in there, trapping me there for all eternity.

This has left me pondering more generally why anxiety has increased for so many at a time when, with technological advances, we have never, in theory, been safer. Ironically, though, the very inventions that make us safer are also those that alert us to a wide range of new dangers we had never even thought of, and this brings a whole raft of potential new dangers into our thinking. Many of these dangers are also not presented to us in relation to the likelihood of them ever occurring. A major unintended consequence.

For example, I've made sandwiches at home for years without giving it a thought. Cut my bread on a wooden board that I then ran under the tap after use. Since owning restaurants, I am now hyper-aware about food hygiene, cross-contamination, bacteria, and safe food storage. This is a good thing, but it has changed my sandwich-making habits forever. It also causes me to drive others mad with my keen interest in their food safety practices, which rarely measure up to my exacting standards.

Likewise, I remember a friend whose romantic partner worked in fraud. You couldn't buy a packet of crisps at the corner shop without being warned to hide your pin, shred receipts, and change your bank password. All great advice, but suddenly, there were countless new factors in the external world that needed my control. Don't even get me started on the risk of leaving fairy lights plugged in at night.

To stay sane, I needed to decide where to draw the line.

The more I tried to control various aspects of the external world, the less I trusted myself to be okay without taking these steps. This was a rabbit hole for me and seriously impacted on my fun.

Should I travel abroad (having risk-assessed the country) and enjoy the experience of eating foods from another culture, or look aghast at the food hygiene and instead eat vacuum-packed sterile food I had brought from home? Clearly not!

I needed to find a balance between my obsession with making everything safe and trusting my intuition to do the job for me. I didn't want to be reckless, but without some trust, life was a bit too fraught to enjoy.

I was talking to my daughter about why young people are more relaxed travellers generally than their adult counterparts. Yes, there is probably a greater naivety about potential danger, but isn't there also a greater trust in their ability to be okay without controlling the bejesus out of everything?

Growing up, children commonly do not have much control over their lives, and I wonder if this acceptance of having less control creates less need for control, freeing them up to do more fun things in a spontaneous way.

'You are as old as the risks you take. In many ways, ageing is not the process of growing old, but rather the slow death of becoming overly protective, scared, and worried about losing what you have. Youth is found in the energy of going for it, taking the risk, and trusting that you'll figure it out along the way.' James Clear, 3,2,1 newsletter, 13 March 2025

In the 1970s, I didn't know about the myriad of things that might cause me future harm, so I didn't allocate any brain space to worrying about them. I cycled with the wind in my hair, sat crammed in the back seat of my mum's car with countless other friends with no seatbelts, drank unfiltered water, and played outside with other children for hours, turning up at home just before dark.

I'm not saying this in terms of rose-tinted glasses. I can see there was so much wrong with the 1970s, and things are clearly safer now. I applaud this, but I do want to find a better balance between trusting myself to ride a bike and needing to cover myself head to toe with protective gear to prevent any possible harm should I fall off. If the gear becomes too onerous, I probably won't bother riding my bike at all.

It is perfectly logical to want to keep myself safe and make the world a safer place. The thing is, so much of life is totally out of my control, and seeing as I don't just want to simply stay at home, I need to develop a new relationship with my sense of trust, such as going for a walk without my mobile phone and Life 360 tracking my precise location.

I'm all for seatbelts, bike helmets, fraud checks, and food hygiene knowledge, but I think society's obsession with pointing out potential danger (to a skewed extreme) is making us all more anxious. I need to balance this by growing my faith to intuitively perceive danger, and trusting that I can make the right call if needed.

I need to remember that I am resilient and capable, and that I have options other than staying at home to keep me safe.

There is very little we directly control, and I'm beginning to understand that that is okay.

'The best way you can find out if you can trust anybody is to trust them.'
– Ernest Hemingway

The person I needed to learn to trust was myself.

Notes

Chapter 42 – Belief Coding

At times, when writing this book, I have run the risk of letting my ego settle in at the laptop, pushing me aside to wax lyrical about all the amazing changes I have so cleverly made.

I've been magnetically drawn to the idea that I'm fixed, as if I was a car that had just had an extensive overhaul at a fancy garage.

Not only am I fixed, but I'm the number one mechanic at the fancy garage.

I did it all myself, and I can now tell others how to get under the bonnet of their cars too. No need for a mechanic. I, Helga, will pass them the spanner. I know what I'm doing.

Then the universe, bored by the braying of my ego, sends me some learning, and back to school I go. This particular lesson was a tough one, and I received it only yesterday.

I will explain more at the end of the chapter, but I now understand why I stumbled across Belief Coding at the eleventh hour, at a time when I thought I was no longer in need of new techniques. My naivety never ceases to amuse me.

I promise I'll come back to the lesson from last night in a moment, but here's how I came across Belief Coding. Going through my chapters at the final editing stage, I realised there had been some duplications in my work and I had, in fact, only written up forty-one different methods.

Darn it. The whole premise of this book was to find out if the answer to life, the universe, and everything was forty-two. How could I have only forty-one techniques? This realisation came moments before I was heading out to meet a new friend, one I had previously only connected with online through a book we are co-authoring together. I turned up late to meet her.

I don't like to keep people waiting. I genuinely believe there is an arrogance in assuming my time is worth more than that of the person I keep waiting. At the same time, I'm also learning self-compassion, and on that particular morning, my boss had called me as I was leaving to offer me an exciting new opportunity. I was caught between being rude to him by rushing him off the phone and being rude to this amazing woman by keeping her waiting. I think I messed up on both fronts in the end, rushing my boss and being late for the meeting, but my intentions were good to all.

So, I arrived at the café, lovely new friend sitting there beautifully calm, me talking way too fast, bags, coats, and hair flying in every possible direction—an air of complete chaos counterposed her zen-like calm. Yin and Yang.

We got talking, and she told me more about herself, her journey, and the fact that she had just completed her Belief Coding practitioner training. Had I heard of it? No. Did it sound interesting? Absolutely.

The old addiction to me getting even better at overcoming anxiety has never quite left me, and dopamine was coursing through me as she talked about improvements to confidence, amongst other benefits, that people experienced from her sessions. Serious catnip for me!

That irresistible urge to get one step closer to whatever nirvana state I believed existed in terms of feeling calm in an anxious world kicked in, and I asked her if she fancied having a go on me. One thing she needed for her training was to get her sessions down to under two hours. Ha! Speed is my middle name and something I can apply to any situation, whether it's wolfing down pizza, inhaling a pint, or speaking. As I was told at school, I'm like a tape on fast forward. I could be useful and get fixed at the same time. Music to my ears.

I hear you questioning where my own zen-like approach to life might have disappeared to, in this instance. This is March 2025, and I'm back to feeling dizzy with excitement at the thought of being 'cured' afresh.

Anyway, we swapped numbers and agreed to meet for an online session the following week. I was nervous and excited in equal measure. The coffee high was also on the wane by the car journey home, and my social anxiety issues kicked in. Did I talk too much? Did she hate me? Was I being an insane show-off? I have never quite understood how to balance that societal need to be interesting with the equally important requirement to be humble; it's a tricky tightrope for an ADHD-me.

I worried about everything. It was classic overthinking. Time to disregard the avalanche of negative thinking bombarding my brain and do a meditation or something equally useful. So, did I do this? Hell, no. I was tired, had been burning the candle at both ends, was a touch hungover (a mere blip, honest), and so the scary thoughts had a potency that was impossible for me to ignore.

When I got home, a message dropped into my inbox. Lovely new friend had sent me an email, explaining how the Belief Coding treatment would work. We would be working on self-limiting beliefs, and I should have a think over the coming days about what I might like to work on. The timing was perfect!

I decided I needed to work on shame, feeling not good enough, and a general low level of confidence that, although immeasurably better than it had been a few years prior, was something that still kicked in with all the accompanying people pleasing and other associated fear-based behaviours.

I logged on to the session, and lovely new friend was there, smiling at me and reassuring me that the list of hideous behaviours I feared most were not the first and overriding thing she had taken from our initial meeting. She said she thought I had good energy. Phew. My ego—that's not supposed to be driving my behaviours—exhaled in relief. We then did some body compass moves. I needed to stand up for this. We needed to establish what was a yes and no response from my body when she asked me a question.

Turned out, leaning backwards was yes and leaning forwards was no. We asked simple questions. I told a lie, and my body responded. I hate lying. I said a true statement, and my body responded entirely differently. We tested it out a few more times, and it was strange how my body would lurch, seemingly without my instruction, one way or another, in response to her queries.

We did the session. She coded in some lovely new beliefs to replace the unwanted ones: I'm not good enough, I'm ashamed of myself, I am too afraid to speak out in case people don't like me.

The session ended, and she asked me not to drink alcohol for twenty-four hours, advised me I might feel tired, and said she would check in over the coming days to see how I got on.

Well…

I went for a walk in the lanes with my dog, and I felt lighter somehow. Joyful even. I kept getting these little bursts of inane grinning. This seems to happen when I have any kind of fear-based breakthrough. I had to read my new belief codes morning and night for seven days. I did this patchily but tried to read them as often as possible. They made me feel good, so it was easy homework to complete.

This brings me neatly back to yesterday.

I posted a message on the wrong group chat on WhatsApp last night.

It was a fairly innocuous message, but if misunderstood (as no doubt it was in the chat I posted it into), had the potential to cause me the kind of attention/potential dislike that I fear most intensely. The person who the comment most closely related to replied in an instant. No option to delete. I had to ride it out.

This was a small comment, a transgression, but in that moment, fear overwhelmed me like a tsunami. My brain went into overdrive. I catastrophised. I sought support from others. I poured myself a massive glass of wine. I drove my family mad seeking reassurance regarding the likely fallout. I wanted to apologise to everyone who might have misconstrued my message. All this habitual anxious behaviour kicked in, but also something a little more interesting.

I laughed about my embarrassment with my daughter. Really laughed, and not just due to the red wine. In fact, I couldn't stop. My daughter and I then went on to have a slightly more serious discussion about why I feel shame so strongly. She asked me to tell her about as many other shame-inducing episodes as I could think of (I left out a few). There were so many. We belly laughed. This major mess-up suddenly felt a bit less important. Still mortifying, but I had managed to laugh about it.

I drank another glass of wine—just to be safe—and decided to try and sleep it off, whilst obviously obsessively checking my phone to measure the degree of fallout. I woke up in the middle of the night, checked my phone again, and yes, definitely some fallout, but the world had not imploded.

The normal pattern for me after such an episode would be to experience waves of anxiety followed by a stressful, sleepless night. Waves of anxiety followed, for sure. Though not the destabilising kind. It was manageable, and I took it on the chin. I waited for the expected insomnia to follow, checked my phone again, and it was 6:19 a.m. Remarkable. I must have fallen asleep. This never happens when I have a shameful episode.

Where were the lost hours of thrashing about, feeling sick, unable to sleep, crying due to the sheer intensity of my embarrassment?

Before going to bed last night, I was convinced that the horror of the messaging debacle would render me incapable of writing for days. I had a deadline, and I was gutted about the potential of all that lost time. In reality, I got out of bed, had another look at the fallout, accepted that I had certainly made an error of judgement, and then went off to walk the dog, feeling fairly okay.

Whaaaaat?

I later sat down to write, with no excessive overthinking, and then it struck me; a lightbulb moment. Something inside me had shifted. Something of seismic proportions.

It was remarkable that I was able to look at what was an embarrassing slip-up and feel okay. This was totally new territory to me. Shame had been with me for so long that I'd never really considered it might go. My focus had always been on managing my relationship with fear. Then, when no one's looking, shame gets up and packs its bags. Crazy!

So, thank you, lovely new friend.

I am glad I did the Belief Coding session with you. I didn't think I needed it. I thought I was doing it as research for the book, but it was clearly my intended treatment number forty-two. Sent as an intergalactic message from who knows where. Maybe from Arthur Dent himself.

A Random Aside – Celebrating the Wins

There are points in life when you need to reflect on the wins. Have a look back over the years and see many things that have gone so much better than anticipated. Weirdly, many of these moments come amidst the chaos. It seems life doesn't have to be perfect for us to enjoy an upside.

When I start to reflect on this, I get this deluge of positive memories and struggle to know where to start. Some are bigger than others, but all have snuck in under the radar, and I realise I, without this prompt to remember, could tell an utterly one-sided story of my life of struggle. Struggle is only part of the tale!

If I hunt hard enough, I realise that my life wins have also come thick and fast.

Cycling to Dawlish Warren, in the summer, midway through some pretty hefty anxiety episode, I remember stopping, looking up at the sky (my young son cycling ahead of me), the sun warming my face and feeling this moment of unadulterated bliss descend upon me. Right out of nowhere.

I had forgotten there was another way to feel. It reawakened something inside me. Took me back to other similar moments of joy. Swaying on my garden swing singing Elvis Costello's *Oliver's Army* at the top of my voice in 1979, for instance. It was a moment when I felt free, bursting with happiness. When I look back on childhood, it is easy to forget these moments (and many more like this) existed, as it's the harsher ones that seem determined to occupy my entire brain space. I can and do choose to rearrange my memories these days.

Other wins have been more obvious. Getting my flat in the Royal Crescent for one. Who gets to live in one of the most prestigious addresses in England for a mere £22 a week?

Then there is that dreaded Glastonbury festival. I dwell on the disaster of the dodgy drugs trip, forgetting that, at the same festival, I found myself lying on the grass behind the Pyramid Stage, shooting the breeze with Feargal Sharkey no less, although I did ruin the vibe by banging on about my loathing for *A Good Heart*, his 1985 solo single. Apologies, Feargal! I have just Googled whether Feàrgal Sharkey was even at

Glastonbury in 1990. There is no internet evidence to back up my tale, but I'll stick to it nonetheless. If it wasn't Feargal, someone was doing a mighty fine impression of him, sporting those luscious locks, famously tossed around on the *A Good Heart* video. I swear it was him (please confirm, Feargal, if you ever read this).

Life threw me other interesting curveballs too. I remember phoning in sick for a restaurant shift in the late nineties, and my manager giving me such a hard time that I had to drag my sorry (hungover) ass into work, only to have Gwyneth Paltrow and Chris Martin sit in my restaurant section. I remember getting caught up in the excitement of smuggling them out the back door to prevent a mobbing from super keen drunken stags in the upstairs restaurant, all thoughts of terrible ill health swiftly forgotten. It was around the time *Yellow* was a huge hit for Coldplay. Gwyneth, portrayed in the media at the time as an obsessive macrobiotic diet fiend, tucked into two rounds of garlic bread and some cheesecake, reassuring me that we are all human, and no one lives up to such lofty ideals 24/7.

Then there were the bigger wins, such as surviving the tear to my carotid artery. It is so easy for me to get caught up in my tragic tale of anxiety and forget that I have been snatched from the jaws of death more times than I care to remember. That might be something worth celebrating, no?

Even ending up on a big night out with Buster Bloodvessel (he was on the mineral water) from Bad Manners, on the one evening that I covered for a journalist on the student newspaper. These things can get forgotten in the melee of bad experiences. It's also just occurred to me that I nearly died 'bustin' a blood vessel' - the times my life throws up these seemingly random connections!

Thinking about it, I'm luckier than I realised. School may have been challenging often, but I did have this burning desire to be on the telly, and it was me they picked to be on the children's game show *Screen Test* in the early eighties. That it was possibly my biggest brush with shame to this day doesn't detract from the fact that they did pick me, out of all the kids, to get the chance.

Likewise, getting to present the weather on the UK daytime TV show *This Morning* in the early nineties. I was truly appalling, but the fact is, I got to prance around that weather map, so all was certainly not doom and gloom.

When I was on a roll, things often went well for me, and good times could appear smack, bang in the middle of times where, either side, I couldn't even get out of bed. I say this because I need to explain that my story is nuanced. Everyone's is. In one month, I might have felt so hopeless and afraid I couldn't even walk into town, yet a few months later, the very same year, I could be found zooming around the stage set of *Supermarket Sweep* (when it was iconic with Dale Winton), having a few too many after show drinks with Dale himself. This led on to me gate-crashing a wedding, but I prefer to stay focused on the positives for now.

I remember working for a Mexican restaurant owner in Exeter in the nineties who was also developing property. At the time, I was working for £5 an hour. This was before minimum wage. Within months, I had bought my first house to do up, and within five years, I also owned a restaurant. It was incredible how life unfolded for me.

I remember moving house in the late nineties and looking at some wish list I had drawn up for things I hoped for from life. They weren't massive things but included living by the sea (tick), having lots of rescue animals (tick) and having my own restaurant business (tick). Basically, everything on the list had become a part of my life. I was exceptionally lucky in so many ways, even if I did have to continue to do battle with my anxiety enemy. It seems I missed this evidence of manifestation in action (laughs).

Life seemed to happen to me in waves; huge upward and downward curves. Over time, this slowly wore me down.

Initially, I could bounce back from episodes of debilitating anxiety (like when I went up to Manchester alone to film *This Morning*. I took my anxiety with me, but I managed to get through that trip) but over time, I lost the courage to keep trying. My fear of fear grew exponentially as my comfort zone shrank.

My husband and I opened many businesses during these years, and I can easily forget that our first restaurant won the RSPCA Good Business Award in 2005. Considering Marks and Spencer and Lush won the retail categories, this was something of a major win. I was far too anxious to attend the award ceremony in London (huge shame as my husband was on a table with an interesting bunch of celebs), but I was still a part of that winning team.

It would be so easy to tell a depressing version of my life, me trapped in a small corner of Devon, but when I did manage to break free, interesting things often happened. Not always fun, but certainly interesting.

Attempting to travel to Germany once, I was one of the few people who has ever broken down in the Channel Tunnel. This may be a surprising story to include in the lucky breaks chapter. The lucky part comes from living to tell the tale. So many times, I have found myself on the fortunate side of a serious life outcome.

And so it goes on. How lucky was I that a scuba diver turned up from under the sea, just as I was taking my last breath in Cornwall?

I have always wanted to work in radio and now find myself with my own afternoon show on local radio. How that happened, I'm not sure.

Even the opportunity to write this book. There have been so many lucky breaks on this particular journey, from the words that simply spilled onto the page when sitting down to write a different book, to the editor I met through a friend (apologies that I didn't ever follow up with that; I was too scared at the time), to the lovely editor (Karen) who is currently working on this book and used to write her own novels in my café. At that time, I was in awe of her as a writer and had no clue that, years later, she would be editing my book. She had zero idea that I was struggling so much with anxiety. Appearances can be so deceptive!

I'm saying all this because it is easy to forget that no human is any one thing. I'm not exclusively anxious any more than I am entirely happy. Both are only a part of my story. For years, I identified with being an anxious person. I didn't see that I merely experienced anxious feelings. I believed I WAS anxious. Now, I see that the anxious feelings were just a part of my humanness that had gotten a bit big for their boots. When I realised they didn't actually define me, when I saw myself as something other than an 'anxiety sufferer,' everything started to shift. Noticing even those small occasions, like the bike ride to Dawlish Warren with my son, when I was able to feel utter joy, were real lightbulb times, indicators that I was not inherently broken. I simply had feelings that passed through me, and for some reason, I had a habit of entertaining the anxious ones.

I like to think of my thoughts like film choices on Netflix. I always seemed to pick the scary ones with the outcome that my brain kept providing more of the same, like Netflix assuming all I like is *Emily in Paris* and *Bridgerton*. Eventually, my entire brain feed filled with scary thoughts, and I forgot that there was a whole raft of other, jollier thoughts flowing equally often through my brain, but I was only focussing on the anxious ones. When I started noticing the lovelier ones, they multiplied too. Genius!

That's the reason for including this slightly more chipper chapter. Given half the chance, I can write an entirely positive account of my past thirty-five years if I only choose to pick out the good bits. That I have chosen to tell you about my anxiety story is because it has been exceptionally hard, and I am so beyond grateful to be over the worst of it, and if even one person could find something in my ramblings that enabled them to see their anxiety differently, this would all be so worthwhile. Perspective is everything. For years, I got caught up in my anxiety story, not realising all the incredible things that were within grasp if I just took the time to notice.

Even in the midst of my anxiety, there were still times when I had amazing, genuinely enjoyable opportunities. I couldn't necessarily see them all at the time, but they were there, hiding in plain sight, just waiting for me to grab them. It's important for me to remember that. This is just one telling of my story. There are so many other ways to remember my past. It all depends on what I choose to focus on.

Taking a Leap – Cambridge April 2025

I just couldn't resist a final leap!

From Lyme Regis, favourite holiday destination during the anxiety years and where The Hitchhiker's Guide to the Galaxy was written, to returning from an anxiety-free weekend in Cambridge (where Adams studied), to avidly reading all four Hitchhiker's books as a teen, to my inability post-university to even read the opening chapters of Dirk Gently's Holistic Detective Agency (the death references freaked me out after my 'out of body' experience), I have always felt this tenuous thread connecting my to the life of the author Douglas Adams.

Even now as I work for the Devon Wildlife Trust, and re-listen to Adams' brilliant speech about the misguided view of humans and their place on this earth (recorded three months before his death), I am curious about my connection to him and his brilliant collection of books, particularly the 42nd anniversary box-set edition of *The Hitchhiker's Guide to the Galaxy* that nudged me to write my very own book, *Don't Panic,* much to the delight of blue baby, who no doubt had this in mind all along.

Heck, I even opened a restaurant in Dawlish, the end of the universe for some (not me, fortunately, as I was marooned there for the best part of the last twenty-five years).

So, what's with this Douglas Adams obsession? All I know is that at the height of my struggles, the craziest concepts in his books seemed to suddenly make sense, none more so than the Total Perspective Vortex, that if turned on, should have blown the brains of the ego-crazed Zaphod Beeblebrox. Had this happened to me at Glastonbury? Did I see myself as this tiny speck of dust in an infinite universe and my ego couldn't take it? Where was my guide with the friendly words, 'Don't Panic' written on the front in big letters? I guess I needed to write it for myself.

It seems apt that Cambridge University, choice of Adams, should be the place where I finally said, '*So Long, and Thanks for All the Fish,*' to my anxiety. The final goodbye after years of faithful duty as my ever-present travel companion.

Cambridge is at the extreme other side of the UK from my home in Devon. Cambridge is not easy to get to from there. It's either a very long drive (6.5 hours on the way there) on busy roads and motorways, or a train journey involving a change and dash across central London. There is not one element of the above journey that would not have filled me with terror even as little as a year ago.

Let me tell you how it was in 2025.

My daughter asked me if I would take her to Cambridge for a long weekend to check out the university (she is one smart girl). I said yes, as I often do, whilst thinking, 'How in the heck will I manage that?' It was January. I'm an eternal optimist, and April seemed ages away. I didn't think too much about it. I couldn't picture me driving there, but I put it out of my mind for the time being.

Strangely, as the event got closer, I still didn't seem to be thinking about it (stark contrast to the anxiety years, when I would have been obsessing about every minuscule detail). It wasn't until the night before that I realised it wasn't a straightforward drive. I was going to have to drive up the M5 via Birmingham, on numerous motorways, all in less than twelve hours' time. Cue the anxiety, surely? I promptly fell asleep. I never sleep when I'm fearful. Where was the insomnia?

I got up in the morning, packed the car, picked up my mum, who was coming on the trip, and set off for the motorway. I was calm. The M5 was at a standstill (normally something I can't bear), ambulances were speeding past, junctions were closed, diversions were in place, and it was four hours before we even got close to Birmingham. The journey was just one long traffic jam after another. All that being stuck and unable to escape, yet there I was, checking out the scenery and waiting for things to get moving.

I kind of expected some anxious feelings to show up, at least for a bit, to allow me to apply all of my newly learned skills of accepting feelings and letting them pass by. Nothing showed up.

There I was, trying to find an exit on a massive and unfamiliar motorway intersection, and no panic.

There I was, on the busy A14, with lorries driving perilously close to me, unsure if I was going in the right direction, and no panic.

There I was at the holiday accommodation, camomile tea at the ready, and you guessed it – still no panic.

This was an absolute first.

Things had become so much easier over the past few years, and there had been many good trips, but not one of them had happened without some insomnia before I left, fear at the idea of the trip, or residual anxiety as I settled into a new place.

Not so in Douglas Adams' Cambridge! I was there, six and a half hours' drive from home, feeling utterly relaxed and excited to explore. I wasn't even concerned about getting lost. I had no bag of tricks for any (let alone every) eventuality. I had shoved some clothes and my medicine into a carrier bag twenty minutes before leaving.

The rest is just the tale of a great weekend away. Punting on the river, eating in waterside cafes, spending hours in bookshops where, of course, the first book I spotted on display at Heffers was *The Hitchhiker's Guide to the Galaxy,* right next to Sylvia Plath's *Johnny Panic and the Bible of Dreams.* It felt like a sign. There was just space for my book to nestle in between the two titles.

I spent two and a half beautiful days in Cambridge and sensed I had passed another invisible barrier.

My mind, body, and spirit had finally accepted that travel was no longer something to fear. With a smartphone rather than the Hitchhiker's Guide to direct me, I could now finally follow in Arthur Dent's footsteps (and possibly Douglas Adams' himself), and get out there and explore the beautiful universe.

It makes sense to me that it would all turn around in Cambridge. I had visited Cambridge shortly before my life had imploded at the age of twenty-one. There I was, at the age of fifty-five, feeling free once more in this special city. It has not passed me by how often my daughter is there, pushing me on at all the key points in my changing relationship with anxiety. Love is a tough opponent for fear.

During the same weekend, we also revisited Manuden, the Essex village where I had run so free as a child. It was forty-five years since I was last there (if only it had been forty-two). As we walked around the village, I lovingly remembered every hidden footpath and tree I had climbed. It was a place I never believed I would be able to see again.

So, what's next for me now? Hitchhiking around the galaxy? It certainly feels like the start of a big adventure in my life. A book signing in New York? *Don't Panic* – here I come!

The Unexpected Leap – Torbay Hospital May 2025

If ever there was a chapter I didn't expect to be writing, it has to be this one. I am currently perching my laptop on a chopping board across a Zimmer frame. Unusual choice, one might think, but needs must, as I have been involved in an accident and am recovering from a hip replacement operation.

I won't bore you with the details, other than I was walking my dog in the narrow country lanes around my home on Friday, when a car reversed into me and threw me to the side of the road. Doggie was thankfully unharmed other than stress. Poor love, trembled for hours.

I am now recovering at my mum's bungalow (unable to manage at home), having just been discharged from hospital.

This in itself is a full circle moment, as the last time I stayed with my mum was when I had the mental meltdown after Glastonbury aged twenty-one, which triggered the start of this whole anxiety journey. Neat plot twist!

This also means I have missed out on a book launch for Start Over, Volume Two, a book that I am a co-author of, and have bypassed the chance to be a key speaker at said launch, which was supposed to give me a platform to launch this book. Sad face.

However, the upside is that I have taken another huge and surprising mental leap, despite all the excruciating physical pain.

Let's get back to the accident.

I don't like hospitals. Does anyone? I have always considered them a huge trigger for my anxiety. I also don't like taking drugs or feeling 'out of it' since my Glastonbury dalliances.

So, the events that transpired have provided interesting challenges for me. A chance to test the exact point I am at on this whole anxiety journey.

Firstly, the ambulance drivers picking me up made the judgement error to use sat nav to find the hospital (I don't have a positive relationship with sat nav, if you remember from being lost in the fog), managing to get the ambulance wedged in a lane unsuitable for motor vehicles. With a broken hip, the bumpy track was quite the barometer for my pain tolerance. The fact that they then kept reinforcing that they had no clue where they were or how they would get the stuck ambulance back out again, would, with all certainty, have set me off, even a year ago, on an anxious thought explosion resulting in panic. This time, yes, I did have shedloads of pain but zero anxiety. It was interesting to observe.

Arriving at the hospital and unable to move my lower body, it didn't take Sherlock Holmes to tell me I was going to be transported by lift to my ward on the fifth floor. I have tested many anxiety-provoking situations, but lifts were one I was happy to leave unchallenged. Stairs are the healthier option anyway. As a result, I hadn't been in a lift for decades. On day one in hospital, I had six trips in a lift. I'd be a liar to say I loved it, but I went with the flow, always delighted when the doors opened again for sure, but another big anxiety no-no ticked from my dwindling list.

Then came the locked wards with security passes to get anywhere. Had I had the physical capacity to walk and that anxiety-fuelled desire to leave, it would have been entirely impossible to do so. In effect, I was locked in a prison on the fifth floor of a tower block, stranded on a trolley, unable to move without extreme pain and much assistance. My younger self would have lost the will to live.

Levered into a bed, unable to do anything for myself, including using the loo, I was entirely at the mercy of the nursing staff and a call bell. Did I mention there were patients screaming on trolleys around the ward?

As if that wasn't enough, I was pumped full of drugs, including morphine, leaving me feeling in a permanently woozy state. Talk about a living nightmare. It was all rather One Flew Over the Cuckoo's Nest.

And you know what? I didn't panic. I kind of expected to and waited to see what feelings would emerge, but panic wasn't one of them. I wasn't using my energy to push all my anxious feelings down. I simply went with the flow and accepted my state. This was not an expected result, despite recent evidence of a new Zen-like me slowly being reborn.

Insane pain aside (think childbirth times a million), there was a part of me that was beyond chuffed at this outcome. Could there have been a better test for my progress?

I guess there was just one biggie left; the actual operation. My past health episodes put me at greater risk of having a stroke, so as the consultant went through the necessary advice on risks (popping off, stroke, paralysis) as I signed the various consent forms. I had no choice but to mull a little on the less desirable outcomes of the operation as I nervously scribbled my name across the papers. Full-blown panic attack, you might think? No. Strangely, just a little normal-level concern.

Then a long five-day wait for the operation, giving me all the time in the world to whip up concerns about the general anaesthetic. I had the misfortune as a child to watch a TV show where the anaesthetic didn't work, with the patient being operated on in agony but unable to move to alert the surgeons. Only through tears rolling from the patient's eyes did they eventually realise what was going on. Was no one monitoring my viewing choices in 1975? Anyhow, the result of this was that I never fully shook off this lurking fear of 'going under' and hoped that I could skirt through life without ever having an operation. No such luck.

Operation day arrived. I was gowned up and ready by eight a.m., waiting on a trolley for my big moment in the theatre. It was 12:45 p.m. when they called me in. I honestly expected to feel surging fear at this point. The anticipation for this moment the night before had brought on some worry. What actually happened on the day, though, was a sense of complete calm descending over me. I even found myself laughing with the nurses. I didn't see that one coming.

I then ended up making friends with a bunch of fellow inmates on the ward. We even managed to persuade the staff to give us a telly for a cinema night. My phone is pinging every few minutes today with the new buddies asking for health updates. We are planning a reunion. There will be cake and cocktails, I'm sure!

So today, I am punching my bruised arm in the air, at yet another huge moment for me.

In terms of triggers for my anxiety, they were all there with bells on, but despite this, I remained calm.

If I needed a test that I was on the mental mend, this one has to get a gold star.

Now to learn how to walk again. What a metaphor for my new life free from fear!

Conclusion

Here I am, thirty-five years after Glastonbury 1990, two years to the day that this book plopped out onto my unsuspecting page, one anxiety disorder lighter, and about to celebrate my fifty-sixth birthday in a few weeks. I didn't see any of the above coming—even the birthday after my health issues—but I am delighted to be here, nonetheless!

A lifetime ago, I walked into an independent record shop just off Nottingham High Street and purchased a ticket for Glastonbury Music Festival, along with 50,000 other wired-for-fun humans.

Chattering excitedly to my gang of friends, buzzing with hope for the rose-tinted vision I held of the life ahead of me, I innocently handed over my collection of ten-pound notes and received my golden ticket. The rest, as they say, is history.

Someone, somewhere, was having a very wry smile that day.

Someone, somewhere, maybe saw that I was indeed going on a big journey, but not the one I imagined as I stood there, leaning on the wooden shop counter, surrounded by a sea of delicious vinyl, dressed head to toe in Indian cotton, DMs laced up, with a many months-old Mohican growing out into a messy bob cut. Could that not have been warning enough that things were going in a suspect direction? I loved that Mohican and only grew it out to avoid grief from my dad.

It was the end of one era and the start of something different. Different is good, no?

You have to smile, in hindsight, coming out the other side of what has been one seriously tough adventure. I can finally sit back and say that it all worked out well in the end.

I guess I can most closely relate the past few decades to one of those epic gap year holidays. The one with the missed flights, hotel rooms riddled with cockroaches, plastered in mosquito bites, dysentery for days that emerges years later as this tale of incredible adventure, the trip of a lifetime that shaped the person retelling the story in the present day. Glastonbury was that 'trip' for me.

There is something almost beautiful about blindly falling into a life experience with no safety tools at your disposal.

Easy to proclaim when you are finally 'out the other side' of this anxiety journey, I appreciate.

Getting through the challenges over the years has been undeniably hard, but without discomfort, I'm certain I would never have delved deep enough into my psyche to clean up the many unattended wounds. I would never have willingly chosen to face my lurking inner demons.

Maybe the scary hypnotherapist was right when she said I was possessed by demons. Perhaps I just didn't understand exactly what she meant. This is a VERY generous interpretation on my part.

And looking back, it's not even true that I jumped into any of my experiences without safety tools at my disposal. That was just how it felt at the time.

I had the best safety tools of all; intuition, inbuilt resilience, and an untapped ability to cope with just about anything. I just had to quieten down the shouty voice of anxiety so I could hear my intuitive voice and learn to read the guiding signs. I would inevitably find myself back on the right path if I trusted my own innate sense of direction. Fat chance, obviously, when I had drunk a bottle of gin and popped a few pills 'just to be safe.'

This was the biggest lesson I needed to learn on my journey. To listen to my intuition and stop looking to the external world for all the answers.

To stop blocking out my feelings with food, alcohol, or anything else. It sounds simple as I type it today.

I'm older as I write this, but not weary as I was for so many anxious years of my youth. Deeply drained and exhausted from all the fear. My limbs may not move with the same fluidity they possessed at age twenty-one, and I can't say being hit by a car in a country lane has helped, but there is a certain lightness to my step that has been missing for a very long time.

The last time I felt truly free was probably when I was eight, building camps in the Essex countryside during long, hot weeks of the endless summer holidays. Just me, the uncomplicated natural world, and with very little thought at all.

It was around this age that I had the audacity to express opinions of my own. That was when things at home began to unravel apace.

I thankfully find myself back in that place again. Not Essex, but the place it represented in terms of my freedom—a freedom that actually never went away—armed with a more certain voice, the confidence to speak, and an unexplored spirit for adventure. I am ready for the life I thought I was all set for back at Nottingham University, on graduation day all those years ago.

My life learning was so much more complex and lengthy than my formal schooling. It was the Open University equivalent of getting a degree. Took a bit longer, had to be fitted around other life events, but was more than worth it in the end. Formal education fed my ego, but my life learning has nourished my soul.

So, here I am today, not perfect, not 'fixed,' but free in a way that I can see I was born to be, hoping to help others too on this twisty journey of life. There has to be a reason why 'blue baby' hurtled through space, fighting so hard to gain her place in this world, to throw her dice of life and see where they landed.

Which brings me back to the question that started this whole, long, forty-two chapter ramble. Is the answer to life, the universe, and everything forty-two?

Maybe…

I could have written this book about forty-two great teachers, forty-two life lessons, or even forty-two monumental cock-ups that got me to the place I am now. A place of calm. A place of acceptance.

The next phase of my life will be forty-two wild adventures! Better late than never.

My anxiety came in with a bang and went out with a whimper. It exploded into my life, taught me what I needed to learn, and then quietly slipped away, leaving me back in control, steering my own ship, so to speak.

At the age of twenty-one, after years of going in the wrong direction, drifting further and further away from who I really was, I needed to take stock of my life. I simply didn't want to. I was scared. I kept looking away and hoping to find the answer at some 'party at the end of the universe.' As with all difficult things in life, from death to taxes, they all have to be faced in the end. We can only look away for so long.

I love the concept of the 'disinfectant of daylight' that Cathy Rentzenbrink talks about in *The Last Act of Love*. The revelations that shining a light onto our darkest fears can bring. Light helps me see things so differently!

Anxiety got my attention as only hideous panic attacks can. It refused to be ignored. In the end, though, I learned the lessons I needed to learn, and on this day in history, I can honestly say I am grateful for the teachings. I think my biggest fear throughout this whole journey, was that I didn't have the capability to get through this. This proved to be categorically untrue!

Life lessons are painful. Life lessons are tough, but the other side of the experience is liberation and freedom, accompanied by a strange realisation that I was always okay. Never broken. Not the real me. The me buried so deeply underneath layers of overthinking. It was all just wonky thinking. Some mine, but much also the cloudy thinking of others, presented to my mind as if they were thoughts my own.

I think back to Arthur Dent in *The Hitchhiker's Guide to the Galaxy* and totally get that the universe looked like one vast, chaotic, and scary place. Arthur never knew with any certainty quite what he might be facing next. None of us do. Armed with a guide emblazoned with 'Don't Panic' on its very cover, though, meant he was always better equipped to deal with the unexpected than he ever realised. Much more so than Zaphod Beeblebrox—now, that's one man caught up in serious denial!

I am no different from Arthur, I suppose, only I wasn't issued with a helpful guide to the universe. I did panic rather a lot as a result.

And all that panic... was it worth it in the end? It's certainly what led me to write this guide for you. So, here it is. *Don't Panic!* A guide to encourage you to get out there and explore our beautiful universe and to ditch the unnecessary panic. If Arthur Dent can do it, heck, if I can do it, I am nothing less than certain that so can you!

'Strange, it is a huge nothing that we fear' - *Storm on the Island* by Seamus Heaney.

Never a truer word said!

From Anxiety 10 to 0

(most of the time)

My Steps to Recovery

I don't have concrete steps you can follow to move you from anxious to okay. It's a bit disappointing because isn't that why we read books like these? To find the one book that says definitively, 'do this and you will feel better.'

I can't promise that, but I will have a crack at highly imperfectly trying to unpick the steps that helped me:

I stopped drinking alcohol (not completely, but to the greatest extent) because alcohol makes me feel shaky and ungrounded. Any numbing benefits are quickly overtaken by the worsening of all my feelings as I sober up.

Drinking water and staying hydrated. With this, I include any sensible steps to improve my nutrition and energy intake. This has involved reducing the junk food I eat and including a range of previously unfamiliar ingredients, including turmeric, kale, quinoa, kefir, and kombucha. You get it. Do what works for you, but my diet and water intake needed an overhaul.

When I feel uncomfortable, I **go out for a walk**, and within twenty minutes, I always feel better.

I have started to notice my inner dialogue and have challenged it. Calling yourself every negative name under the sun is in no way helpful. Likewise, reliving every shameful moment and then stuffing it back down once you have fully submerged yourself in the self-loathing feelings is, again, not useful. Who knew? I now feel more uncomfortable being mean to myself than I used to feel saying nice things to myself in the mirror.

Practising gratitude. No, I hear you cry. That sounds so like I have been brainwashed by the well-being industry. Maybe, but there is a genuine benefit to looking for things in life to appreciate. My mind is forced to focus on the good stuff and has less time to tell me that I'm a weak and useless being with no right to draw even a breath... which neatly segues me onto...

Breathing. Who knew this was something I had to think about? The truth is, I don't, as breathing for those in good health handily happens anyway. If I do choose to focus on it, though, I often notice that my body appreciates a slightly larger intake of oxygen, and my raspy, shallow gasps can be replaced with big, calming breaths. Remarkably, watching my breaths works better than counting sheep to help me sleep.

Sleep... my old nemesis. I have yet to triumphantly declare that I have built a solid relationship with you, dear sleep, but I am actively working on it. I now have earlier nights, which seems to suit my body marvellously.

Creativity. It doesn't matter whether I'm dancing around the kitchen like a demented llama (that's a thing), singing like an outtake from *Britain's Got Talent*, or sitting at the laptop, banging out my latest genius insight. Being creative on any level makes me feel better. I lose myself in the moment and handily lose my anxious feelings too. Result!

Novelty. I have a brain that enjoys novelty. No need to put a label on it, but my mate calls me 'magpie,' possibly because of my badly dyed hair —black with white roots determinedly pushing up through—but more likely because I love nothing more than a shiny new thing. This is not great when developing addictions, but handy when determined to get to the bottom of an anxiety issue by testing out forty-two methods. I now ditch addictions in favour of more wholesome pursuits and am currently planning my forty-two next big adventures. Novelty, when directed at my passions, lifts the spirits and calms my mind in a brilliant way. I can find passion projects even in the depths of challenge. When I felt I couldn't go out, I could still write a short story, paint a bad painting, or listen to a new genre of music. Try it. Following your passions is a winner.

Curiosity. Have a go at swapping curiosity for fear. You don't have to take big steps, but taking a gentle peek at what might be around the next corner with a curious interest creates an entirely different bodily response to imagining a rabid dog hiding around the corner about to rip you to shreds. Having become way more curious, I have yet to meet any rabid dogs!

Truth. Just because you think it, doesn't mean it's true. That blew my mind. I assumed what went on in my head was a mine of useful safety information that needed to be acted on at all times. This has proved to be completely false. Dare I say, I have thought the most incredible amount of nonsense and believed it, to my detriment. I love this quote from Lewis Carroll.

'Why, sometimes, I've believed as many as six impossible things before breakfast,' says The White Queen in *Through the Looking Glass.* For me, this can be multiplied by any big number you can imagine.

Having a curious poke at the thoughts I believed to be true (number one being 'I can't cope with having a panic attack') and asking myself two vital questions. Is this true? Is this useful? Was it William Morris who said to keep only things that are either beautiful or useful in your home? I would change that to keep only thoughts that are true or useful in your head. Be open to noticing your thinking and ask yourself over and over again, is this true? A handy trick for me is to see how I feel. My feelings are a direct reflection of my thinking. If I'm feeling anxious, the quality of my thoughts will be poor. I will then take a look at what I'm thinking about and say to myself, 'Based on all previous occasions, these thoughts are likely to be nonsense,' and distract myself by going for a walk. I might also check if there is something I could usefully do to calm the anxiety, like open a letter I've been avoiding. The anxious thoughts then move on. What I used to do was throw a 'bad thoughts party' where I invited more and more bad thoughts to come and join any initial anxiety. This was not helpful and increased the likelihood of me having a panic attack.

Take uncomfortable steps. The only way to prove to yourself that you can cope with anxious feelings is to be willing to feel them. To stand up to them. Lucky for me, so many things close to home brought on my anxious feelings, so picking off the easier ones gave me ample opportunity to practice. If this is not the case for you, pick a scenario that is tough but not terrifying and feel the feelings for a moment. Build up your tolerance to them. I say to myself, 'Make this as bad as you can. Dial up the anxiety to the max. Is this all you've got?' and the feelings always, without fail, get better rather than worse.

Time a panic attack. They don't last long. I always imagined I was panicking continuously, but that was not true. It was just a story I told myself. Now, I admit, there were times when I was making toast or painting my nails when I was not anxious. Start noticing the reality of how anxious you are. Is it actually only one hour in total over a twenty-four-hour period? It may be way more, but there will be gaps. Start paying attention to the gaps without panic and make a point of noticing them.

Get a few supportive people to be your cheerleaders. Ditch looking for support from people who don't even try to understand. There are people out there who will want you to do well. I'm not saying the support I got was always what I wanted - i.e. phoning a friend at breaking point and saying, 'I can't go to Nice,' and my lovely (always kind) friend said, 'Bullshit. Grab your bag and get in the car. You can do this, and you will do this.'

What? I was hoping for a nice, calm word and the permission to give up, which I then got from someone else. The tough words did bounce around my head, though, as I knew this person definitely had my back. I went to Nice and had an amazing time!

Take your time. If you're anything like me, you'll want to be fixed 'right now.' Having been truly useless at PE, I now see I needed to apply a kind of Olympic training regime to overcoming my anxiety. It was not going to be an overnight fix (well, maybe if you're very lucky and can shift your thinking in an instant as some do), but my new thinking would have to be a 'muscle' I developed. My old thinking was engrained, much like Scooby Doo's habit of eating gigantic Scooby snacks. To get Scooby onto a macrobiotic diet is not going to happen overnight. Take small steps, but take a step every day and you will make progress. Think tortoise and the hare. You will finish the race.

Constantly look for areas to **practice being resilient and stepping out of your comfort zone.** Try to notice the difference between the voice of fear (rather shouty) and the voice of your intuition (way quieter). Try and tune into your intuition as much as you can.

Celebrate the small wins. I remember walking around a circular walk near my house for the first time without turning around and running home. I reached the 'mythic' mid-point of the walk and pushed through and kept walking. There was no point in turning around, as home was now closer if I kept going. This took years to achieve. It was an interesting symbol for pushing through anxiety. These are the wins you should celebrate, and these were as significant as going abroad for the first time to me.

I have no idea if any of the above will help. There's probably more. I wanted to try and give an honest breakdown of my progress. Yours will be different. New steps are hard to take, but I cannot begin to describe the incredible feeling on the other side. Some people have to climb Everest to get that feeling. One of the perks of anxiety is that I can feel it by getting on a train and travelling just one stop. Every cloud…

Q & A – Me and my Younger Self

Younger me

Are you truly
happy?

Me

Wow, that's a big question to kick off with. Yes, I would say I am most of the
time, but how we both define happy might be different.

Younger me

What do you mean?

Me

I'm happy with the little things in life. I've turned into a tree hugger for real
now. (laughs)

Younger me

I secretly always wanted to try that
(laughs)

Me

Absolutely! What is different now is that I don't care as much about what
other people think. I'm more willing to try things that might make me look
stupid in the eyes of others.

Younger me

That scares me rigid. Face facts, everything scares me rigid
(laughs nervously)

Me

What do you
mean?

Younger me

I don't want to be happy with a small life. I want adventure. I want to make a difference in the world. I want to shake things up.

Me

Me too, actually. I just go about it a different way. I wonder how happy you really are. You use alcohol as a prop. I don't need to do that anymore. I barely drink.

Younger me

That sounds dull.

Me

Is it, though? You do know you're fine without the booze? You don't need it in the way you think you do. People will like you when you're sober. Some possibly more.

Younger me

Old people like you, you mean?

Me

I'm not convinced you mean that. When you down a bottle of wine in a few minutes flat to go out, how does that really feel?

Younger me

F**king amazing. I get off my head so quickly and I just want to get out there and find the party.

Me

How do you feel if you can't have a drink?

Younger me

Bad, awkward, like I want to shrink away.

Me

That doesn't sound that great. How do you feel the next day?

Younger me

Horrible every time. I always have to phone people to find out what I did and feel this incredible shame and that I'm not good enough. I just want people to like me. It scares me if I think they don't or if I've f**ked up in some way.

Me

Maybe the right ones like you anyway. Could it be that you're not finding the right friends because you're permanently drunk?

Younger me

Maybe, but not entirely. That's way too simplistic. I think you've forgotten what it's like to be young! What about the anxiety? Does that get any better?

Me

Yes. It isn't a thing for me now. I'm no longer scared of feeling anxious. Maybe sometimes I get a little unsure if I'm doing something new, but I realise that's normal. Everyone feels scared to try new things.

Younger me

How on earth did you do that? I can't see how I'm ever going to get over it. How can I get on a plane? That's never going to happen, surely. The thought of it makes me sick.

Me

Those thoughts change. I don't feel scared of having an anxiety attack anymore. I know I can survive it. It doesn't have the power to stop me from doing things anymore because I no longer fear the feelings.

446

Younger me

I think you've forgotten what it feels like. I can't take that horrific feeling. I can't bear it.

Me

You can. You are incredibly strong underneath. Once you see that you're so much more than your panicky feeling, it recedes. A bit like standing up to someone you fear. You reach a point when you don't care about the feelings anymore. You don't love them, but you know they're just feelings, and you can get through them every time. That's when they start to disintegrate. Your fear of them is what's making them stronger. The fear fuels the panic.

Younger me

So, how do I get less scared of them, then?

Me

You might not like this, but you learn to let them pass through you. You stand firm and let the feelings wash over you. You experience a few panic attacks without running away and see it's okay on the other side. Like floating in a riptide rather than trying to swim against it, or opening a door when you don't know what's on the other side of it. You refuse to open the door because you imagine that what lies behind it is terrifying, dark, and horrible. When I eventually open that door, it's a gateway to a beautiful new world.

Younger me

You're losing me now with your door nonsense.

Me

I guess I'm trying to say that how you look at life now, and how I look at life, are different. Our lens changes focus. You see a plane and tell yourself lots of scary stories about it, and that makes you afraid. I look at a plane and see a way to get to a new place. It might make me nervous, but the nervousness is something I can cope with. I am no longer afraid of the fear.

Younger me

You keep saying that. We have the same eyes, although I notice you wear glasses, so how do we see things differently?

Me

I'm not scared of dying, for one.

Younger me

I'm terrified of it. It's all I think about. I spend so much time pushing those scary feelings away.

Me

I stopped pushing feelings away, and I had a few interesting experiences. It all changed how I feel about dying.

Younger me

You're scaring me now by talking about death. And you're bloody old, way nearer to it than me.

Me

How about thinking of something a bit easier, then? Remember when you believed in Father Christmas?

Younger me

Yes, briefly, until Heidi pulled off Uncle Trevor's beard.

Me

Once she had done that, could you go back to believing in that story?

Younger me

No. She ruined it for me.

Me

Same with me for anxiety. I'm not scared of the worst-case scenario, which was always having a massive panic attack. I'm not frightened of it, so I can do all the things you stopped doing because you were too frightened it might happen.

Younger me

So, how did you learn not to be scared?

Me

I tried loads of different therapies, which calmed me down over time. I know you think they made no difference, but I learned more than I realised along the way. Some of that hypnotherapy definitely gave me the confidence to try new things. I also met some important people on this journey.

Younger me

I can't stand the thought of doing things that make me feel anxious. I think you've forgotten how shit it feels.

Me

That is probably true to an extent. The less I panic, the harder I find it to feel those panic feelings in my body. I am no longer the 'Master of the Panic Attack.'

Younger me

Are you saying I want to be 'Master of the Panic Attacks'? I bloody hate them.

Me

No, I promise I would never be that crass, but I have wondered over the years if there wasn't a value to us having panic attacks. Ways that it served us.

Younger me

That makes me so angry. You have forgotten how hard it is to be in my situation.

Me

Possibly, but hear me out. What is the one surefire thing to stop you from going out and wildly partying and getting yourself into dodgy situations? What is the one thing that can get people to back off when you're being pressured to do things you don't want to do?

Younger me

That is so not true.

Me

Really? I remember going to bed and staying there for weeks, recovering. I remember you getting at least two key people to back off by telling them you had panic attacks.

Younger me

But I truly, truly hate this feeling. Tell me more about getting better and when it happens.

Me

I wish I could say we have a speedy recovery, but it takes time. You do lots of incredible things, though, despite your panic attacks. Possibly because of them.

Younger me

Like what?

Me

Because you feel you can't travel, you plough your incredible energy into opening successful businesses. Restaurants, shops, and cafes.

Younger me

> So, do you still do that
> now?

Me

I found a list you wrote of all the things you liked and were important to you.

No, because I want to follow my purpose and do the things I feel passionate about. I love to write.

Younger me

> Me too.

Me

I found a list you wrote of all the things you liked and were important to you. It was a blueprint for life. If I had followed your advice, I could have had the life of my dreams earlier.

Younger me

> Why didn't you, then, you
> eejit?

Me

I had to learn a few lessons along the way, and there's nothing like a challenge to teach me a lesson.

Younger me

> You are freaking me out
> now

Me

We have a good life. We learn the lessons we need, and we are able to find a genuine freedom and confidence without needing to get plastered. We know what's good for us and stop asking the rest of the world what we should do. Actually, that's not entirely true. I have seen two psychics called Sarah this year alone.

Younger me

You truly are a flaky,
tree hugger.

Me

Right back atcha, H! You are just too scared to be yourself. You need time to learn it's okay to be you, just as you are.

Younger me

You're making me tear up.

Me

Learning you're okay as you are is a big part of learning to deal with the anxiety. Learning to trust in yourself and believe in your own strength and value gives you the power to turn around to your fear and say, "That's not who I am."

Younger me

That sounds nuts.

Me

I mean that when you realise you don't need to fear yourself, when you get brave enough to look at who you are, to not run away from that, you find that you're fine, and there is nothing to run away from. The panic attacks are the same. When you get brave enough to stand there and withstand whatever they have to throw at you, you find again that you're incredibly strong. Once you know that, you can do anything. Things might be scary, you might feel anxious, but it doesn't undermine your belief in yourself that you can cope.

Younger me

You mean I learn that I'm Wonder Woman?
(laughs)

Me

Yes. You've hit the nail on the head.
(laughs too)

Glossary of Random References

BOOKS

Author	Title	Page
Douglas Adams	The Hitchhiker's Guide to the Galaxy	20, 21, 41, 417, 420, 434
Emily Brontë	Wuthering Heights	255
Katherine May	Enchantment	15, 25
Michael Rosen	We're Going on a Bear Hunt	136
Patrick Holford	Beat Stress and Fatigue	152
Patrick Holford	Optimum Nutrition for the Mind	152
Philip Larkin	An Arundel Tomb (poem)	165
Vonnie Winslow Crist	Quote about mystery and magic	10

MUSIC

Artist	Song/Album	Page
A-ha	Single mentioned	156
Blondie	Maria	262
Bob Marley	Various works	261
Bonnie Tyler	Total Eclipse of the Heart	158
Brian Ferry	Love is the Drug	160
Destiny's Child	Survivor	262
Elvis Costello	Oliver's Army	407
Frankie Goes to Hollywood	The Power of Love	158
George Michael	Careless Whisper	158
Huey Lewis and the News	The Power of Love	158
Indigo Girls	Closer to Fine	262
Irene Cara	Flashdance	155

MUSIC

MUSIC

TV SHOWS & FILMS

Title/Show	Type	Page
Altered Images on Top of the Pops	TV Show	124
Calamity Jane	Film	180
Downton Abbey	TV Series	156
Gregory's Girl	Film	124
Heathers	Film	164
Kill Bill	Film	156
Screen Test	TV Show	123, 409
Strictly Come Dancing	TV Show	184
Supermarket Sweep	TV Show	103, 410
The Good Life	TV Series	97
The Goonies	Film	60
This Morning	TV Show	103, 409, 410

TED TALKS

Speaker/Creator	Title	Page
Kelly McGonigal	How to make stress your friend	54, 280
Sir Ken Robinson	Do schools kill creativity?	280
Shahina Jaffer	Art and Perception	281
Tim Box	How to Stop Feeling Anxious about Anxiety	281, 347, 349

APPS & TECHNOLOGY

App/Technology	Purpose	Page
Calm app	Meditation (The Daily Trip)	23
CD Walkman	Music listening device	167

ACADEMIC & RESEARCH

About the Author

Her almost lifelong battle with anxiety has not stopped **Helga Beer** from turning her little corner of Devon into a merry-go-round of entrepreneurial activity. She has owned and run three successful restaurants, an ice-cream parlour, two cafes and a gift shop over the years while holding down a multitude of jobs in between.

Helga is a devoted, some would say over-devoted, mother of two, or five if you count the rescue cats and dog that share her ancient thatched cottage that sits well off the beaten track.

As well as working for the county's leading wildlife charity, she juggles a hectic family life with hosting a local radio show and running her creative writing workshops 'Feel the Fear and Write it Anyway'. She has even found the time to co-author a best-selling book.

Now the genie is firmly out of the bottle, she plans to make up for lost time by cramming in as much travelling as possible – starting with a speaking tour of 42 local village halls and building to an epic 42-country trek around the world. Ideally on a global book tour, but if all else fails, a tasting trail of the world's best veggie dishes wouldn't go amiss either!

If the number 42 is, indeed, the answer to life, the universe and everything, then Helga is on a mission to share the inspiring secrets and, yes, some of the mis-truths she has unearthed during her 35-year quest for inner peace.

Connect with Helga: helgakbeer@gmail.com

Notes

Notes

Printed in Dunstable, United Kingdom